Eastern Africa Series

THE ERITREAN
NATIONAL
SERVICE

Eastern Africa Series

Women's Land Rights & Privatization
in Eastern Africa
BIRGIT ENGLERT
& ELIZABETH DALEY (EDS)

War & the Politics of Identity in
Ethiopia
KJETIL TRONVOLL

Moving People in Ethiopia
ALULA PANKHURST
& FRANÇOIS PIGUET (EDS)

Living Terraces in Ethiopia
ELIZABETH E. WATSON

Eritrea GAIM KIBREAB

Borders & Borderlands as Resources in
the Horn of Africa
DEREJE FEYISSA
& MARKUS VIRGIL HOEHNE (EDS)

After the Comprehensive Peace
Agreement in Sudan
ELKE GRAWERT (ED.)

Land, Governance, Conflict & the Nuba
of Sudan
GUMA KUNDA KOMEY

Ethiopia
JOHN MARKAKIS

Resurrecting Cannibals
HEIKE BEHREND

Pastoralism & Politics in Northern Kenya
& Southern Ethiopia
GUNTHER SCHLEE
& ABDULLAHI A. SHONGOLO

Islam & Ethnicity in Northern Kenya &
Southern Ethiopia
GUNTHER SCHLEE
with ABDULLAHI A. SHONGOLO

Foundations of an African Civilisation
DAVID W. PHILLIPSON

Regional Integration, Identity
& Citizenship in the Greater Horn
of Africa
KIDANE MENGISTEAB
& REDIE BEREKETEAB (EDS)

Dealing with the Government in
South Sudan
CHERRY LEONARDI

The Quest for Socialist Utopia
BAHRU ZEWDE

Disrupting Territories
JÖRG GERTEL, RICHARD ROTTEN-
BURG & SANDRA CALKINS (EDS)

The African Garrison State
KJETIL TRONVOLL
& DANIEL R. MEKONNEN

The State of Post-conflict Reconstruction
NASEEM BADIEY

Gender, Home & Identity
KATARZYNA GRABSKA

Remaking Mutirikwi
JOOST FONTEIN

Lost Nationalism
ELENA VEZZADINI

The Oromo & the Christian Kingdom of
Ethiopia
MOHAMMED HASSEN

Darfur
CHRIS VAUGHAN

The Eritrean National Service
GAIM KIBREAB

Ploughing New Ground*
GETNET BEKELE

Hawks & Doves in
Sudan's Armed Conflict*
SUAD MUSA

*forthcoming

The Eritrean National Service

Servitude
for 'the Common Good'
and the Youth Exodus

GAIM KIBREAB

JAMES CURREY

James Currey
is an imprint of Boydell & Brewer Ltd
PO Box 9, Woodbridge, Suffolk IP12 3DF (GB)
www.jamescurrey.com

and of

Boydell & Brewer Inc.
668 Mt Hope Avenue, Rochester, NY 14620-2731 (US)
www.boydellandbrewer.com

British Library Cataloguing in Publication Data
A catalogue record for this book is available from the British Library

ISBN 978-1-84701-160-2 (James Currey cloth)

Typeset in 10 on 12 pt Cordale with Gill Bold display
by Kate Kirkwood Publishing Services

In memory of those who fled the indefinite national service in search of a dignified life, but perished en route.

And I have to also mention my brave daughter, Reema, who spent the previous year travelling the world alone and gaining invaluable life experience and the type of autonomy that could never be matched. YOU MAKE ME PROUD! ☺

Contents

List of Figures and Tables   x
Foreword by Professor Christopher Clapham   xi
Acknowledgements   xii
List of Acronyms & Abbreviations   xiv

1 Introduction   1

The Goals of the Eritrean National Service: Origins and Rationale/s   2
Outline of the Structure of the Book   3
Methodological Procedures of Data-Gathering   6
The ENS: A Synopsis   11
The Common Good and the ENS   15
The Rationales of the ENS   17
The Magnitude of the ENS   19

2 National/Military Service in Africa: Theories and Concepts   22

National/Military Service: The Highest Good and Fountain of Virtue   23
War, Solidarity and Social Capital   26
Compulsory Military/National Service: The Antithesis of   28
   a Free Society
The Institution of National/Military Service in Africa   33

3 The Government and the Structure of   36
the Eritrean Defence Force

National Service and Preparation for War   44
National Service and the Border War   47
The Narratives of Conscripts   49

4 The Nature of the Eritrean National Service and   52
its Effectiveness as a Fighting Force

Indefinite Nature of Service   55
Coercion, Indefinite Service and Flight Propensity   60

Indefinite Service without Remuneration   64
Mismanagement   66
The ENS: Mechanism of Enrichment   67
The Impact of the Conflicts between *Yikealo* and the *Warsai*   69
    on Defence Capability

5 The Eritrean National Service as a Mechanism of Preserving   75
**   and Transmitting the Core Values of the Liberation Struggle**

Conscription as a Vehicle of Homogenisation and   84
    National Integration
Political Socialisation as Opposed to Political Education   86
The ENS as a Mechanism of Transmission and Preservation   88
    of Core Values: Deserters' Narratives
Vices Learned in the ENS and the WYDC   91

6 The Eritrean National Service: A Vehicle for National Unity   94
**   and Cohesion**

National Service: A Form of Mass Mobilisation against   98
    Imagined Foreign Threat
The ENS: Instrument of National Integration   99
The ENS: Mechanism of National Unity and Cohesion: 100
    Respondents' and Informants' Perceptions
Dissenting Opinions   109

7 The Eritrean National Service and Forced Equality   112

Respondents' Perceptions as to whether the ENS Ensured Equality   116
      among Conscripts
Equality, Religion and Women's Participation in the ENS   118
The ENS, Wealth, Class and Corruption   120
From Badge of Honour to Unbearable Burden   126

8 The Overarching Impact of the Eritrean National Service   128
**   on the Social Fabric of Eritrean Society**

The Impact of the ENS on the Country   128
Sexual Violence   132
Militarisation and Securitisation of Education   135
The Plight of Deserters and Draft Evaders   141
Mistreatment of Eritrean Asylum-Seekers in Israel and Remittance   144
Asylum and the Eritrean Diaspora   145

9 Impact of the Open-Ended Eritrean National Service on   153
**   Families and Conscripts**

Dissenting Minority Voices   175

10 Conclusion   177

The Building of Eritrea's Defence and Fighting Capability   177
Preservation and Transmission of the Core Values of the   180
    Liberation Struggle
Fostering National Unity   183
Promotion of Equality   186
Overarching Impact on the Social Fabric of the Polity   188

Postscript: The UK Upper Tribunal (Immigration and Asylum
    Chamber) Country Guidance on Eritrea   191
References   193
Index   209

List of Figures and Tables

Figures
1   Map of Eritrea & the Sawa Mililtary Camp   13

Tables
4.1 Total number of Eritrean asylum-seekers and refugees in the   59
    EU+ countries 2008–2015
6.1 Friendships among conscripts (by ethnicity)   107
6.2 Friendships among conscripts (by religion)   107
6.3 Friendships among conscripts (by region)   108
7.1 Prevalence of corruption in Eritrea, 2005–2015   122

Foreword

In this important and innovative book, Gaim Kibreab examines one of the most secretive states in the world, Eritrea, through the prism provided by its system of 'national service', which subjects a very large proportion of the population, and especially the youth, to an indefinite period under the control of the state. Drawing both on the analysis of reports in the country's state-controlled media, and especially on interviews with a large and varied number of refugees who have – at the risk of their lives – fled from Eritrea, he is able to provide an insight into many aspects of Eritrean life that have hitherto evaded the attention of researchers. In many ways, the findings of the study confirm what might have been expected. Even though two of the key objectives of national service have been to strengthen the country's defensive capabilities and promote its economic development – its official title is the 'Warsai-Yikealo Development Campaign' – the actual effects have been quite the opposite. An army of disgruntled conscripts is unable to replicate the heroism and sense of purpose that drove the epic liberation struggle that culminated in Eritrea's independence in 1991, while the impact on 'development' has been disastrous. Particularly important here is the impact on subsistence agriculture and the complex survival mechanisms that have enabled families to spread their risks in an extremely uncertain environment. The gender equality that characterised the liberation struggle has given way to the widespread exploitation of women within the national service system. Yet it is a tribute to the professionalism of the research – in a field often marked by a high level of partisanship on either side – that the author shows how some of the objectives of national service have been achieved. In particular, it has indeed served to promote an enhanced level of national identity and helped to bridge ethnic and religious differences within a country with nine distinct ethnic groups, divided roughly equally between Christianity and Islam. This is ground-breaking research, essential to the understanding of modern Eritrea, and with much to teach us beyond its boundaries.

Christopher Clapham
Centre of African Studies, University of Cambridge

Acknowledgements

This research project has spanned nearly two decades and benefitted from the generosity and wealth of knowledge and experiences of a large number of people. I corresponded with and interviewed many people, too many to name in the book. Given the state of fear and risk permeating present day Eritrea, a substantial proportion of the respondents and key informants interviewed for the study, including many in the diaspora, do no want to be identified by name. I thank them warmly just the same. I hope their voices are presented clearly and loudly in the book. Without their help, this book would have never seen the light of day.

Samuel Gebrehiwet was always ready and willing to provide any information I asked of him and patiently answered what must have seemed an unending stream of questions. Mihret Haile and he opened their house to me and welcomed me as kin. In no small way, this book owes its existence to them. Dr David Styan has heard a good deal about this book and has read some of the chapters and made very useful if not always gentle comments. Our daughter, Fanus, an English Literature student at Durham University, has read the whole manuscript and advised me to learn how to write short sentences. Even though I am aware of the proverb that 'old habits die hard', I have promised her to try. I owe a debt of gratitude to Professor Christopher Clapham, who in spite of his tight schedule wrote the foreword to this book. Hannah/Azieb Pool/Asrat has read and edited Chapter 1. She also used her dense social network to find a suitable photo for the cover of the book. Without her help, this would have been impossible. It is comforting to have a cousin who is always ready and willing to help.

I owe a big thank you to Fessehaye Solomon, Dawit Fessehaye, Abdella Adem, Solomon Noray, Zerai Gebrehiwet, Elias Mewes Chine, Moges Berhane, Yohannes Berhe, Ellien Haile, Efrem Ariaia, Aster Gebreselasse, Isaias Tsegai, Kemal Ibrahim, Asefaw Gebrekidan, Suleiman Hussein, Salah Aboray, Selam Kidane, Laurie Lijenders, Kahsai Habtay, Woldegebriel Kidane, Merhawi Habtay, Bereket Kidane, Selam Gebrehiwet, Tesfalem Araya, Kidane Tuku, Medhanie Kifletsion, Kflehans Teweldebrhan (Gordm) and Isaac Kiflay. A debt of gratitude is due to Dr Mebrahtu Atewebrhan for drawing the map of the Sawa Military training camp. Nadia Imtiaz undertook the unenviable task of collating and checking the references and painstakingly reading the whole manuscript. Melany Wagestroom has carefully formatted the whole manuscript and I am grateful to her.

The two anonymous reviewers have provided some useful comments and suggestions, which have helped me to prepare the final copy. I acknowledge a debt of gratitude. Last but by no means least; I would like to thank my Commissioning Editor, Jaqueline Mitchell, for her detailed and highly constructive help. A debt of gratitude is also due to the Managing Editor, Lynn Taylor.

In spite of all the assistance and encouragement generously provided, I remain entirely responsible for all the shortcomings as well as the views expressed.

Acronyms & Abbreviations

Agelglot	National service conscripts
AI	Amnesty International
BBC	British Broadcasting Corporation
COI reports	Country of Origin reports
EDF	Eritrean Defence Force
ELF	Eritrean Liberation Front
ELM	Eritrean Liberation Movement
ENS	Eritrean National Service
EPLA	Eritrean People's Liberation Army
EPLF	Eritrean People's Liberation Front
EPRDF	Ethiopian People's Revolutionary Democratic Front
FAO	Food and Agriculture Organisation
G-15	Fifteen leading members of the ruling Front who issued an open letter in May 2001 accusing the President of acting illegally. Eleven of them have been held in unknown place without being charged since 18 September 2001
Gedli	Liberation struggle
HRW	Human Rights Watch
IMF	International Monetary Fund
NUEW	National Union of Eritrean Women
NYSC	Nigerian Youth Service Corps
PFDJ	People's Front for Democracy and Justice
PGE	Provisional Government of Eritrea
PLF	People's Liberation Forces
Tegadalai (sing.)	Freedom fighter
Tegadelti (plu.)	Freedom fighters
UNDP	United Nations Development Programme
UNHCR	United Nations High Commissioner for Refugees
UNICEF	United Nations Children's Fund
Warsai	Inheritor of the core values of the liberation struggle
WFP	World Food Programme
WYDC	Warsai-Yikealo Development Campaign
Yikealo	Former combatants (to whom nothing is impossible)

I

Introduction

People are so docile right now. It is almost as if good government means when the politicians lie to us for our own good, for the public good...

James Bovard

The Eritrean National Service (ENS) constitutes the nerve centre of post-independence Eritrean polity without which it is difficult to understand and analyse the causes of the successes and failures of the Grand National projects, such as nation building, nurturing of national unity and common Eritrean national identity, post-conflict (re)construction and the building of efficient defence capability. During the liberation struggle, also called the thirty years' war (1961–1991), the idea of 'the common good' in which individual interests were sacrificed in pursuit of the grand cause – independence – was the single most important lynchpin. Its pursuit created a politically and socially acceptable moral justification for the sacrifice of individual interests.

Although the war ended, the ENS continued and has become open-ended; though intended as a common good, it has degenerated into indefinite forced labour or a modern form of slavery. Consequently, thousands of citizens are forcibly held in endless servitude against their will, under the threat of severe punishment. It affects every aspect of the country's economic, social and political situation, as well as the lives of hundreds of thousands of households and conscripts.

There has not, to date, been any in-depth and critical scrutiny of the ENS's achievements and failures. There is also a dearth of data on its overarching impacts on the social fabric of Eritrean polity. This book is a partial attempt to fill the lacunae. The main aim of this book is to examine the extent to which the stated goals of the 'national service', as stipulated in the proclamation on the ENS, various government policy declarations and practices, have been, or are in the process of being, achieved. Unlike other wide-ranging national service programmes discussed briefly in the book, in which the main focus is on citizenship, independence, equality, responsibility and participation, in Eritrea the main emphasis has been on control, loyalty and service. Since 2004, hundreds of thousands of young men and women have fled the country, risking their lives in order to disentangle themselves from an indefinite state of entrapment.

The other core purposes of the book are to: state the goals and objectives of the ENS; discuss briefly the historical backdrop to it; provide the rationale/s underlying the programme; examine the national service's transformative effects, as well as its impact on the country's defence capability, national unity, national identity construction and nation building. It also examines the extent to which it is able to function as an effective mechanism of preserving and transmitting the core values of the liberation struggle to the *warsai* (conscripts). The impact of the national service on the social fabric and livelihood systems of the society, families and conscripts are also critically examined. Equally, the book aims to give voice to the voiceless conscripts who are forced to serve indefinitely without remuneration and against their will under the menace of punishments.

THE GOALS OF THE ERITREAN NATIONAL SERVICE (ENS): ORIGINS AND RATIONALE/S

Proclamation No. 11/1991 on the ENS was among the first proclamations enacted by the Provisional Government of Eritrea (PGE). It was enacted soon after the Eritrean People's Liberation Front (EPLF) seized power by throwing out the Ethiopian forces of occupation from the country on 24 May 1991. The fact that the PGE enacted the proclamation on national service before the country's future was to be determined in a referendum nearly two years later shows the extent to which the compulsory, but then not yet universal, national service was perceived as a critical instrument of national unity, nation building and post conflict national (re)construction.

All Eritreans – women and men – between the ages of eighteen and forty are required to perform national service.[1] However a few categories were exempt from national service, and three categories of people could gain exemption, subject to meeting the required criteria. Proclamation No 11/1991 was repealed in November 1995, 18 months after its implementation, and replaced by Pro. No 82/1995. The latter abolished all exceptions stipulated in the first proclamation on national service and turned the compulsory national service into an almost universal obligation. After 1995 only veterans of the thirty years' war (1961–1991) of independence were exempted.[2] Those who are declared unfit mentally and/or physically by the Board[3] established by the government are exempted from military training, but are required to perform national service 'in any public or government organ according to their capacity.'[4] Even when they complete the required eighteen months service they will continue to have the compulsory duty to serve according to their capacity

---

[1]   See Article 2 of the National Service Proclamation 11/1991; Article 8 of the National Service Proclamation 82/1995.
[2]   Art. 12 (2) Proc. 82/1995.
[3]   Art 11 (3) Proc. 82/1995
[4]   Art.13 (1) Proc. 82/1995.

until they reach fifty years of age.[5] The universality of the ENS is clear from these provisions. Even conscientious objectors such as Jehovah's Witnesses are forcibly conscripted in violation of the canons of their faith (AI 2004).

Although the first proclamation on the ENS was enacted in 1991 primarily to overcome widespread youth unemployment, military training was implemented for the first time in 1994. Prior to 1994, students at secondary and university levels took part in summer development work programmes without taking military training (Kibreab 2008, 2009b). The ENS consists of six months military training at the Sawa Military Camp and twelve months participation in development work[6] under the auspices of the Ministry of Defence or other ministries, regional administrations or the firms of the ruling party. During the first six months, all conscripts receive intensive military and physical training. All citizens who complete the required eighteen months of active national service also 'have the compulsory duty of service until the age of 50.'[7]

The objectives of the ENS according to Proclamation No 82/1995 are to:

(1) establish a strong Defence Force...to ensure a free and sovereign Eritrea;
(2) preserve and entrust [to] future generations the courage and resoluteness, heroic episodes shown by the people in the past thirty years;
(3) create a new generation characterised by love of work, [and] discipline ready to participate and serve in the reconstruction of the nation;
(4) develop and strengthen the economy of the nation by investing in development work...;
(5) develop professional capacity and physical fitness by giving regular military training and continuing practice to participants in Training Centres; and
(6) foster national unity among our people by eliminating sub-national feelings.[8]

One of the central aims of the book is to examine the extent to which some of the goals are achieved or are in the process of being fulfilled.

OUTLINE OF THE STRUCTURE OF THE BOOK

Having stated the aims and objectives of the book, this introductory chapter will now present the goals and structures of the national service. It will then describe the structure of the book and the methodological procedures used for data gathering. The chapter also provides some initial

---

[5] Art. 13 (2) Proc. 82/1995.
[6] *Ibid.*
[7] Art. 23 (2) Proc. 82/1995
[8] Article 5, Pro. No. 82/1995 (Published in the *Eritrean Gazette* No.11 of 23 October 1995).

historical and contextual background to the ENS, including its rationale, as well as its magnitude. Chapter 2 then presents different theories on national service and the philosophical perspectives which, on the one hand, view compulsory national service as being the highest good or fountain of virtue and on the other, as being the antithesis of a free society and a form of forced labour or a modern form of slavery. Chapters 3 to 9 draw on original data from research interviews with former conscripts who deserted from the national service after serving on average six years rather than the eighteen months required by the law on national service in the country.

Chapter 3 examines the relationship between the government and the military and the extent to which the former's constant interference has stifled the development of an institutionalised and professionalised military which serves the interest of the state and the polity rather than the government of the day. Based on the narratives of former conscripts, Chapter 4 examines the extent to which the ENS has built the country's defence or fighting capability. If the evidence suggests otherwise an attempt is made to identify the constraints on building effective defence and fighting capability. The chapter also examines the extent to which the institution of national service (which, due to its open-ended and compulsory nature, has forced tens of thousands of conscripts to 'vote with their feet' in search of opportunities for a livelihood and international protection against forced labour) is able to contribute to the building of Eritrea's defence and fighting capability. Inasmuch as the contribution of the ENS on Eritrea's defence capability is to a large extent influenced by the degree of professionalism, technical capability and autonomy of the Eritrean military, the chapter examines the constraints on the development of an effective system of defence in the country.

Chapter 5 examines the extent to which the national service preserves and transmits the core values developed during the liberation struggle to the present generation, the *warsai*. It also discusses the impact of war fought against an external enemy on internal solidarity and on citizens' willingness to serve and sacrifice their lives in the service of the nation. In view of the fact that the former combatants, the *yikealo*, are perceived by the Eritrean government to be the repository and conduit of the core values engendered during the liberation struggle, the chapter assumes that their ability to transmit these values to the *warsai* is to a large extent dependent on the nature of their relationship with the latter. The chapter therefore devotes considerable space to examining the relationship between the *yikealo* and the *warsai* and how this affects the process of transmission of the values and norms of the liberation struggle. The chapter also identifies the virtues and vices the conscripts developed and internalised in the process of participating in the national service. Some abuses unrelated to the aims and objectives of the ENS, such as exploitation of conscripts' labour power for commanders' personal gain and how these corrupt activities and practices reduce the effectiveness of the ENS to preserve and transmit the core values produced during the liberation struggle, are also discussed.

Based on the former conscripts' perceptions, Chapter 6 discusses the extent to which the ENS functions as a vehicle for national unity and social cohesion. In view of the fact that Eritrea is a multi-faith and multi-ethnic polity, it examines whether the national service has enabled the conscripts who hail from disparate ethno-linguistic, religious and regional backgrounds to bond across the social cleavages of religion, ethnicity and region on the basis of shared values and secular national Eritrean identity. The chapter also discusses the factors that enhance national unity and trans-cultural understanding, such as enhanced knowledge of different places and communities in the course of performing national service, and the development of trans-ethnic, trans-religious and trans-regional friendships among the conscripts. Some space is also devoted to the dissenting opinion of a few respondents concerning whether the ENS promotes national unity and social cohesion.

Chapter 7 examines the extent to which the national service is executed with equality independent of religion, sex, ethnicity, class, wealth, power and family connections. The chapter also examines the prevalence of corruption and the extent to which it is possible to buy oneself out of national service and/or to influence the decision concerning location of assignment in the post-six-month military training at Sawa.

Chapter 8 examines in detail the impact of the national service on the social fabric of Eritrean society and the government. Drawing on the perceptions of respondents and in-depth interviews with key informants and on studies conducted by United Nations agencies, the International Monetary Fund, the World Bank, the African Development Bank and independent analysts, the chapter assesses the overarching impact of the national service on all aspects of Eritrean society. The extent of the militarisation of Eritrean polity and the securitisation of the educational system are also discussed in the chapter. In view of the fact that the former conscripts, in spite of their common experience at Sawa and after, do not speak with a single voice, the chapter also considers the dissenting opinion of a few respondents. Eritrean society is socially, economically and politically differentiated and therefore it is unrealistic to expect that the service would affect all citizens in the same way irrespective of their connections to the corridors of power and wealth. The chapter therefore attempts to identify the winners and losers. It also briefly discusses the plight of the conscripts who suffer at the hands of ruthless traffickers and smugglers en route to Israel via eastern Sudan and the Sinai desert, as well as to the EU+ countries through Ethiopia, Sudan, the Sahara, Libya and the Mediterranean Sea.

Chapter 9 presents an in-depth analysis of the impacts of the ENS on the livelihoods of families, and conscripts' careers, survival and wellbeing. Further, the dissenting opinions of a few respondents who see the ENS as the ultimate good and worth sacrificing one's own and one's family's present and future interests are considered briefly.

The main findings of the book are presented in Chapter 8.

METHODOLOGICAL PROCEDURES OF DATA-GATHERING

The data on which this book is based are derived from diverse sources. A detailed questionnaire comprising of 117 questions was administered to 190 respondents.[9] The ethnic composition of the respondents is as follows: Afar (1.1 per cent), Saho (4.7 per cent), Tigre (15 per cent), Tigrinya (64 per cent) and Blin (15 per cent). Among the 190 respondents, 30 per cent are Muslims. Among the respondents, 27 per cent were female and 73 per cent male. Of the total, 7 per cent, 30 per cent, 36 per cent, 24 per cent and 4 per cent, respectively were under 25 years, 26–30 years, 31–35 years, 36–40 years, and 41–45 years. Among the 190 respondents, 55 per cent, 37 per cent, 4 per cent, 3.2 per cent, respectively were single, married, divorced and cohabiting. Among them, another thirty-eight key informants were interviewed in depth. Of the latter, ten were Muslims, excluding the seven family members on whom information was acquired and eleven were female.

Researching Eritrea is not an easy undertaking. This is, *inter alia*, due to government restrictions on independent research activities and travel restrictions on foreigners and independent-minded researchers outside of Asmara, without which no meaningful fieldwork is conceivable. This is exacerbated by the dearth of research-based and official publications on the prevailing socio-economic reality of the country (see for example Reid 2009). Under these circumstances, there are no opportunities for empirical research in the country (see Hirt and Mohammad 2013). The restriction on research does not only apply to rural areas, but also throughout the country, including in the urban centres. It is not only foreigners who are unable to undertake research in urban and rural Eritrea, but all independent-minded Eritreans within and outside of the country who do not work under the auspices of the ruling party or the government are unable to obtain research permits. The process of application and approval of research permits, even for those who reside in the country, is highly securitised and restricted.

The problem of sources in the country is eloquently described in a brief report of the Norwegian Country of Origin Information (COI) Centre (Landinfo) (2015) that states:

> It is very difficult to uncover facts about the social conditions in Eritrea, including National Service. Until recently, the government has not published information on the conditions of national service, the number of conscripts in service [...] Therefore most of the information on National Service comes from statements from Eritreans who have left the country or consists of anecdotal information passed on to representatives of the international community in Asmara. [...] The majority of our sources are anonymous at their [informants'] request. The disadvantage of anonymous sources is [...] readers cannot verify whether or not the sources and information are reliable.

Norwegian Country of Origin Information Centre continues:

[9]   The term respondent refers to those who were interviewed in the survey and key informant refers to those who were selected systematically for an in-depth interview.

> Another problem Landinfo [the team from the Norwegian Country of Origin Information Centre] experienced [in obtaining information about] Eritrea is the likelihood of 'round tripping' or false confirmations, i.e. two sources say the same thing which seemingly confirm certain information when really they are referencing the same source. This can occur because there are few independent international sources in Eritrea. *The international community in the country is quite small and representatives Landinfo met with over the years have been up front about the fact that much of the information they share is not fact-based, but are points of view and sometimes speculation.* (2015: 5, emphasis added)

This honest revelation is edifying. Notwithstanding this fact, some of the so-called fact-finding missions, by organisations such as the Danish Immigration Service (2014) and the UK Home Office (2015), present these 'round-tripped' or 'false confirmations' as facts and as a basis for policy change. Not only do Landinfo's insightful and honest observations indicate the extent of the inaccessibility of sources, but they also demonstrate that COI reports based on data gathered from interviews with diplomats, government and other informants in the country, where the opportunity to scrutinise, interrogate and countercheck the information gathered openly and transparently is impossible, is of insignificant value. In spite of the potential weaknesses in the quality of data gathered from Eritreans who have fled or left the country, under the present repressive political system in the country there is no other better option. Although it is important to acknowledge the weaknesses of the data gathered from conscripts who have fled the country in search of protection and a better life, if the necessary measures are taken to countercheck the different sources against each other, the risk of collecting inaccurate or wrong information may be minimised or avoided.

The data on which this study is based are derived from diverse sources. In Eritrea the introduction of new policies, no matter how profoundly significant, is seldom preceded by a debate, as is commonly practiced in democratic societies. For example, in the UK the publication of white papers (final policy) is sometimes preceded by publication of a green paper in the process of consultation and debate, intended to inform the public in order to reach general understanding and consensus. In Eritrea this is never the case. However, more often than not, the introduction of new policies is preceded or accompanied by in-depth interviews conducted by journalists working for the government and PFDJ-owned TV station, radio, newspapers, magazines and websites, with the personal ruler, Isaias Afwerki, the former Defence Minister, Sebhat Ephrem, and army commanders. These vital sources include Eri TV, *Dimtsi Hafash*, Hadas Eritra, *Eritrea Profile, Hidri, Sagem, Hiwyet, Ta'atek, shaebia.com* and *shabait.com*. These sources are indispensable for anyone writing on post-independence Eritrea. The aim of most of the interviews is to inform and ensure public compliance rather than to encourage debate and to arrive at a general consensus.

Nearly all of these interviews are in Tigrinya, save a few of the press statements translated into English and published on *Shabait*.com, the ruling party's website, and in the government's English newspaper, *Eritrea Profile*. Sebhat Ephrem's many and detailed interviews, some of them lasting up to eight hours at a time, published in the Defence Ministry's magazine, *Te'ateq* (Be Ready), are indispensable sources on the ENS. *Ta'ateq* also occasionally interviews the President and the military commanders at Sawa, especially during inductions and graduation ceremonies. I have used these sources extensively while researching this book.

In order to update the data, I have interviewed deserters in Geneva and London who left Eritrea in 2015. I have also conducted in-depth interviews with ten former EPLF combatants in the last five years who currently reside in the UK. The data gathered from the latter have been useful for comparative purposes. All the names of the people I have interviewed for this study have been changed to ensure anonymity and their safety. Whenever this was deemed inadequate their characteristics have been altered. Muslim, Christian, female and male names indicate the religion and sex of interviewees.

I would have been unable to gather all the data I needed to write this book had it not been for the wealth of data derived from interviews with the President, the Defence Minister and the commanders at Sawa military camp published in government and party owned newspapers, magazines and websites. This task would have also been very difficult, if not impossible, to accomplish if Tigrinya were not my mother tongue.

This book attempts to provide a qualitative understanding of the ENS, which, besides sinking hundreds of thousands of Eritrean households into abject poverty, has been an important driver of forced migration in post-independence Eritrea. By utilising structured and semi-structured interviews and by scrutinising primary sources such as policy documents, newspapers, pamphlets, and interviews and speeches of government officials, especially, as noted earlier, the Head of State, Isaias Afwerki, the chief architect of the national service, as well as the former minister of defence, Sebhat Ephrem, the book examines the extent to which the stated goals of the ENS have been, or are in the process of being, achieved. Some of the data are derived from interviews with those who are directly affected by the national service. These data are also supplemented and enriched by data generated from in depth interviews conducted with systematically selected key informants who prior to their flight had served in the ENS for an average of six and a half years.

In the course of researching for the book, I have also gained in-depth insights into the organisational structure and leadership of the Eritrean military, as well as the factors that previously motivated the combatants, the *yikealo*, during the liberation struggle; furthermore, I have gained a greater understanding of the changes and transformations they have undergone in the post-independence period and the extent to which these changes constrain their ability to maintain and transmit the core values they internalised in the liberation struggle to the *warsai* (conscripts). It is not suggested here that the quality of the data and the methods of data gathering are free of weaknesses. In an ideal world, the quality and reliability of the data would have been substantially improved had it been possible to replicate the study inside Eritrea to compare and contrast the two data sets. Unfortunately, this is not possible under the prevailing political, human rights circumstances and the severe restrictions on research in the country.

The idea of random sampling was ruled out from the outset because there was no sampling frame from which a representative sample could be drawn. Post-independence Eritrean asylum-seekers and refugees are scattered all over the world and are permanently on the move. For example, in 2011 they lived in eighty-five countries,[10] and it was impossible to use a representative sample that reflected accurately the characteristics of the total population. Methods include the survey method in which structured and self-completed questionnaires written in English and Tigrinya (an Arabic translation was abandoned because all ENS participants were fluent in Tigrinya or English) comprising open and closed-ended questions, were administered to respondents selected on the basis of chain referral or snowball sampling. This was supplemented by unstructured in-depth interviews conducted with systematically selected individuals guided by an inventory of issues; focus group interviews; interviews with key informants; narrative analysis; personal histories; and government policy documents. President Isaias Afwerki's and Sebhat Ephrem's (former Defence Minister) numerous interviews in the Eritrean mass media, including state owned television, and magazines of the ruling party and the Ministry of Defence, nearly all of them in Tigrinya, are indispensable sources. Without delving into such rich Tigrinya sources in detail, it would have been difficult, if not impossible, to gain in-depth insights and understanding of the rationales, meanings, aims, objectives and philosophy underlying the ENS.

In situations where no sampling frame exists or is difficult to create (this is generally the case in studies concerning refugees and asylum-seekers), the snowball sampling approach has been widely used by social scientists, especially in the area of hard to reach and deviant populations (see Bryman 2008). The population covered in the study is neither hard to reach nor deviant, but is scattered and hard to recruit. Alan Bryman, the author of the acclaimed book *Social Research Methods*, used snowball sampling in his study of Disney theme park visitor because of the lack of an accessible sampling frame. By the same token, the only feasible approach to the study of Eritrean deserters and draft evaders covered in this study has been snowball sampling. However, the use of this approach has by no means been straightforward. This was because the chain referral method of sampling was far from being a self-propelled process as once it was initiated it did not proceed smoothly. The success of the approach depended on active and deliberate engagement of the researcher and his assistants who organised, developed and controlled the sample's initiation and progress throughout the process. For a variety of reasons, including fear of the Eritrean state and its agents, and others which for lack of space cannot be presented here,[11] at the initial stage, the general tendency among potential respondents has been to say 'no' to being interviewed or included in the survey.

---

[10] UNHCR, Statistical Online Population Database.
[11] This will be presented in detail in a forthcoming work.

After undertaking an exploratory pilot study, it became clear that unless well-connected locators with easy access to potential respondents in their respective residential areas and cities were selected, the research project was unlikely to succeed. The locators were selected carefully, taking into account their gender, religion, ethnicity, political views, social positions in their respective communities, past experiences, connections through multiple and dense webs of networking, educational status and reputations. Not only did the locators develop referral chains but, more importantly, they spent an immense amount of time convincing and reassuring each potential respondent that the process was totally anonymous and the whole *raison d'être* of the study was academic and intended, *inter alia*, to advance knowledge and understanding of the different aspects of the national service and the Warsai-Yikealo Development Campaign (WYDC), including the plight of conscripts and their families, as well as their positive and negative effects on the Eritrean economy and society. The locators were already known to the author and were selected on the basis of strict criteria that included consideration of ethnic and religious identities and political affiliations and/or views. The purpose of such criteria was to ensure inclusion of women and men, different levels of education, ethnic and faith groups, as well as individuals representing an array of political views.[12] The central aim of the methodological procedure was, as far as possible, to include respondents, which in qualitative, if not, statistical terms might indicate the general characteristics of the subjects of the study.

As indicated earlier, a sample drawn up using a snowball sampling approach is unlikely to be representative of the whole population and, as a result, the findings of the survey are indicative rather than conclusive. Although this study has been underpinned by such an assumption, it is worth noting that there are specialists who emphasise the relevance of the snowball sampling approach to quantitative research. For example, referring to Coleman's classical work, Alan Bryman, after discussing the limitations of data gathered using snowball sampling, states: 'This is not to suggest that snowball sampling is entirely irrelevant to quantitative research: when the researcher needs to focus upon or to reflect relationships between people, tracing connections through snowball sampling may be a better approach than conventional probability sampling' (2008: 185). In our case, it is due to lack of choice that the snowball sampling approach has been used, but, although contested, this approach is commonly used in the study of unstable and mobile populations, such as refugees, asylum-seekers and internally displaced people (IDPs). Nevertheless, given the relative homogeneity of participants of the ENS and WYDC, the survey data may indicate, albeit not conclusively, the general characteristics of the population. Alice Bloch argues that sampling frames may exist for sub-groups residing in settlements or camps, but not in countries of settlements: 'The consequence of the paucity of data on refugees and asylum-seekers from which to sample is that surveys are usually based

---

[12] The identity and other details of the locators are withheld as agreed with them.

on non-probability techniques and are almost always reliant on access to refugees through community-based organisations [...] or pre-existing contacts from which to snowball sample' (Bloch 2007: 233). But there are other analysts who call for a return to traditional sampling methods without offering an effective solution to the dilemma of dearth of sampling frame (Jacobsen and Landau 2003).

In this study the chain referral sampling method was used to select respondents in the UK, Switzerland, Sweden, Norway, South Africa and Kenya in 2012.[13] For no other reason than convenience and consideration for cost and time, the large majority of the respondents are in the UK. There is also no particular reason why 190 respondents rather than 200 or 300 were interviewed. It is important to state that although the data derived from the structured questionnaire are important, other qualitative methods of data gathering used in the study have also resulted in a vast amount of useful data, which informs the arguments in the overall research project.

Given the paucity of data, this study addresses the research question on the basis of perceptions of former conscripts who fled Eritrea, first to seek asylum in Ethiopia and Sudan, and later moving on to Kenya, South Africa, United Kingdom, Switzerland, Sweden and Norway after serving in the ENS/WYDC for an average of about six years. The data based on the experiences and subjective perceptions of the respondents should be read bearing the following caveat in mind: the respondents, in spite of their experiences, do not speak in a single voice. In order to do justice to their diverse voices and to maintain the authenticity of their voices their narratives are presented verbatim as far as possible.

THE ENS: A SYNOPSIS

The synopsis of the ENS is preceded with a succinct historical background to the provisional government of Eritrea (PGE). After Ethiopia's defeat, a provisional government of Eritrea (PGE) was established and, after an interim period of two years, a national referendum was held 23–25 May 1993, in which 99.9 per cent of the population voted in favour of independence (see Styan 1996). In May 1993 Eritrea became a member of the United Nations as an independent state and a government was formed, pursuant to Proclamation No. 37/1993 published on 19 May 1993 (see Provisional Government of Eritrea 1993). The proclamation stipulated that the government was to comprise three branches: (a) legislature known as 'National Assembly,' (b) executive known as 'Cabinet of Ministers,' and (c) a judiciary.[14] The National Assembly comprises members of the EPLF's Central Council and sixty others. The latter comprised thirty members from the regional assemblies, namely,

---

[13] Twenty-five completed questionnaires from the Sudan arrived late and were not processed, although part of the data in the open questions is used in the discussion.

[14] Article 3 (1[a, b, c]).

the chairmen and secretaries of all the regional assemblies and a female member of each regional assembly elected by the latter. The remaining comprised ten women and twenty other nationals selected by the EPLF's Central Council.[15]

The National Assembly elects the Head of State and the latter is the chairman of the executive and the national assembly (legislature).[16] Because the chairman of the executive is also the chairman of the national assembly, the notion of division of power and the principle of checks and balances were ignored from the outset. In hindsight, it is possible to argue that Proc. No. 37/1993 laid the foundation for one-man rule in the country. It is also worth noting that since then, out of the seventy-five members of the Central Council, eighteen have been arrested, five died in office, seven are in exile and another seven are frozen (Awate Team 2014), that is they have been told to stay at home until further notice (many have been in such a frozen state for more than a decade).

According to Proclamation 37/1993, the maximum duration of the transitional government was to be four years. Nevertheless, the provisional government has been in power for twenty-three years. The PGE established a Constitutional Commission headed by Professor Bereket Habte Selassie and the draft constitution was completed on schedule. It was ratified by a Constituent Assembly in May 1997. However, not only has the president refused to implement the constitution but eighteen years after its ratification, he declared it void on 30 December 2014 (Isaias Afwerki 2014). The elections that were supposed to take place in 1997 and 2001 were never held and no explanation was provided. The border war against Ethiopia that broke out a year after the ratification of the constitution provided a convenient retroactive pretext to the Eritrean government's failure to implement the constitution and hold the promised two elections. Although the book does not delve into this issue, the degeneration of the ENS into forced labour is inextricably linked to the nature of the governance in the country.

The ENS constitutes the nerve centre of post-independence Eritrean polity, without which it is difficult to understand and analyse the causes of the successes and failures of the Grand National projects, such as nation building, nurturing of national unity and common Eritrean national identity; post-conflict (re)construction and building of efficient defence capability. During the liberation struggle (1961–1991), the idea of a common good in which individual interests were sacrificed in pursuit of the grand cause – independence – was the lynchpin. The pursuit of the collective common good created a politically and socially acceptable moral basis, which justified the sacrifice of individual interests. As demonstrated throughout the book, the incumbents have become habituated to making endless demands on citizens at the expense of their own and their families' livelihoods and careers notwithstanding the fact that the country no longer faces an existential threat as was the case during the thirty years' war of independence.

[15] Article 4 (2).
[16] Article 4 (3).

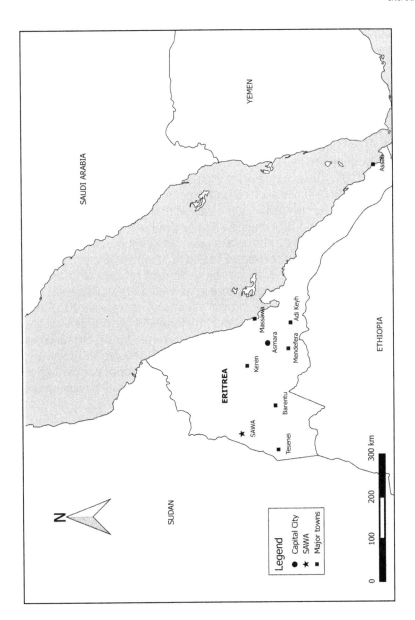

Map 1.1: Map of Eritrea showing the location of the Sawa Military Camp
Source: Dr Mebrahtu Ateweberhan

Although the national service, which over time has become open-ended, affects every aspect of the country's economic, social and political situation, as well as the lives of hundreds of thousands of households and conscripts, hitherto there has been no in-depth and critical scrutiny of its achievements and failures vis-à-vis its goals. There is also dearth of data on its overarching impact on the social fabric of Eritrean polity. This book is a partial attempt to fill the lacunae.

As we shall see throughout the book, when the Provisional Government of Eritrea introduced the ENS soon after the defeat of Ethiopian rule in Eritrea in May 1991, the large majority of the Eritrean people embraced the idea not necessarily because each citizen expected to derive personal gain from it, but because its success was considered to be an ultimate common good for the country and its citizenry. As we shall see later, the Eritrean people's commitment to the national service was not open-ended.

Before delving into the main text of the book, it is necessary to present a general background to the ENS for the benefit of readers who are not familiar with its complexity and structure, as well as the changes it has gone through over time. The first cohorts of conscripts were sent to Sawa military training camp (see Map 1.1) in May–June 1994 at the peak of the malarious rainy season without proper preparation. During the first six months, all conscripts receive the same kind of intensive military and physical training. At the end of the six months, all conscripts are assigned to work in the different ministries, departments, regional governments and the military, namely, the army, the navy and air force. Some are also assigned to work for the firms of the ruling party, the PFDJ, for the remaining twelve months. Before the border war between Eritrea and Ethiopia broke out in May 1998, the Eritrean government complied with the eighteen months duration as stipulated in the proclamation on national service. Accordingly, the first four cohorts that joined the national service before the border war (1998–2000) were demobilised when they completed the required eighteen months.

When the 1998–2000-border war broke out between Eritrea and Ethiopia, the government recalled all those who were demobilised and embarked on extensive nation-wide mobilisation. The intensity of mobilisation varied depending on the level of threat posed by the Ethiopian army. All those who were mobilised during and after the border war were not demobilised unless they were older than fifty-four when they were mobilised during the state of emergency. In May 2002, the government introduced yet another policy known as the WYDC which rendered the national service indefinite and open-ended on the pretext that war might break out at any time in the future and the reconstruction of war-torn economic, social and physical infrastructure of the country required labour intensive development approach. Thus in the overwhelming majority of cases, those who joined the ENS after May 1998 have never been demobilised.

The open-ended service was very unpopular among conscripts and citizens approaching the age of conscription. Consequently, tens of thousands began to flee the country after or before they received call up papers (see Table 4.1, Chapter 4). In order to prevent school leavers from leaving the country to evade participation in the national service, the government introduced a new policy in mid-2003 that required all final year secondary school students to be transferred to the Sawa military training camp in Western Eritrea to complete 12th grade and receive military training simultaneously. Although the national service was supposed to begin at the age of eighteen, the transfer of secondary school students after 11th grade to the military camp meant that many of them were conscripted before reaching that age. The students received military training for the first three months and later combined both military training and secondary education. At the end of the academic year, they were assigned to the military until the results of School Leaving Certificate (matriculation) were announced. Those who succeeded were transferred to the now defunct University of Asmara before it was closed down in 2006 on the alleged grounds that it had become a breeding ground for dissent and protest. After the closure of the University, those who passed the School Leaving Certificate examinations were transferred to the different colleges scattered around the country. Until recently, students in college were part of the armed forces and kept the organisational structure and military discipline that they had experienced at Sawa Military Training Camp. Those who failed the School Leaving Certificate examinations were assigned to the military and to different ministries, departments, regional governments and firms of the ruling party within the framework of the ENS.

Since the most important organising principle underpinning the philosophical foundation of national service in general and the Eritrean national service in particular is the idea of the common good, there follows a brief discussion of the concept.

THE COMMON GOOD AND THE ENS

Generally, the meaning of the concept of the common good is highly contested. Notwithstanding the contestations, however, Amitai Etzioni argues that it '... has survived as a meaningful concept for well over two millennia, and continues to serve as a very significant organising principle of civic and political life' (2015: 1). For Amitai Etzioni, the concept of the common good 'denotes those goods that serve all members of a given community and its institutions, and, as such, includes both goods that serve no identifiable particular group, as well as those that serve members of generations not yet born' (Etzioni 2015). From this perspective, the common good is pursued to serve the interest of all citizens regardless of class, gender, sexual orientation, political opinion, religion or ethnicity.

However, it is not only the meaning of the concept of the common good that is contested, but the question of who defines what constitutes the common good is equally disputed. Some analysts argue that inasmuch as the normative concept of the common good prescribes that all citizens must adhere to a pre-existing 'common way of life' (Kymlicka 1997: 226), it is inimical to a pluralistic democratic society. Barry (1964: 1), for example, argues that 'appeals to the common good are nothing more than a handy smoke-screen employed by political agents to ensure support for their particularistic goals; apart from this merely rhetorical function the concept is too vague to serve any normative role in political discourse.'

There are also those who deny the existence of the common good. Edward Younkins, for example, writes that whatever allegedly constitutes the common good must be good for everyone in the community concerned. The common good 'consists in treating each person as an end and never solely as a means. This simply means respecting the autonomy of each individual' (2000: 49). Younkins further states: 'A proper social system should not force a particular good on a man, nor should it force him to seek the good. It should only maintain the conditions that leave him free to seek it' (Younkins 2000). People contribute to the common good not because they expect to derive any direct personal benefit, but rather because 'they consider it a good that ought to be nurtured. They consider it the right thing to do – by itself, for itself' (Etzioni 2015: 5).

During the liberation struggle in Eritrea, the notion of sacrificial nationalism (on the latter see Hogan 2009, 2014; Bernal 2014) reflected in the readiness and willingness of citizens to lay their lives down for the common good of the country and its citizenry was a norm. This was perceived as the single most important organising principle throughout the liberation struggle. When the country faced an existential threat, the need to sacrifice one's interests and life *n'rebha hager* (in pursuit of the common good) was implicitly embraced by the overwhelming majority of the population. The idea of the common good was perceived as a sacrosanct principle and every worthy citizen should contribute to its promotion and achievement. There was no critical assessment of what constituted the common good. All efforts were exclusively focused on throwing out the enemy from the country. With the benefit of hindsight, it is easy to see that not much forethought was expended on the question of: what happens when the shooting stopped?

Questioning of the official discourse or the conventional wisdom was considered traitorous. As we shall see throughout the book, these trends developed during the war, have persisted in the post-independence period. The leadership's power to make demands on citizens' resources, time and life was a norm during the liberation struggle. Eritreans expected these powers to cease once independence was achieved without realising that the ruler, Isaias Afwerki, and his inner circle's agenda was to run the country as they ran the liberated areas during the war of independence. Herein lies Eritrea's tragedy (see Kibreab 2009a). The open-ended national service, which requires nearly all able-bodied Eritreans to work for the state and the party indefinitely without rumination, only makes sense when conceived in this perspective. The ENS, which was initially destined to bring change and transformation, has become the source of anguish. The majority of Eritreans are no longer willing to pay the price for no return indefinitely. The question of who pays the price and who benefits is on every citizen's lips.

THE RATIONALE FOR ERITREA'S NATIONAL SERVICE

One of the critical factors that decisively determined the outcome of the thirty years' war of independence was the ability of the EPLF leadership to create a highly organised, disciplined, committed and cohesive army with an impressive track record of organisational and fighting capabilities (Habteselasse 2004; Pateman 1990; Connell 1997; Kibreab 2008). What makes the victory of the Eritrean people even more astonishing is that the country is inhabited by disparate ethno-linguistic and multi-faith communities that can be described in the same way Charles Moskos described America, as a nation that 'does not claim solidarity and unity by virtue of a claimed common ancestry or some divine foundation myth' (1988: 9). In light of this, he perceptively contended, '[o]ur cohesion depends upon a civic ideal rather than on primordial loyalties' (1988: 9).

The leaders of the EPLF considered the substantial stock of social capital produced during the thirty years' war, fought against a more populous and stronger enemy, as the single most important factor for the triumphant outcome of the liberation struggle (see Isaias Afwerki 1994, 1995, 2003, 2004; Sebhat Ephrem 1995, 2008). The powerful sense of patriotism, sacrificial nationalism, common national identity, social norms of solidarity, unity and mutual trust were partly the result of the need to stand together against a 'mightier' enemy and partly due to the development of social capital engendered during the liberation struggle (Kibreab 2008).

Notwithstanding the successful outcome of the war, there was no guarantee that the powerful feelings of camaraderie, social cohesion, unity of purpose and mutual trust engendered under conditions of war would necessarily endure *ipso facto* in peace time and once the external enemy was removed (James 1943 [1910]; Carr 1942). As we shall see, the leader of the ruling party, the EPLF (now PFDJ), and Head of State, Isaias Afwerki, the prime architect of the ENS, feared that after the common enemy's removal from the country, not only might the stock of social capital, or the glue that held Eritrean society together during the war, dissipate but also, in the worst case scenario, the society might disintegrate (Afwerki in Kaplan 2003). The Eritrean national service is therefore conceptualised and implemented by its architect as a substitute for war and as a means of promoting national unity and social harmony in the multi-faith and multi-ethnic Eritrean society.

Eritrea, in spite of its small size both in terms of population and geography, is inhabited by nine disparate ethno-linguistic groups, namely, the Afar, Blin, Hedared, Kunama, Nara, Rashaida, Saho, Tigre and Tigrinya. As neighbouring and economically interdependent and competing communities these disparate ethno-linguistic groups sometimes cooperated with each other and sometimes fought against each other in pursuit of common and divergent interests, respectively. Nevertheless, it was during the Italian colonial period (1890–1941) that they were all brought under the same rule for the first time, as was the case with many pre-colonial African societies. Richard Reid (2011) challenges the dominant narrative among Eritrean scholars who assume Eritrean history or identity was the result of Italian colonialism. Although the suffering and exploitation commonly experienced by the different ethno-linguistic groups and the common struggles they waged together to extricate themselves from the yoke of colonial oppression and racism had laid the edifice of the foundation on which the construction of common national Eritrean identity rested, the process of construction of the Eritrean nation and national Eritrean identity were far from complete.

The process that began during the colonial period, and in Reid's view much earlier, was further broadened and deepened during the thirty years' war of liberation in which all Eritreans, setting aside their religious, ethnic and regional differences, fought together single-mindedly against a common external enemy. Had it not been for the ability of the disparate ethno-linguistic groups to set aside their differences, they would have been unable to defeat sub-Saharan Africa's strongest army. In the process of fighting for a common cause, not only did Eritreans bond across the social cleavages of ethnicity, religion, gender, class and region, but they were also able to develop shared values that cemented their unity and led to the development and gradual consolidation of sacrificial nationalism, dedication, and a sense of common purpose and commitment to public causes (Bernal 2014). These core values were viewed by the leadership of the EPLF as the most important factors that determined the successful outcome of the war of independence, as well as being considered indispensable to the process of nation-building and post-conflict (re) construction.

However, when the EPLF assumed state power and began to lay down the rules for governing the country and the people, they were caught unaware by the perceived, or actual, high level of attitudinal differences between the civilian youth, namely, those who grew up and lived in the areas controlled by the Ethiopian government and the fighters of the EPLF, and the populations that lived in the areas they controlled during the liberation struggle. The youth, especially those in cities, were perceived as being too self-interested, individualistic, indulgent, noncommittal, and lacking a powerful sense of nationalism, dedication and common purpose. In the immediate post-independence period, some of my ex-combatant friends referred to them as the 'lost generation' that needed to be salvaged for Eritrea's and their own sake. The task of bridging the alleged gap between the two apparent worlds was, therefore, considered a vital national interest. Reshaping the civilian youth by instilling in them the values of the liberation struggle developed during the thirty years' war was considered a pre-requisite for building a viable and cohesive national community in a multi-faith and multi-ethnic polity.

The ENS was therefore conceived as a grand scheme of social engineering intended to influence and shape popular attitudes and social behaviours by transmitting the values and culture of the liberation struggle to present and future generations. The former EPLF combatants are referred to as the *yikealo*, which in Tigrinya means someone capable of achieving a miracle, and are said to be the repository of the cherished values of the revolution.

Those who participate in the ENS are referred to as *warsai*, which means the heirs of the legacy of the revolution. The *yikealo* are perceived by the EPLF, its successor, the PFDJ, and the government as the incarnation of the treasured values of the revolution, as well as the conduit through which the phenomenal values and character that drive an individual citizen to embrace the moral obligation to serve their nation, even by laying down their lives, are transmitted to the *warsai*. Furthermore, it is assumed that the latter would go on to disseminate the treasured values they inherit from the *yikealo*. In return, in the process of serving in the ENS, the *warsai* are expected to transmit these values to the rest of society via different means, including through the military, families, communities, schools, workplaces, theatres, music, sports, a variety of activities undertaken in pursuit of the common good and through dense social networks developed in the course of training, learning, working and living together at Sawa twenty-four-seven, and thereafter. Consequently, the country, the state, the government, society, families and the *warsai* themselves are expected to benefit not only from increased industrial, agricultural and service production, as well as the development of the infrastructure, but more importantly also from the transformative effects of participation in the service.

The architects of the ENS believe that youth participation fosters common national Eritrean identity and commitment to the project of national unity and nation building, and there is a well thought out philosophy underpinning this approach (see Chapter 2). Although the colonial experience under Italy (1890–1941), British Military Administration (1941–1951) and Ethiopian occupation (1962–1991) had brought the disparate ethno-linguistic and faith groups closer to each other, and this was further deepened during the thirty years' war of independence, the protracted process of nation building and common national identity construction are considered far from complete: the ENS is therefore conceived of as a critical instrument for this. In the following, the goals and structure of the Eritrean national service are presented.

THE MAGNITUDE OF THE ENS

In view of the fact that the ENS has become indefinite and open-ended, in the sense that whoever joins is never allowed to leave, it is important to discuss its magnitude. When considered within the context of Eritrea's small population, which was estimated in 2011 at 5,415,000 (WHO 2013), the proportion of nationals participating in the ENS is significant. Statistics on the total number of conscripts are difficult to come by. However, during the 23rd Round National Service Graduation and 4th Eri-Youth Festival held at Sawa on 13–15 July 2010, the Commander of the Sawa Military training, Colonel Ezra Woldegebriel, said that the total number of conscripts during the last sixteen years (1st to 23rd rounds), namely, between July 1994 and July 2010 was 400,000 (quoted in Shabait

2010).[17] This suggests that, on average, 25,000 are conscripted per year. Since 2010, there have been four rounds. Between July 1994 and July 2013, 475,000 ENS conscripts have graduated from Sawa. The cohorts in the 27th round graduated in July 2014. This brings the total to 500,000. To this must be added those who are rounded up, including those who drop out from the *warsai* school at Sawa, who receive military training at Wi'a, Meiter, Kiloma, Gergera, Himbirti, Gahtelay, Asmara and Hasheferay in Barka. The members of the People's Militia are also trained in the last five sites together with rounded up conscripts. The number of those who are trained in the other sites outside Sawa is large, but their number is unknown.

During the 6th Youth Festival and 27th Round National Service Graduation held on 18 July 2014, the commander of the Sawa military training centre, Colonel Debesai Gide, stated, 'the participants of the 27th round were from eighty-three secondary and seven technical Schools across the nation.' He also stated that they received the set military and academic training, in addition to development activities. Colonel Debesai also stated that about 500,000 youths have participated in national development and national resistance tasks over the past twenty years since the launching of the national service (Shabait 2014).[18] It is not clear whether this figure includes those who received military training at Meiter, Wi'a, Kiloma and other training camps. Without taking into account the substantial number of the *agelglot* who have been fleeing the country, 9.2 per cent of the total population has been conscripted over a period of twenty years (1994–2014). It is important to underscore the fact that the 9.2 per cent of the population tied to the ENS indefinitely is the most productive and the extent of loss to the country's labour force is substantial. In light of the rudimentary nature of the technology in use, labour is the single most important factor of production and hence the cost of the labour power lost to the country's economy and households' livelihoods is by any measure enormous.

Every year about 25,000 youths from all religions, ethnicities, regions, classes and political opinions, and of both sexes, are brought to the Sawa military training camp. An unknown number of youths are also brought to Wi'a, Meiter and Kiloma military training camps where they eat, live and work together, as well as receiving military training and political socialisation in their respective mother-tongue without distinction due to religion, ethnicity or place of origin. At the end of the six months of military training, each cohort tours the whole country on foot, known as *guüzo* (the hike). The aim of this excruciating trek is partly to acquaint

---

[17] 23rd Round National Service Graduate and 4th ERI Youth Festival Officially Opened, 16 July 2010, available at http://www.shabait.com/news/local-news/2465-23rd-round-national-service-graduate-and-4th-eri-youth-festival-officially-opened (last accessed 14 September 2010).

[18] Members of 27th National Service Students back home to their families, 18 July 2014. Available at http://www.shabait.com/news/local-news/17601-members-of-27th-national-service-students-back-home-to-their-families (last accessed 14 September 2010).

the *agelglot* with the diverse geographical features of the country and its cultures, the ways of life of the people and the country, and partly as a rite of passage (on rite of passage see van Gennep 2010[1909]). The long and agonising hike as a rite of passage marks, in the government's conception, the transition of the *agelglot* (conscripts) from their status of fragmented identities and loyalties to a single national Eritrean identity that is expected to constitute the edifice of the foundation on which national unity and social cohesion rest.

After eight months those who complete 12th grade in combination with military training at Sawa and who pass the post-secondary entrance exams (matriculation) are transferred to the different colleges located in different parts of the country whilst remaining in the ENS. The organisational structure of the colleges was originally the same as in the army, but this is gradually changing. The students are regimented in military units, platoons and battalions headed by military commanders. The colleges operate under strict military discipline and non-compliance results in severe punishment and detention (Reid 2008). The majority of the *agelglot,* including those who fail matriculation, are assigned directly to the military (army, naval and air forces). Others are assigned to work in different ministries, departments, regional governments and the enterprises of the ruling party all over the country, including in remote and hard to reach places within the framework of the ENS. Those who are rounded up do not go to the Sawa military training camp, but instead receive military training in Kiloma, Wi'a and Meiter and after six months they are assigned to the military. Regardless of the specific assignments after the six months following military training they all remain within the ENS.

Despite the proclamation on the ENS, that the second phase should last twelve months after the six months of military training, as already mentioned, after the border war between the governments of Eritrea and Ethiopia broke out in May 1998 and following the introduction of the WYDC in May 2002, the ENS has become open-ended (see AI 2004; US Department of State 2011; HRW 2009; Kibreab 2009b, 2013). Those who have not fled abroad to seek asylum are still serving in different capacities within the framework of the open-ended ENS two decades later without being remunerated, save the pittance of pocket money.[19]

---

[19] On 9 January 2016, it was falsely reported on East Afro, a pro-government website, that the conscripts who previously earned 500 Eritrean Nakfa (ERN) would now receive 2,000 ERN (US $83) gross and 1,700 ERN (70 US $) net per month. Those who graduate from the colleges, such as Mai Nefhi, within the ENS will receive 3,500 ERN (US $ 145.8) gross per month. See East Afro, 9 January 2016, https://de-de.facebook.com/eastafro/posts/1325132124179161 (last accessed 14 September 2010). The figures are wrongly given in US dollars in the website. Meskerem.net has corrected this. See also http://www.madote.com/2016/01/eritreas-national-service-salary.html (last accessed 14 September 2010).

2

National/Military Service in Africa: Theories and Concepts

This chapter presents different theories and perspectives on national service. It also briefly discusses the philosophical foundations of national/military service. Some analysts perceive compulsory and universal national service as the ultimate good, benefitting not only conscripts, but also the whole society where such a policy exists. Others view compulsory national service as the antithesis of a free society, because citizens are forced to relinquish their freedom in order to perform the obligation. The exponents of the latter school of thought equate compulsory national service with forced labour or a modern form of slavery. Some analysts also equate compulsory national service with the feudal institution of *posse comitatus* (the inherent power of the state to call upon its physically fit citizens to serve their country).

Opinions among political theorists and other analysts are so divided that no other topic in social and military history is probably as controversial, and perhaps none arouses such strong feelings of sympathy or antipathy as that of compulsory military and/or national service. Scholarly opinions on national/military service are fervently divided into two mutually opposed schools of thought. One perceives national/military service as a civic duty and as an expression of political and civic rights, which create and reproduce values that are amenable to greater cross-cultural understanding, mutual respect, national unity and greater commitment to the common good. The prominent exponents of this school of thought postulate that well thought out national service programmes engender democratic values, promote good citizenship, national cohesion, a common sense of purpose, mutual trust and commitment to the common good. These values are said to be valuable to the national community and to the individual participants themselves. The latter is said to be due to the changes and transformations servers are expected to undergo as a result, as well as the fundamental contributions they are likely to make to their national communities.

The other school of thought perceives compulsory national/military service as antithetic to a free society, because individuals are forced against their will to undertake compulsory national/military service at the cost of their interests and future careers. The exponents of this school of thought argue that not only does compulsory national service represent a gross violation of liberty and freedom, but they also associate it with forced labour or a modern form of slavery whose genesis, they argue, can be traced back to an institution of the late Roman Empire. The following presents the two schools of thought and their conceptions of compulsory national/military service.

NATIONAL/MILITARY SERVICE: THE HIGHEST GOOD AND FOUNTAIN OF VIRTUE

Historically, the point of departure of the exponents of national/military service is avid opposition to the standing army in favour of the civic militia. Jean-Jacques Rousseau, one of the most influential thinkers during the Enlightenment in eighteenth-century Europe, was, for example, fervently opposed to the institution of the standing army which, he argued, besides being costly to maintain was not fit for purpose. He said, '...I do not see that this army has ever safeguarded against any invasion...' (2005 [1761]: 217), and further stated that the army is:

> ...good for only two ends: either to attack and conquer neighbours and to enchain and enslave Citizens. These two ends are equally alien to you: therefore renounce the means by which they are attained. *The State must not remain without defenders, I know it; but its true defenders are its members. Every citizen ought to be a soldier out of duty, none ought to be one by profession.* (Rousseau 2005 [1761]: 217–18, emphasis added)

This clearly indicates that conscription lay at the heart of his entire political philosophy (Hippler 2007: 33). That is the reason Rousseau's *Social Contract* directly links military service to the right to vote (Hippler 2007: 191–2). The corollary is that a citizen-soldier would be virtuous and represent the moral values of civil society. The institution of the civic militia or national service was therefore perceived as a moral counterforce to the military. However, as we shall see later, in the context of the developing world, there are analysts who perceive the military as a critical vehicle of modernisation and a repository of social virtues (see Lerner and Robinson 1960; Krebs 2006).

The conception of the 'citizen-soldier' as quintessence of virtue and patriotism featured in Montesquieu's writings. He observed, '...in a popular state there must be an additional spring, which is virtue' (Montesquieu 1989 [1748]: 22). He defines virtue '...as love of the laws and the homeland. This love, requiring a continuous preference of the public interest over one's own, produces all the individual virtues...' (p. 36). He also defines political virtue as 'a renunciation of oneself, which is always a very painful thing' (p. 35). Thereby only the 'citizen-soldier' can be the bastion of virtue and consequently safeguard public interest. Montesquieu argues, '[v]irtue, in a republic is a very simple thing: it is love of the republic; it is a feeling and not a result of knowledge...' (p. 42). He further states, '[l]ove of the homeland leads to goodness in mores, and goodness in mores leads to love of the homeland. The less we can satisfy our particular passions, the more we give ourselves up to passions for the general order' (1989: 42–3).

The corollary is that renunciation of self-interest is *sine qua non* for pursuit of the common good or public interest, including willingness to sacrifice one's life in defence of one's country and its cause. This is said only to be possible when one relinquishes personal interests in favour of the common good. In Montesquieu's conception, the extent of love and commitment to one's country is proportionally related to the intensity of hardship endured in the service of the common good. Herein lays the central plank of the logic of compulsory military or national service. Montesquieu uses the analogy of monks who, in spite of the unbearable hardship intrinsic to a monastic life, love their order. He wonders, 'Why do monks so love their order?' 'Their love,' he observes, 'comes from the same thing that makes their order intolerable to them.' He further states, '[t] heir rule deprives them of everything upon which ordinary passions rest; what remains, therefore, is the passion for the very rule that afflicts them. The more austere it is, that is, the more it curtails their inclinations, the more force it gives to those that remain' (1989: 42–3).

It follows that those who are called upon to serve and/or die for their country will, in the process of providing such service and forfeiting their interests, love their country more than they would have otherwise. This is notwithstanding the fact that their country is the cause of their affliction. The more severe the affliction or deprivation the greater becomes the attachment or feeling of love of one's country. That is why Thomas Hippler (2007: 31) perceptively observes, '[a]ll the elements for a coherent theory of military service are present in Montesquieu: a republican equation for virtue, a perfect equality by means of austere abnegation of the self, and a constitutional concern for an effective control of the armed forces and subordination to the principle of popular sovereignty.'

Policy analysts, politicians and academics debated the idea of national service during the eighteenth century (see Montesquieu 1989 [1748]; Rousseau 2005 [1761]), the nineteenth century (see Bellamy 1888) and around the turn of the twentieth century (see James 1943 [1910]; Bourne 1982 [1916]). In spite of the plethora of literature on the subject, the debate continues unabated. William Evers (1990) states that the three most renowned philosophers who provided the moral foundations for political activists and policy analysts, who passionately advocated for universal and compulsory national service programmes were Edward Bellamy (1888), William James 1943 [1910] and Michael Walzer (1983). However, as discussed above, Montesquieu and Rousseau had already laid down the philosophical edifice of the foundation of compulsory national service.

Evers (1990) argues that Edward Bellamy (1888) was the first to intro- duce the idea of an 'industrial army' based on compulsory youth service as the central plank of his new social order. James (1943 [1910]), regarded by many writing on the subject as the most passionate advocate of national service, wrote that every citizen must be compelled to serve the state for a 'certain number of years' (1943 [1910]). He referred to this as 'blood tax' (1943: 325). However, James was not the first to refer to compulsory service as 'blood tax': during the French Revolution, military service was defined as '*impôt de sang*' (a blood tax).

The citizens who are called to military service pay a veritable tribute that could be called the tribute of blood: as all the others, its goal is the conversion of the social body; but it is essentially unique since it affects the first of all properties; i.e. the person and the most precious of all liberties, the liberty of the individual. (Desmousseaux VIII: 2, cited in Hippler 2007 [1757]: 109)

The idea is that all citizens who are either in early adulthood or approaching adulthood should perform compulsory national service for a limited period of time (James 1943 [1910]; Etzioni 1983; Janowitz 1983; Walzer 1983; Elberly 1988; Moskos 1988). James argued of the need for a 'moral equivalent of war' in which all young men would be compelled to serve their communities. Randolph Bourne (1982 [1916]) was the first to propose that men and women between the ages of sixteen and twenty should participate in some form of public service for two years (in Bandow 1990). William James wrote, 'martial virtues, although originally gained by the race through war, are absolute and permanent human goods,' with the national service being seen as an instrument of inculcating such virtues in peacetime. He said, 'I spoke of the "moral equivalent of war." So far, war has been the only force that can discipline a whole community and until an equivalent discipline is organised, I believe that war must have its way' (1943: 326). He further wrote, 'The martial type of character can be bred without war. [...] The only thing needed henceforward is to inflame the civic temper as past history has inflamed the military temper' (1943: 326). In his view, compulsory national service would accomplish this.

David Hart refers to martial virtue as *'first and foremost, moral theory about the good character required in military theory and practice'* (1994: 7, emphasis in original). Hart defines martial virtue as 'those qualities of civic character that impel individual citizens to accept their moral obligation to prepare, support, and fight in defence of the republic which means to fight for the primary values of their polity.' He further observes, '[i]t assumes that the virtues necessary for good citizenship are also the virtues necessary for both military service and welfare. In other words, martial virtue sets the moral parameters for the soldiers of the republic' (1994: 7). National service is therefore conceived of as an instrument of breeding, perpetuating and transmitting in peacetime the 'martial type of character' normally developed during wartime. As we shall see later, at least theoretically, this constitutes the single most important *raison d'être* of the Eritrean National Service (ENS).

A closely related theory to the above presented philosophical foundation of national service which is intimately linked to the rationale and objectives of the ENS is the theory of social capital, particularly in relation to war fought against a common enemy. National service programmes have been adopted in different countries either to heal wounds inflicted by intra-state wars by reconciling previously feuding groups or to transmit the values and norms engendered during wars of liberation and resistance against common foreign enemies. The relationship between war and social capital and how national service can function as a mechanism of maintaining and transmitting these values is discussed in the following.

WAR, SOLIDARITY AND SOCIAL CAPITAL

The theory of social capital postulates that where people of different ethnic, geographic, religious and occupational backgrounds interact repeatedly with each other, over time, they are able to know and trust one another, to interconnect with each other and share experiences, values and norms that encourage cooperation, openness and compromise (Putnam 2000; Kibreab 2008). James Coleman, for example, states that social capital facilitates 'the achievement of goals that could not be achieved in its absence or could be achieved only at a higher cost' (1990: 304). People involved in such interactions are able to engage in mutually beneficial cooperative activities in pursuit of goals that they could not achieve by themselves or could only achieve at greater costs (Putnam 2000). In the process, a series of webs of social networks based on mutual trust are developed that interconnect people across social cleavages such as race, class, sex, ethnicity, religion and region that over time produce shared experiences, values and norms that people can draw upon in pursuit of goals of mutual and national interest. Just as physical capital and human capital do, social capital constitutes a resource that the members of given social networks tap into in different settings. Such social networks are 'part of the wider set of relationships and norms that allow people to pursue their goals, and also serve to bind society together' (Field 2003: 3). The fighting of a war against a common external enemy is said to provide fertile ground for the development and consolidation of social capital, or the glue that holds a society together.

That war's ability to engender a set of values and a sense of common purpose among citizens are necessary conditions for solidarity and the unity of present and future generations is recognised by various theorists and analysts (see Carr 1942; James 1943 [1910]; Moskos 1988). Edward E. Carr in his book, *Conditions of Peace* (1942) states that war provides a sense of meaning and purpose, which are absent in modern societies, and that as a result it is a powerful weapon of social solidarity and cohesion. In the developed world, he argues, '...war or preparation for war is to-day the only moral purpose with the recognised capacity of inspiring the degree of self-sacrifice in all classes of the community necessary to keep the political and economic machine in motion.' He further points out that in the English-speaking world, war has become 'a moral purpose which has revived the national will, increased the sense of cohesion and mutual obligation...' (1942: 124), and argues that, '[i]t is essential to recognise [...] this purpose is the product of war, that it is directly inspired by the needs of war, and that it is animated by the potent forces of a common enmity and a common fear' (1942: 124).

However, Carr also argues that there is no guarantee that the powerful sense of common purpose and willpower engendered by a war fought against a common enemy will necessarily endure in the post-war period or in peacetime, but he observes that in spite of this, a society that has been through war will not be the same after (1942: 125). In the same vein, Bernard Crick wrote, '[a] communion of oppression can create a community of passionate intensity. The only question now is, the past being past, will this intensity tolerate diversity once the alien is gone?' (2000: 82). He further noted, '[t]he struggle against imperialism [read any external enemy] has to be continued, long after the imperialists have gone, because the enemy alone creates the unity by which the governing party can hope to perpetuate itself in office' (2000: 82–3). The potency of this theorising will be clear when we discuss later the institution of national service in the context of post-conflict Eritrea.

The German sociologist S. Rudolf Steinmetz argued that wars fought against common enemies in the past 'hammered and welded people into unified political communities "cohesive states" and that human beings can only develop their capacities in such political communities' (cited in Evers 1990: xxxi). Charles Tilly also famously stated, 'war made the state, and the state made war' (1975: 42). Steinmetz was equally concerned that, once the shooting stopped, the society that was unified by the need to stand up together against a common enemy may face the risk of disintegration, and consequently wondered: 'What, in a future era of peace, would replace the fear of the enemy? Would the people of cohesive states degenerate and disintegrate in the absence of military foes?' (cited in Evers 1990: xxxi). It is, *inter alia*, to overcome the danger of post-war societal disintegration, disharmony and apathy that philosophers, policy analysts and politicians advocated for the institution of compulsory national service as the 'moral equivalent of war', so that the strong sense of patriotism, martial virtues – courage, wisdom, compassion – common purpose, solidarity and discipline engendered and necessitated by war would endure in peacetime. Wilhelm von Humboldt, in his *Limits of State Action* (1792), argued that war was the most salutary phenomenon for the culture of human nature (cited in Hippler 2007: 177).

Edward Carr argues that any post-war situation requires a substitute moral purpose or a new creed that '...will lay more stress on obligations than on rights, on services to be rendered to the community rather than benefits to be drawn from it' (1942: 123). Herein lays the importance of compulsory national/military service. This principle constituted the central plank of the ENS in which conscripts are socialised into the values of the liberation struggle, where personal interests are sacrificed for the so-called common good. William James wrote, '[m]artial virtues must be the enduring cement; intrepidity, contempt of softness, surrender of the private interest, obedience to command must remain the rock upon which states are built' (1943: 323). He further notes:

> If now – and this is my idea – there were, instead of military conscription a conscription of the whole youthful population to form for a certain number of years a part of the army enlisted against *Nature*, the injustice would tend to be evened out, and numerous other goods to the commonwealth would follow. The military ideals of hardihood and discipline would be wrought into the growing fibre of the people... (1943: 325)

As a substitute to the discipline of war, William James argued that the government should conscript young men to serve in:

> ...coal and iron mines, to freight trains, to fishing fleets in December, to dishwashing,

> clothes-washing, and window-washing, to road-building and tunnel-making, to foundries and stoke-holes, and to the frames of skyscrapers, would our gilded youths be drafted off [...] to get the childishness knocked out of them, and to come back into society with healthier sympathies and soberer ideas. They should have paid their blood tax. (1943: 325)

After national service, James stated, participants 'would tread the earth more proudly, the women would value them more highly, they would be better fathers and teachers of the following generations' (James 1943: 322–3). The values learned from mandatory and universal national service, he argued, are 'order and discipline, the tradition of service and devotion, of physical fitness, unstinted exertion, and universal responsibility' (1943: 327). This was his conception of the 'moral equivalent of war'.

According to Donald Eberly, one of the important results of national service is that participants gain common experience that enhances social cohesion and unity (in Evers 1990: 218). Morris Janowitz maintains that national service helps individuals achieve 'civic consciousness [...] the process by which national attachments and obligations are molded into the search for supranational citizenship' (1983: xi). Proponents of national service argue that participation in such programmes integrate citizens from different racial, ethnic, class and religious groups into one nation with a sense of common citizenship (Etzioni 1980; Walzer 1983: 170). Such an outcome has been the single most important attraction to the architects of the ENS. National service is perceived as a force that unifies Eritrean society (Afwerki 2008; Ephrem 2008; Proc. No. 82/1995). Michael Walzer also states '...what is being shared is the burden of service: the time spent, the difficult training, the harsh discipline' (1983: 170). As we shall see, the conscripts interviewed for this study cite these experiences as the most memorable and enduring, and those that cemented their relationships in spite of their disparate backgrounds.

National service is also said to contribute to character building by eliminating 'tempting vices' (Evers 1990: xxix). William James was convinced that young men who take part in national service, especially those from the 'luxurious classes', needed a harsh, challenging environment in which to develop their characters (Evers 1990: xxiv). According to James, '[a]ll the qualities of a man acquire dignity when he knows that the service of the collectivity that owns him needs them. If proud of the collectivity, his own pride rises in proportion' (1943: 322). In spite of his fervent advocacy for compulsory and universal national service, William James belonged to the 'anti-militarist party', and in his view a permanent peace is unachievable without 'elements of army discipline,' *inter alia*, engendered by the institution of compulsory national service.

COMPULSORY MILITARY/NATIONAL SERVICE: THE ANTITHESIS OF A FREE SOCIETY?

Liberal analysts reject compulsory military service on the grounds that it is imposed on citizens against their will, which they construe as representing a clear and present violation of the fundamental rights of servers. Others are opposed to compulsory military/national service on the grounds that servers are required to risk their lives and careers for the sake of the state which more often than not is incompatible with the fundamental end of the politics of liberal societies, namely preservation of life and property (Cohen 1985). Eliot Cohen further states, '[m]ilitary service means forfeiture of normal rights and submission to martial law... The instinctive obedience inherent in the military induced by drill and severe punishments and harassment produces no beneficial effects on the recruit' (p. 139). George Nasmyth argues:

> The whole object of military training is to secure instantaneous obedience without thought, to make men a part of an autocratic military machine, so that if he is ordered to sink the Lusitania or destroy the city of Louvain, he will obey instantly and unquestionably. Surely unthinking obedience is far removed from the self-imposed discipline, that respect for laws because they have been enacted by common consent and for welfare of the people. (Cited in Cohen 1985: 140-1)

Michael Walzer also observes that '[i]ndeed, the great advantage of liberal society may simply be this: that no one can be asked to die for public reasons or on behalf of the state' (1983: 89).

In what follows the central thrust of the other school of thought that essentially perceives compulsory military/national service as a vestige of the depraved institution of the past is discussed. There are analysts who trace the origin of the history of the institution of compulsory and universal national and military service to the feudal tradition of *posse comitatus*. They refer to compulsory national and/or military service as a modern form of slavery. These analysts perceive national/military service as an oppressive and regressive institution that leads to flagrant loss of liberty. David Dawson, an avowed opponent of compulsory national service, for example, traces the historical roots of conscription to the late Roman institutions of *patricinium* and *precarium*, as well as to the Germanic barbarians' institution of *posse comitatus* (1982: 4). In Republican Rome, and later the Roman Empire, the institution of *patricinium (precārius)* referred to the 'exercise of a function of a *patromus*, patronage. A *patronus* is an influential person who has undertaken the protection of another person...' (*Oxford Latin Dictionary* 1982: 1311). The *International Encyclopaedia of the Social and Behavioural Sciences* defines *patricinium* as a patron-client relationship which involves 'asymmetric but mutually beneficial, open-ended transactions based on differential control by individuals or over access and flow of resources in stratified societies' (2001: 11118).

In Great Britain, France, Prussia and North America, the system of compulsory military service was derived from the feudal tradition of *posse comitatus* stemming from the inherent power of the state to call upon its physically fit citizens to serve their country in different capacities as the need arose. For example, in North America, when the petitions and appeals of the rebelling colonies for redress produced no results, they issued a document in which they declared, 'all men are [...] endowed [...] with certain unalienable Rights, that among are Life, Liberty, and the pursuit of Happiness' (cited in Dawson 1982: 6). In 1777 Massachusetts and Virginia introduced compulsory military service based on the feudal tradition of *posse comitatus* to pursue the values enshrined in that document. *Posse comitatus* was assumed to embody the responsibility of citizens within a particular age group to serve their communities or country (Dawson 1982). Thomas J. DiLorenzo considers compulsory national service incompatible with the principles on which the American republic was grounded. He states:

> The American republic was founded on the belief that individuals have inalienable rights to life, liberty, property, and the pursuit of happiness, not some vague obligation to become indentured servants for the government. This aspect of the American heritage suggests that citizens should strongly resist any national service schemes. True voluntarism is a legitimate part of the American heritage, but that's not what national service is about. National service under the auspices of the federal government is necessarily coercive. (1990: 1)

Exponents of the second school of thought are strongly opposed to the idea of universal and compulsory national/military service on the grounds that it constitutes forced labour which they argue is incompatible with the fundamental principles of freedom, fairness, justice and human rights. Bruce Chapman (2002: 1) for example, states, '[u]niversal service never was a good idea, and it grows worse with time. It fails militarily, morally, financially, and politically.' Forced labour is severely proscribed in international law. The conventions that outlaw forced labour are signed by nearly all states worldwide.

Article 2(1) of the ILO Forced Labour Convention (CFL) (1930) defines 'forced or compulsory labour' as '...*all work or service which is exacted from any person under the menace of any penalty and for which the said person has not offered himself voluntarily*' (Art. 2(1), emphasis added). Involuntary exaction of labour or service and the use or threats of penalty are the two critical elements in the definition of forced labour. The approach of international efforts to prohibit governments, state agencies, private companies, political parties, military officers and individuals from recourse to forced or compulsory labour have been inextricably linked to the efforts of the international community to eradicate slavery and other institutions and practices that are either associated with or are similar to it. One such practice is the institution of forced or compulsory labour referred to as 'slavery-like practice' (ILO 1998). The Slavery Convention, 1926, *inter alia*, states, '[t]he High Contracting Parties recognize that recourse to compulsory labour or forced labour may have grave consequences and undertake [...] *to take all necessary measures to prevent compulsory or forced labour from developing into conditions analogous to slavery*' (Art. 5 Slavery Convention 1926, emphasis added). The Convention limits the conditions under which forced labour may be exacted and vests the responsibility for exacting forced labour in 'competent central authorities of the territory concerned' (Art. 5 (3) 1930).

Article 25 of the Convention, 1930 states, '[t]he illegal exaction of forced or compulsory labour shall be punishable as a penal offence and it shall be an obligation on any Member ratifying this Convention to ensure that the penalties imposed by law are really adequate and are strictly enforced.' This assumes that the offender is a private firm, a group or an individual. The framing of this stipulation clearly indicates the international community's resolve to eradicate the 'slavery-like practice' of forced labour. The General Conference of the ILO's adoption of the Convention Concerning the Abolition of Forced Labour in June 1957 reinforced the provisions of the 1930 Convention which, *inter alia*, stipulates that states that ratify the Convention are required to 'suppress and not to make use of any form of forced or compulsory labour: (a) as a means of *political coercion or education* [...] (b) *as a method of mobilizing and using labour for purposes of economic development; as a means of labour discipline....*' (emphasis added). This is the main aim of the ENS that is proscribed in international law.

The fact that other international instruments proscribe such a practice reinforces that the international norm against forced or compulsory labour is deeply embedded in international human rights law. The Report of the Commission of Inquiry on Forced Labour in Myanmar, for example, states, '[t]he prohibition of recourse to forced labour, including the right to the free choice of employment, is closely related to the protection of other basic human rights: the right not to be subjected to torture or to other cruel, inhuman or degrading treatment...' (ILO 1998). The Year Book of the International Law Commission, 1980 concluded:

> ... there exists now in international law a peremptory norm prohibiting any recourse to forced labour and that the right not to be compelled to perform forced or compulsory labour is one of the basic human rights. A state which supports, instigates, accepts or tolerates forced labour on its territory commits a wrongful act for which it bears international responsibility; furthermore, this wrongful act results from a breach of an international obligation that is so essential for the protection of the fundamental interests *of* the international community that it could be qualified, if committed on a widespread scale, as an international crime under the terms of Article 19 of the draft articles of the International Law Commission on state responsibility. (Cited in ILO 1998: 70)

The importance attached to the eradication of forced labour is also clearly reflected in Article 1 (1) of the Convention, 1930 which posits that any state ratifying this Convention 'undertakes to suppress the use of forced or compulsory labour in all its forms within the shortest possible period.' States are therefore compelled not to exact forced labour, nor to tolerate or condone directly or indirectly its exaction by individuals or agencies within their territories and to repeal all laws that allow such practices. The Eritrean government clearly violates this proscription inasmuch as it is the main beneficiary of forced labour. The ruling party and high-ranking military officers are equally guilty of exacting the labour of conscripts by force (Kibreab 2009b; HRW 2013; Keetharuth 2014). States are also required to ensure that '[t]he illegal exaction of forced or compulsory labour shall be a penal offence...' and '...that the penalties imposed by law are really adequate and are strictly enforced' (Art. 25 CFL 1930).

Eritrea ratified both the Forced Labour Convention, 1930 (No. 29) and the Abolition of Forced Labour Convention, 1957 (No. 105) on 22 February 2000.[1] Consequently, it has at the minimum an obligation to prohibit the

---

[1]   See List of Ratifications of International Labour Conventions, Eritrea, available at http://webfusion.ilo.org/public/db/standards/normes/appl/appl-byCtry.cfm?lang =EN&CTYCHOICE=2100 (accessed 22 March 2007).

practice within its territory let alone to cease to commit it itself. This responsibility, as pointed out by the International Law Commission, is 'a peremptory norm' – *Jus Cogens* – 'A norm accepted and recognised by the international community of states as a whole as a norm from which no derogation is permitted' (Rozakis 1976: 73). Therefore all states, regardless of whether or not they are signatories to the conventions on slavery and forced labour, are required to comply with the unconditional principles and norms of international law. The extent to which the Eritrean government abides by these treaties will be examined throughout this book.

The meaning of forced labour is synonymous with modern forms of slavery in international law (see UN News Centre 2014). For example, the anti-slavery organisation observes, '[t]here are many different characteristics that distinguish slavery from other human rights violations, *however only one needs to be present for slavery to exist.* Someone is in slavery if they are: forced to work – through mental or physical threat; ...physically constrained or has restrictions placed on his/her freedom of movement.' As we shall see throughout the book, although the large majority of the former conscripts who were interviewed for the study do not object to participation in the ENS for eighteen months, as stipulated in the Proclamation on national service, nearly all respondents and key informants reported that they would not have served even a day beyond the statutory requirement of eighteen months which suggests that their participation in the ENS beyond this is involuntary and is performed under threat of degrading treatment in the context of highly restricted freedom of movement. The requirement to serve beyond eighteen months, in the absence of an imminent threat to national security or state of emergency, therefore falls within the purview of forced labour or a modern form of slavery.

The ENS is also characterised by the ILO as forced labour (ILO 2010). The hundreds of thousands of conscripts are seldom involved in military-related activities, as there has been no war in the country since June 2000. As the findings of this study show the overwhelming majority of conscripts are involved in manual labour on construction sites, agricultural farms, housing projects belonging to the government and the PFDJ, as well as to senior military officers. Many also work in the civilian sector of the administration, infrastructure projects, education and construction. The ILO Committee of Experts has examined the extent to which the exaction of compulsory work or services from citizens in the ENS is limited:

> ...to genuine cases of emergency, or force majeure, that is, to circumstances endangering the existence or the well-being of the whole or part of the population, and to ensure that the duration and extent of such compulsory work or services, as well as the purpose for which it is used, is limited to what is strictly required by the exigencies of the situation.

The ILO Committee of Experts has pointed out that the existing large-scale and systematic practice of imposing compulsory labour on the population within the framework of the national service programme is incompatible with ILO Abolition of Forced Labour Convention No. 105, which prohibits the use of forced or compulsory labour as a method of mobilising and using labour for purposes of economic development (referred to in Kibreab 2009b; Keetharuth 2014).

The right of the Eritrean government to require its citizens to undertake national service within the spirit and letter of the relevant international conventions on human rights, including the conventions against forced labour is not in doubt. It is rather its failure to abide by the terms and conditions of its own law in terms of limiting the duration of the ENS to eighteen months, and the scale and nature of the activities the conscripts forcibly engage in, as well as its consequent degeneration into indefinite obligation that has turned it into forced labour. The latter is strictly prohibited by international law to which the Eritrean government is a signatory. As will be seen, not only are the hundreds of thousands of men and women required to serve indefinitely without remuneration, but also the duty to serve is enforced under the menace of severe punishment.

THE INSTITUTION OF NATIONAL/MILITARY SERVICE IN AFRICA

The institution of national service is not only used as an instrument of maintaining and transmitting social values and traits developed in wartime, but it also serves as a means of producing a set of values and shared norms of solidarity and cooperation that promote trans-ethnic and trans-faith cooperation and trust. The set of civic virtues and values created and reproduced through the institution of national service are critical in the process of healing wounds and reconstructing or counteracting the erosion of social norms of cooperation and trust resulting from the deleterious effects of intra-state wars. For example, one of the main reasons the Federal Military Government in Nigeria introduced the National Youth Service Corps (NYSC) programme in 1973 was to foster national unity and trans-ethnic and trans-faith cohesion in a country recovering from a violent intra-state civil war where there were over 374 ethnic groups. As Ebenezer Obadare (2010: 20), for example, observes:

> Faced with a total breakdown of social harmony following Nigeria's thirty-month Civil War (1967-70) [...] the then Federal Military Government realised that having won the war, it was imperative that the peace – of solid and voluntary national unity – be won...true feelings of loyalty and solidarity that produce national cohesion and unity [...] could only be an outcome of a deliberate social process.

Writing about the Nigerian National Youth Service Corps (NYSC), Gregory Enegwea and Gabriel Umoden (1993: 2) state that one way in which the problems of inter-ethnic diversity can be addressed is by engaging '...in deliberate social engineering, designing programmes and pursuing policies meant to promote national unity, de-emphasise point of discord amongst the constituent groups, and foster greater inter-ethnic understanding and harmony.' They further note, '[t]hese programmes may entail both compulsory elements and voluntary incentive systems, either to discourage certain types of conduct deemed inappropriate, or to promote healthy behaviour and interaction across ethnic divides' (1993: 2).

Drawing insights from William James' famous and widely-quoted essay, 'The Moral Equivalent of War', in which he argues that a democratic nation can foster and maintain social cohesion without going to war, Obadare states that for post-civil war Nigeria, '...the way to avoid another relapse into the ugly past was to engineer "new citizens" united in common allegiance to the nation-state through service' (2010: 21). As stated earlier, national service can play a critical role in fostering social cohesion and harmony in a divided society that lacks common bonds of lineage or mythology of common ancestry. This is even true of the United States of America. Charles Moskos (1988: 9), for example, wrote,

> America does not claim solidarity and unity by virtue of a claimed common ancestry or some divine foundation myth. America is the immigrant society par excellence. Our cohesion depends upon a civic ideal rather than on primordial loyalties. At stake is the preservation in the United States of a shared citizenship that serves to knit this increasingly ethnically diverse society together as a nation.

Enegwea and Emoden (1993: 22) note that the NYSC was therefore developed in the context of an important challenge that faced the country in the immediate post-civil war period. The NYSC established by decree No. 24 on 22 May 1973 is still in force. No university graduate can gain employment without producing a certificate to show they have performed the obligation. Both men and women are affected regardless of marital status. Only graduates over the age of thirty are issued certificates of exemption.

Other African countries, such as Zambia, Kenya, Ethiopia, Botswana, Gambia, Ghana and post-Apartheid South Africa have also experimented with different forms of national and military service programmes. However, the purposes of such programmes throughout Africa, with the exception of Nigeria and South Africa as well as Eritrea, have been to address widespread youth unemployment in cities, stem the flow of rural-urban migration and to impart skills in the growing youth population in post-colonial Africa. McBride and Sherraden, for example, observe:

> The idea of national service emerged within the context as a way to stem the unhealthy rural-urban drift, impart useful skills in the bourgeoning youth population, and provide temporary employment for the increasing number of high school graduates. Thus, national service was seen, not as something possessing any intrinsic value, but as a possible solution to identified problems in the rural-urban migration interface. The allied social project of using national service as a tool for national integration amid the fierce articulation of rival ethnic identities appears, in this light as an afterthought. (2006: 40)

They further state,

> [t]his is not to deny that there were objective problems in the nascent political space that national service might have definitely helped in obviating. The point is that the idea of national service seems to be stumbled on and adopted for its sheer utilitarian value as opposed to a clear recognition of its innate potential for enhancing citizenship. (2006: 40)

Some African countries, such as Ethiopia and Ghana, adopted national service schemes as a requirement to pay back the taxpayer who footed the bill for university education. As we shall see throughout this book, although the idea of citizenship was not one of the declared aims of the

ENS, it is unique in the continent not only in terms of its inclusiveness and open-ended duration but, more importantly, because it is conceptualised as a tool of nation building and national integration, and as a bridge interconnecting communities across the social cleavages of ethnicity, religion, gender, class and region.

As we shall see, unlike Nigerians who suffered from a fratricidal intra-state war that divided their communities on the basis of ethnicity, the multi-ethnic and multi-faith Eritrean society was held together by a war fought against a common external enemy. Therefore, whilst in Nigeria the national service was initiated, on the one hand, to heal the deep wounds afflicted by the civil war and, on the other, to bring together the communities that were fragmented by the civil war, in Eritrea the national service was introduced, among other things, to preserve and transmit the powerful sense of common purpose, unity and martial virtues produced during the thirty years' war (1961–1991) to the present and future generations. In the Nigerian case, the aim of the national service was to erode the powerful sense of enmity of the 'Other' engendered during the civil war, but in Eritrea the converse is true. In Eritrea, the *raison d'être* of the national service is, among other things, to celebrate, safeguard and transmit the national core values developed during the liberation struggle (Art. 5, Proclamation No 82, 1995). This suggests that the effect of war on society is dependent on the nature of the war concerned. In Nigeria, the civil war divided Nigerian society and hence the national service was introduced to heal wounds inflicted by the war and overcome division. Whether the architects of the ENS have read this literature or not, the stated objectives of the ENS are identical with the objectives set by the philosophers who were protagonists of national service (see Chapter 1).

The following chapter examines in detail the extent to which the ENS builds Eritrea's defence and fighting capability, as stipulated in the proclamation on national service and other policy declarations.

3

The Government and the Structure of the Eritrean Defence Force

The only defence against the world is a thorough knowledge of it.
John Locke, 'Some thoughts concerning education', 1693

As seen in Chapter 1, according to the proclamation on the Eritrean National Service (ENS), all able-bodied Eritrean nationals aged between eighteen and forty are required to perform eighteen months of national service. Following the 1998–2000 border war against Ethiopia and the introduction of the WYDC, the ENS has become open-ended. Since then, with few exceptions, no demobilisation has taken place. At the end of 2012, the President intensified the process of militarisation by establishing the so-called *Hizbawi Serawit* (people's militia) comprising citizens up to the age of seventy for men and sixty for women, who were directly accountable to him. The level of militarisation in the country is unparalleled in modern history (see Hirt and Mohammad 2013; Pool 2013; Tronvoll and Mekonen 2014). The reality in Eritrea is almost identical to the archaic feudal institution of *posse comitatus* which, as seen in Chapter 2, refers to the intrinsic 'power of the country' to call upon a *posse*, that is, able-bodied men and women, to provide military service and to serve in national defence, law enforcement, maintenance of peace and so on against their will and without remuneration. Herein lies the link between the ENS and the old tradition of *posse comitatus*, or bondage. The accounts of the respondents interviewed in this study clearly show that Eritrean citizens are required by law to relinquish their rights over their labour power, and indeed their lives.

This chapter discusses the background of the Eritrean military, especially the state of the military and its relationship with the government before and after the implementation of the ENS. The organisational structure of the Eritrean military and the constant changes it has been undergoing over time are also discussed. The rationales underlying President Isaias Afwerki's decision to constantly reshuffle the higher echelon of the army and to alter its organisational structure erratically are analysed. Notwithstanding the fact that in May 2016 the government had just celebrated its twenty-fifth anniversary, ironically, the organisational structure of the Eritrean military still remains in a state of flux. Its leadership has been shifting constantly since independence, which has hampered its institutionalisation and professionalisation. Continuous political interference has thereby killed the autonomy and dynamism of the military.

In 1992 the president established an expert working group (WG) on the infrastructure of the Eritrean Military. In an unprecedented manner, the WG was comprised exclusively of former Eritrean professional military officers of the Ethiopian armed forces. Some members of the WG were former generals and the rest were colonels in Ethiopia before they joined the liberation struggle and the independent Eritrean State. The president, without the knowledge of or consultation with the Defence Minister, established the WG, which worked from the president's office. After studying and comparing different experiences, the WG developed a model of the organisational structure of the military, and recommended the specific rules and regulations that would govern it and its relationship with the state. The WG recommended that the military should have three autonomous branches, namely, ground force, navy and air force. They also recommended that the army be organised along divisions. The head of the military should be a major general and the rank of the heads of the divisions should be colonels. If the minister of defence was a civilian, a chief of staff should head the army.

In the WG's view, Eritrea, a small country with limited resources, would only need one brigadier general, but also the size of the army should be small. The WG recommended that an institutionalised, professional and autonomous military system should be established that served the state rather than the specific regime of the day. Taking the country's limited resources and size into account, the WG recommended that the emphasis should be on quality and professionalism rather than quantity. The WG finished its assignment and handed its blueprint and its recommendations to the president's office.

When the president announced the structuring of the military, not only did he ignore the blueprint developed by the WG, but also, contrary to the recommendation of the latter, he promoted thirty-seven former combatants to the ranks of brigadier and major general, some of whom did not even have secondary school education. When the president lavishly distributed such high ranks, his main pre-occupation was with reward and loyalty rather than operational efficiency. The presence of thirty-seven generals enabled him to play them off against each other and to co-opt each of them. Since then, the organisational structure of the military has remained unstable and at times chaotic.

The single most important *raison d'etre* of this is to facilitate President Isaias Afwerki's personal rule, partly by eliminating the pre-existing, and stifling the emergence of new, institutions. As Hirt observes, '...the President [...] rules with an iron fist and has weakened or obliterated all significant institutions – including the judiciary, the legislature and the ruling party' (2013: 5). Robert Jackson and Carl Rosberg (1982: 10) argue that in an institutionalised state, conduct is governed by rules: 'Rules are the tools of a civil society. In an institution the rule of its authority always stand above the person and his power or ability.' (1982: 10) They further observe, '[i]n an effectively institutionalised state, the rules are respected by all persons no matter how important they may be; indeed the rules in a well-established state with a strong institutional tradition appear entirely natural,' whilst in 'a state without effective institutions rules are defied or ignored; they appear artificial and without value and meaning' (1982: 10).

> The opposite of institutional rule – obviously – is non-institutionalised government, where persons take precedence over rules, where the office holder is not effectively bound by his office and is able to change its authority and powers to suit his own personal or political needs. In such a system of personal rule, the rulers and other leaders take precedence over the formal rules of the political game: the rules do not effectively regulate political behaviour, and we therefore cannot predict or anticipate conduct from a knowledge of the rules. To put this in old-fashioned, comparative government terms, the state is a government of men and not of laws. (1982: 10)

The fit between this insightful description and the reality of the Eritrean government is astonishing. One way in which President Isaias Afwerki creates and perpetuates his personal rule is, *inter alia*, by destroying the pre-existing traditional institutions and by stifling the emergence of new ones. This is demonstrated by the constant reshuffling of high-ranking military officers, including the chiefs of staff, defence ministers and commanders, as well as constantly changing and shifting the organisational structure of the armed forces. This has enabled the president to suffocate the process of institutionalisation of the military and these measures have, over time, facilitated his ability to rule the country without any form of institutional constraint.

Given the severe restrictions in Eritrea, there is no opportunity to conduct fieldwork in the country: official documents are also either inaccessible or don't exist. Therefore it is not easy to document accurately the organisational structure of the military, or the constant shifts and changes it has undergone in the past quarter of a century. The data for this part of the chapter are therefore gathered from interviews conducted with people who served in different senior positions in the EPLA and later in the EDF. Unfortunately, however, the dearth of documentation and the length of time seem to have affected the accuracy of the interviewees' memories. As a result, some of the information is fragmented and at times contradictory. In a situation where oral history is the major source, the risk of memory decay can be a threat to reliability and consistency. In order to minimise the impact of memory decay among former high-ranking military commanders during the war of independence and after, I have interviewed different informants and counter-checked and compared the information gathered from different individuals.

It is important therefore to bear this in mind when reading the following paragraphs on the positions occupied by different military officers at different times and the organisational structure of the military. The EDF being a continuation of the EPLA, its predecessor has influenced its organisational structure in the post-independence period. In October 1984, seven years prior to Ethiopia's defeat in Eritrea, the EPLA was re-organised along *kifle serawit* (divisions). This organisational structure was abolished in February 1991 and replaced by four corps, namely Corps 161, 271, 381 and 491, headed by Teklay Habteselassie, Haile (China) Samuel, Saleh Hiruy and Mesfin Hagos, respectively.[1] The office of chief of staff was also established in 1988, and Sebhat Ephrem was the first to hold the office. During that time, the heads of the divisions, Saleh Hiruy, Mesfin Hagos, Teklay Habteselasse and Haile Samuel, served as deputies of chief of staff.

The EDF was reorganised after independence and Petros Solomon became minister of defence, with Mesfin Hagos appointed chief of staff in November 1992. The latter served in the same position until the third organisational congress of the EPLF. In the same year, *meselteni haileat mklikal Eritra Sawa* (The Training of Eritrean Defence Force, Sawa) was established, headed by Teklay Habteselasse. Immediately after the third congress, Petros Solomon was removed from his position and Mesfin Hagos replaced him as minister of defence. After the third congress, the office of chief of staff was abolished by the president without consultation or forethought, and Teklay Habteselasse, Halibay Iyob and Haile Samuel were appointed heads of logistics, intelligence and operation, respectively.

By that time President Isaias had perfected the game of playing off the high-ranking commanders against each other by constantly reshuffling them and privileging some and depriving others of money-spinning positions. The purpose was to make them jealous of each other so they would vie against each other. For example, according to one informant, Isaias loathed Musfin Hagos' popularity among the rank and file members of the army. Mesfin received almost the same number of votes as President Isaias Afwerki during the 4th Congress of the EPLF. In spite of this, the president left no stone unturned in undermining him. For example, nine months after Mesfin was appointed as minister of defence, President Isaias created a counter ground force headed by Berhane Gerezgiher without informing or consulting with him. Mesfin Hagos rejected this counter force and was replaced by the ever compliant Sebhat Ephrem in 1995. By the time the border war broke out in May 1998, President Isaias had effectively marginalised and excluded the seasoned heroes of the liberation struggle, thereby depriving the country of its competent military leadership developed under the severe conditions of the struggle. If Isaias had not prioritised the survival of his regime at the expense of the security of the state, he would not have marginalised and excluded the heroes of the war of independence. It was the individuals he targeted who led the liberation struggle to the victorious end, 'against all odds' withstanding the severe test of time.

During the border war, the *kifli serawit* (divisions) were abolished and replaced by five *ginbarat* (fronts), namely Ali Tena Mereb Front, Mereb-Setit Front, Burie Front, Central Front and the Reserve Army headed by Gerezgiher (Wuchu) Andemariam, Filipos Woldeyohannes, Haile (China) Samuel, Omer Towil and Berhane Gerezgiher, respectively. Towards the end of 2001, that is after the suppression of the change-seeking forces and

---

[1]   Key informant's name and place withheld, 2 December 2015. Commando 525, mechanised brigade were also established in the same year headed by Gerezgiher (Wuchu) Andemariam and Awliyay, respectively. Soon after the navy and air force were also created, headed by Kakay and Habtezion, respectively.

the incarceration of the eleven members of the G-15 and the journalists,[2] plus the banning of independent newspapers, the short-lived organisational structure of the army was abolished and replaced by a new organisational structure comprising five military operation zones or command zones, namely Gash-Barka (Zone 1) commander Tekle (Manjus); West (Zone 2) commander Filipos; South (Zone 3) commander Omer Towil; East (Zone 4) commander Haile (China); and Centre, including Asmara (Zone 5) commander-Gerezgiher (Wuchu) Andemariam.

Not only was each of these sycophant commanders subservient to the president but also they could not agree with each other. Because of his insecurity, the president and his cronies ceaselessly sowed seeds of dissonance among them without any regard to the corrosive effect such disharmony may have on the country's defence capability. Each of the commanders reported directly to the president, circumventing the titular minister of defence, Sebhat Ephrem.[3] Other unknown junior, or even non-commissioned, officers also reported to the president behind their backs. This engendered an atmosphere of fear and uncertainty among the high-ranking echelons of the military and facilitated the machinations of the president.

To undermine the civilian administration and the regional governors, the commanders of the five military operational zones were allowed to usurp the powers of the regional governors. The latter were effectively marginalised and excluded from any power of decision-making. As Nicole Hirt states, '...the four [read five] military operational zones [...] gained considerable influence over the civilian administration and the economy. They have become increasingly involved in illegal activities such as smuggling and human trafficking [...] the economy has been monopolised by the party and the military – both of which use national service conscripts as unpaid labourers' (2013: 8). Her assertion is consistent with the data I gathered from most of the respondents and key informants. In an attempt to reduce the haemorrhage and to mollify the international community, the government has detained some high-ranking military officers in CZ1, Tekle (Manjus) Samuel's office. These are suspected of

[2] In September 2001, some of the founding members and leaders of the EPLF and former members of the cabinet and the central council of the ruling party, the People's Front for Democracy and Justice (PFDJ) formed the G-15 and published an open letter to the members of the party and the president calling for democratic dialogue and change. The Open Letter was leaked to the private press and was publicised widely. On 18 September the government arrested eleven members of the G-15. Three were out of the country and escaped arrest. One was in the country, but was not arrested. Simultaneously, the government closed down all the private newspapers and most of the journalists who worked for the private newspapers. The government accused the members of G-15 of treason and of crime against national security. The journalists were accused of being spies. All have been held in incommunicado detention without being charged.
[3] Ironically, the latter organisational structure is the same as the one established by the Supreme Council of the ELF in 1965, which the EPLF leadership condemned on the grounds of tribalism and sectarianism.

engaging in smuggling and human trafficking (ICG 2014: 11).[4] Currently there are only three operational command zones (CZ) with commanders, namely, CZ 2, 3 and 4 (Central, Eastern and Western fronts) headed by Tekle (Manjus) Samuel, Haile China and Mussa Raba'a, respectively. Wodi Lebsu has replaced the Sawa Military Trainining Centre's commander, Teklay Habteselasse. Filipos Weldeyohanness has been appointed as chief of staff.

After 2001, and the indefinite detention of the members of the G-15, '[i]n effect, the government has been the Office of the President ...' (Reid 2008: 213). According to Reid's informant, 'The president has periodically switched power between the Party and the army, in some ways playing one off against the other, creating a situation which we might describe as functioning confusion which has effectively rendered the various ministries marginal to policy making' (Reid 2008: 213). This is consistent with the findings of this study. It is important to state, however, that the so-called 'Party' refers to a few individuals, such as Hagos, Yemene, al-Amin, Zemheret, Osman Saleh, Fozia Hashim and Sebhat Ephrem. The central council of the party has not met since 2001. In the post-2001 period, the Party has been reduced to a shadow of what it was. As Reid says, '[n]o doubt this situation stems from Isaias' sense of insecurity immediately following the arrest of his most prominent critics in September 2001, when he relied on the army – and in particular such key commanders as Wuchu and Filipos ...' (Reid 2008: 213).

Apart form suppressing its potential for institutionalisation and professionalization, the purpose of these constant rotations of the commanders and the ceaseless changes of the organisational structure of the army is also to fetter the military's stability, efficiency, technical capability and autonomy. The overall purpose is to make the military amenable to personal control. The Eritrean head of state also does not want congenial relationships to develop between commanders and soldiers based on mutual trust: he perceives such a stance as a threat to his personal rule. As stated in Global Security (2015), 'EDF units are frequently rotated among the regional commanders to combat the formation of loyalty between soldiers and commanders.' It is further stated that:

> [i]t has also been reported that President Afwerki routinely shifts zone commanders around, apparently to encourage rivalries between them, distribute profits, and prevent them from building up too close a rapport with the units under their command. Similarly, deputy commanders are reportedly carefully selected for their loyalty to the President, who maintains control over zonal commanders through them. (Global Security 2015)

One way in which the president blackmails the zonal commanders is by gathering incriminating information against them from their right hand men. For example, Tekle Manjus' right hand men, Idris Mohammad and Girmai Mesgina (with five others), and Haile China's right hand man,

---

[4]   According to the ICG, these are Major General Fitsum (Wedi Memhir), Girmai Mesgina, head of Manjus' office and the border guard head, Idris Muhammad. The information about Major General Fitsum's detention is inaccurate. In fact, he is one of the heads of the president's bodyguards.

Mussie, have been in detention. Not only have their patrons been unable to protect them, but also the confessions obtained under torture and duress are used by the president to blackmail the patrons and keep them under enduring anxiety and insecurity to ensure their absolute subservience and loyalty to his personal rule.

The fit between the measures the Eritrean head of state has been taking to stifle the growth and consolidation of a professional, institutionalised, autonomous and technically capable military and the actions most post-independence African heads of state took in the immediate post-independence period is astonishingly close. As Herbert Howe insightfully observes, '... personalist rulers since independence have feared their militaries' armed might and so developed strategies of controlling the military' (2001: 27). He further states, '[s]ensing a tension between military capabilities and political loyalty to the regime, these rulers often emphasised the armed forces' allegiance at the expense of operational effectiveness. Loyalty appeared more important than efficiency, given the domestic occurrence of post-independence coups ...' (2001: 28).

As has been the case in many other post-independence African states, the single most important preoccupation of the Eritrean personal ruler has been his regime's survival at the expense of long-term institutionalisation and professionalisation of the military. According to Howe, '[p]rofessionalism usually requires an institutionalised system of stable and widely accepted political values that exist independent of a specific regime. Implicit is the distinction between the state (on-going) and the regime (temporary). In other words, the value and interests of the state, including the military, claim precedence over any other temporary powerful group or leader' (2001: 9). As seen earlier, the converse is the case in Eritrea. Making their interests, rather than the interests of the state, paramount Howe argues that personal leaders often 'create personally loyal, parallel militaries as counterweights to the national armed forces' (2001: 35). This is precisely what Isaias has done in Eritrea, through, for example, the creation of the ground force outside the control of the Ministry of Defence. In 2012 the president also established the people's militia as a counterforce to the army:

> [t]o protect himself and his regime from assassination, coup d'etat, army mutiny, or a foreign commando strike, Isaias has created three separate Presidential Guard units of about 2,000 troops each. These elite soldiers get extra pay, have modern equipment, and receive specialized training. Most are stationed in or near Asmara, including a sizeable group lodged about 800 yards from the DCM's residence. The three units are nominally led by a Major General, but in reality Isaias personally commands each one. In addition, Presidential Guardsmen also serve as jailors for the G-15 (senior Eritrean officials arrested in 2001). Isaias' right-hand man commands the 70-man presidential bodyguard detachment. (Global Security 2015).

President Isaias' compulsive preoccupation with the short-term survival of his personal rule at the expense of Eritrea's long-term interests has suffocated the development of professional, autonomous, efficient and technically capable military in the country. This has wantonly squandered the invaluable knowledge and experience gained during the thirty years of liberation struggle (1961–1991), when the EPLA was considered among the best in the world. 'As the second largest army in Africa, Eritrea's Army is well staffed, well trained, and compared to the vast majority of African armies, well funded. Indeed, during Eritrea's fight for independence from Ethiopia, the Eritrean military was once widely admired as one of the most effective fighting organizations in the world' (Pateman 1990). Not only has Isaias's excessive preoccupation with the desire to ward off the threat of an imagined coup d'état thwarted the development of state institutions, but it has also crippled the Eritrean army, rendering the country and its citizens defenceless against potential dangers. In Eritrea, there is no distinction between the military and civilians. Military matters regarding selection, promotion, demotion, dismissal, policies of command and control, manpower, weapons, intelligence, communications, logistics and organisation lie in the hands of President Isaias Afwerki who micro-manages every aspect of Eritrean society with an iron fist.

In view of the fact that the ruler, Isaias Afwerki, dominates every aspect of Eritrea's political landscape and his regime fears the military, and consequently leaves no stone unturned to stifle its operational effectiveness, *inter alia*, his destabilising and micromanaging of it means it is unrealistic to expect the ENS would build Eritrea's defence and fighting capability. Such an outcome is incompatible with the interest of the country's ruler. This caveat is vital in the assessment of the ENS's contribution to post-independence Eritrea's fighting and defence capability.

Notwithstanding the fact that the head of state and the defence minister, allege that building the country's defence capability was not a major aim of the ENS, this undoubtedly was one of the central objectives, as stipulated in the proclamation on national service and in the series of statements and declarations issued by the government and its representatives, including the president (Isias Afwerki, 1994, 2002b; Sebhat Ephrem 2008). Based on the narratives of former conscripts and key informants, as well as other relevant data derived from diverse sources, including extensive sources based on a series of interviews conducted over time by the state media and different magazines and websites belonging to the ruling party and the government, this chapter examines the extent to which the ENS has built the country's defence or fighting capability. If there is no evidence to show this to be the case, bearing in mind the important caveat presented above, an attempt will be made to identify the factors that have discouraged or hindered the building of an effective defence or fighting capability. In light of the fact that tens of thousands of conscripts and draft evaders have been fleeing the country to evade the open-ended national service, an effort is made to examine whether the ENS has boosted or eroded the country's defence capability. Towards its end, the chapter also examines how factors such as mismanagement, corruption and incessant conflicts between the commanders (ex-combatants), the *yikealo*, and the conscripts, the *warsai*, impinge on the efforts of building robust defence capability.

NATIONAL SERVICE AND PREPARATION FOR WAR

There is evidence to show that not only was building the country's fighting or defence capability at the heart of the policy on national service, but it was also a critical element in the government's overall efforts of preparation for war. The president was asked in 2004, by a group of journalists working for *Te'atek* (Be ready/vigilant or literally 'get armed'), to explain why the 'exceptions' and 'exemptions' provided in the first proclamation (Proc. No. 11/1991) were rescinded by proclamation No 82/1995. He said that the original aim of the ENS was not preparation for war. 'When war broke out, not only did we rescind the exemptions, but we were also forced to ignore the upper age limit of 40 years stipulated in the proclamation. This was done to avert the threat to our national security,' he said (2004: 5). He further stated that '[t]he original aim of the ENS changed fundamentally when war broke out resulting in the invasion of Eritrea by Ethiopia. This necessitated a change in the set of criteria enshrined in the proclamation on national service' (2004: 5). The president is grossly economical with the truth in this regard. When Proclamation No. 82/1995 was enacted in November 1995, rescinding all the exceptions and exemptions, there was no indication that war would break out between the two friendly countries three years later. The universalisation of the national service had nothing to do with the border war in spite of his claim. There was no indication of a border war when this decision was taken.

When Proc. No. 82 was enacted in November 1995 Eritrea had not been invaded by a foreign force. On the contrary, it was Eritrea that invaded the disputed Hanish Archipelago and shelled Djiboutian positions in 1995. It was four and a half years after the 'exceptions' and 'exemptions' were eliminated from the proclamation on the ENS, in May 2000, that the Ethiopian army invaded undisputed Eritrean territories. In fact, it was only the first and second cohorts of national service who were assigned to build dams and roads without being integrated into the army. All the other cohorts, the third, fourth, and all those conscripted subsequently, were integrated into the regular army. The reasons the president and the defence minister gave concerning the rescinding of the broad categories that were previously excepted and exempted from the ENS in the first proclamation would appear to be blatantly untrue.

They both retroactively used Ethiopia's invasion of Eritrean territory as a justification for universalising the obligation to perform national service and for turning the same into a never-ending cycle of forced labour (Kibreab 2009a, 2009b, 2013). The defence minister said, '... the Woyane's [read Ethiopian government's] invasion has shown the centrality of the national service.' 'But', he continued, 'the original aim was not for such a purpose' (2004: 7). The president said that the invasion of sovereign Eritrean territories by the Ethiopian government has fundamentally changed the dimension of the national service. 'Out of the 13 years, we spent the last six either fighting against an invasion or in a state of no-war-no-peace.'

The question that arises, however, is how did the Eritrean government know that Ethiopia was going to invade Eritrean territories four and a half years later? Four and a half years before the border war broke out, the two governments were the best of friends (see Tekle 1995). Their relationship was so amiable that the Eritrean president stated that their goal was beyond borders and even suggested that the two countries may form a confederation of some sort. Leenco Lata (2006: 17), for example, wrote that five years before the border war broke out, '[i]t looked as if the two parties were determined to close once for all the old chapter of spite and acrimony and write a new one of cooperation. The talk in some circles was not only of federation or confederation but even of possible eventual union.' The reality that prevailed on the ground when the Eritrean government universalised the obligation of national service in November 1995, about two and a half years before the border war against Ethiopia broke out in May 1998, shows that the elimination of the exceptions and exemptions had nothing to do with the border war.

In spite of the Eritrean government's hue and cry about being invaded, there is evidence to suggest that it was Eritrea rather than its neighbours that initially instigated the skirmish, although it was Ethiopia that declared the war, which may suggest that at the heart of the decision to universalise the national service by eliminating the categories that were exempted and excepted in the first proclamation on national service (Proc. No. 11/91) lay preparation for war rather than expulsion of non-existent foreign invaders from Eritrean territories. For example, on 19 December 2005, the Eritrea/Ethiopia Claims Commission made a decision on Ethiopia's claim that Eritrea had violated the principles of international law. In para. 14 of the Partial Award, it was stated:

> The evidence showed that, at about 5:30 a.m. on May 12, 1998, Eritrean armed forces, comprised of at least two brigades of regular soldiers, supported by tanks and artillery, attacked the town of Badme and several other border areas in Ethiopia's Tahtay Adiabo Wereda, as well as at least two places in its neighbouring Laelay Adiabo Wereda. On that day and in the days immediately following, Eritrean armed forces then pushed across the flat Badme plain to higher ground in the east. Although the evidence regarding the nature of Ethiopian armed forces in the area conflicted, the weight of the evidence indicated that the Ethiopian defenders were composed merely of militia and some police, who were quickly forced to retreat by the invading Eritrean forces. Given the absence of an armed attack against Eritrea, the attack that began on May 12 cannot be justified as lawful self-defence under the UN Charter. (Eritrea Ethiopia Claims Commission 2005: 467)

In para. 15 the Commission further stated:

> The areas initially invaded by Eritrean forces on that day were all either within undisputed Ethiopian territory or within territory that was peacefully administered by Ethiopia... In the same Partial Award, the Commission explained why it must hold Eritrea liable for violations of international humanitarian law committed by it within such territory and why such holdings concerning conduct during the war have no effect on the international boundary as subsequently determined by the Eritrea-Ethiopia Boundary Commission. (Eritrea-Ethiopia Claims Commission 2005: 467)

There are, however, analysts who argue that the Claims Commission had overstepped its jurisdiction. Christine Gray, for example, states, '[t]he first and most important criticism that may be made of the partial award on the *jus ad bellum* claims is that the Claims Commission lacked jurisdiction to go into the difficult issue of responsibility for the start of the war and that it should not have decided the case' (Gray 2006: 704). However, Eritrea did not contest the decision, and seems to have accepted it (see Dybnis 2011, footnote 137).

The president's assertion that it was the imperatives of war and the need to expel foreign invasion that forced Eritrea to eliminate the 'exceptions' and 'exemptions' that were stipulated in the first proclamation on national service (Proc. No. 11/1991) is therefore disingenuous. Although Eritrea was involved in several disputes with its neighbours, Sudan (see Cliffe 1999; Gunaratna 2002; Kibreab 2009c) and Djibouti (see Gettleman 2008b; Shinn 2012), soon after its independence in May 1993, in November 1995 when the changes in the provisos of the proclamation on national service were introduced there were no major wars in which Eritrea was involved that could justify total mobilisation of the population without provisions for exception and exemption. Eritrea laid claim to a 500 square kilometre piece of territory in northern Djibouti on the basis of an Italian colonial map of 1935, and consequently, a minor Eritrean military incursion occurred in late 1995 and a subsequent frontier post was shelled by Eritrean forces in 1996. None of these small incidents could justify the elimination of 'exceptions' and 'exemptions', as well as the upper age limit of forty years stipulated in the proclamation on national service, however.

Eritrea was also involved in a dispute with Yemen over the Red Sea archipelago. In November 1995 Eritrean forces overran the Greater Hanish Island resulting in the death of six Yemeni soldiers and the capture of 200, who were released soon after. The dispute with Yemen was amicably settled through international arbitration which awarded most of the disputed islands to Yemen, a decision Eritrea accepted as final and binding. At a press conference held in Asmara on 21 December 1999, Foreign Minister Haile Woldense stressed:

> The legal settlement of the dispute will not only pave the way for a harmonious relationship between the littoral states of the Red Sea, but also opens a new window of opportunity for the consolidation of peace and stability in the region and the creation of a zone of peace, development and mutual benefit. (Cited in Kwiatkowska 2000: 67, emphasis in original)

The Vice-Minister of Foreign Affairs of Yemen, Abdulla Mohammed Al-Saidi, also stated that the Award 'represents a culmination of a great diplomatic effort and an important historic development in political and diplomatic relations between two neighbouring countries' and 'a way that should be followed for resolving Arab, regional and international disputes' (cited in Kwiatkowska 2000: 67) The governments of the two countries expressed their commitment to fully comply with and to implement the two Awards.

Eritrea also broke off diplomatic relations with Sudan in December 1994 in protest against Sudan's provision of support to the Eritrean Islamic Jihad Movement (EIJM) which aimed at toppling the government in Asmara (see Iyob 2004; Connell 2007; Kibreab 2009d). The forces of the two countries clashed intermittently between July 1996 and March

1998, but the situation did not degenerate into full-scale inter-state war. With the exception of the dispute with Sudan, the Eritrean government was responsible for starting the armed offensives against its neighbours, Djibouti and Yemen, and later Ethiopia. Hence, it was preparation for war rather than self-defence or the need to expel invaders that underpinned the decision of the Eritrean government to universalise the duty of performing national service, as well as to militarise the whole society and to turn the duration of the ENS into an open-ended obligation.

NATIONAL SERVICE AND THE BORDER WAR

One of the astonishing findings of this study is that a large minority, 44 per cent, of the respondents interviewed for the study stated that had there been no ENS, there would have been no border war between Eritrea and Ethiopia. The respondents were asked whether the outcome of the border war would have been better or worse had there been no ENS. They were also asked 'Do you think the May 1998–June 2000 border war between Eritrea and Ethiopia would have taken place had it not been for the ENS?' Although 50 per cent thought that the border war would have happened regardless, 44 per cent of the respondents thought that the ENS was a major contributor to the outbreak of the border war between the two countries. Those who thought so were asked to explain.

R #001 said that the outcome of the war would have been better in the absence of the ENS, because if there were no national service, 'the Eritrean government would have been forced to seek diplomatic solution to the crisis and would have invested all its capability in dialogue, compromise and negotiation. This would have given the government enough time to reflect and consider the unnecessary potential losses.' The corollary is that the size of the Eritrean army soared and the authorities in Eritrea overestimated their fighting capability and took victory for granted without carefully weighing the balance of power between the two countries.

R #074, who had a university degree and joined the ENS in 1996 voluntarily, said, 'without the ENS, there would have been no border war against Ethiopia.' He further stated: 'The President said it himself when our round (5th 1996) was starting' [induction at Sawa], he said "from now onwards, we are not scared of any one in the region."' The assertions of the president and his ministers, especially the former defence minister, that the sole aim of the ENS was peaceful in terms of socialising the youth into the values of the liberation struggle is without empirical backing. Although the latter was a major goal of the ENS, building the country's fighting capability and preparation for war were equally important. The fact that the president said that after they established the national service, none of the neighbouring countries would threaten Eritrea may indicate that one of the goals of the ENS was to build the country's defence and fighting capability. R #160 also said, 'there would have never been a border war against Ethiopia. In hindsight, I have come to realise that it was Isaias [the Head of State] and his clique who started the war.' This respondent's prophetic views are vindicated by the Eritrea-Ethiopia Claims Commission, which concluded that Eritrea started the border war (Eritrea-Ethiopia Claims Commission 2005).

In hindsight, it may be possible to argue that the ENS, instead of building the capacity of the Eritrean Defence Forces, seems to have become its gravedigger. During the so-called Ethiopian third offensive in May 2000, which resulted in the illegal occupation of large swathes of Eritrean sovereign territories by the Ethiopian armed forces, the Eritrean Defence Forces, which had an impressive track record, were thrown uncharacteristically into disarray and there is no evidence to show that they have recovered a decade and a half later. Even though the president and the defence minister had earlier stated that the reason Eritrea established the national service had little to do with building the fighting or defence capability of the country, they seem to contradict themselves by presenting it as a matter of life and death. Notwithstanding earlier claims, official discourse presents the national service as constituting the edifice of the foundation on which Eritrea's survival as a sovereign state rests. In the defence minister's words, '[o]ne of the pillars upon which the very existence of this country stands, is the national service' (Sebhat Ephrem 1995). When the commander of the Sawa military camp, Colonel Debessai Ghide, was asked, 'What would you say to those who question the necessity of Sawa?' he said in unequivocal terms, 'They are people who want our people to be wiped out from the face of the earth. Sawa is a matter of life and death. Without Sawa, we would not have been able to defeat external invasion [...] Even now whoever wants to see our people defeated would question the importance of Sawa' (2004: 47).

When the defence minister was asked; 'What would Eritrea be like as a state and government without a national service?' he said, 'In other words, you are asking "what would happen to Eritrea if it did not have an army?"' The corollary is Eritrea's army comprises the national service conscripts. He said, '[a] country without an army is a monkey' (Sebhat Ephrem 2008: 43). He further pointed out that without the national service Eritrea would be vulnerable to invasion. He said, '[w]e saw what happened to the Eritreans who were deported from Ethiopia during the 1998–2000 border war. They lost all their capital, land and property. They have nowhere to seek redress from. If Ethiopians could take all the possessions of Eritreans in Addis Ababa, what would stop them from taking everything if they invade Asmara?' (Sebhat Ephrem 2008: 43). He said that without the national service Eritrea would be defenceless and at the mercy of its enemies. Such views are typical of what Enloe refers to as 'core beliefs' of militaristic individuals, groups or states. One of these 'core beliefs', she says, is the assumption that 'a state without military is naïve, scarcely modern and barely legitimate' (2004: 219).

In the opening ceremony of the Festival the president noted that, 'Sawa signifies a permanent symbol for our continued existence as a people and nation' (Isaias Afwerki 20 July 2006). The defence minister also said, '[t]here are malicious attempts to asphyxiate the national service and if our enemies were to succeed, that would sound the death knell of Eritrea.' He further stated that '[t]here can be no armed forces in Eritrea without the national service. Those who fought in the war of independence are getting old. No human being can remain young forever' (Sebhat Ephrem 2008: 43). The *agelglot* (conscripts) should take their place. In his view, in matters of national defence and security, Eritrea has no alternative to the national service (Sebhat Ephrem 2008: 43). The claims by the president and the defence minister that the institution of the national service had nothing to do with preparation for war or national defence is therefore bizarre.

In the following, the narratives of the conscripts who deserted from the ENS are used to examine the extent to which the national service has built Eritrea's defence and fighting capability or whether the ENS has degenerated into forced labour, thereby demotivating the conscripts.

THE NARRATIVES OF CONSCRIPTS

Since one of the central aims of the ENS is to build Eritrea's military power and fighting capability, and consequently to guarantee the sovereignty and territorial integrity of the country, as stipulated in the proclamation on national service and as stated by the head of state and the defence minister (see Isaias Afwerki 1995, 2002a, 2004, 2008; Sebhat Ephrem 1995, 2008), I asked the respondents who had deserted from the national service after serving on average nearly six years the following question: 'Has the national service built Eritrea's military manpower?' By focussing on the narratives of conscripts it may be possible to evaluate the extent to which the national service has built the country's military power, which was one of the stipulated goals. The narratives can also serve as a prism for examining the extent to which the ENS, which began as a civic duty and an instrument of realising civic and political rights, has degenerated into forced labour or a modern form of slavery, a variety of the old institution of *posse comitatus* (on the latter see Chapter 2).

Building the country's military human resources may not necessarily be a function of what the former conscripts think about the extent to which the institution of the national service has bolstered or undermined Eritrea's military manpower. However, since, as we saw earlier, the defence minister, Sebhat Ephrem, and the president, Isaias Afwerki, stress that the backbone of the Eritrean defence force is the national service; the conscripts' narratives concerning their own evaluation of the role the national service plays in building Eritrea's defence capability is critical in understanding and evaluating the extent to which the national service has built the country's military manpower or fighting capability. The findings of the survey show that the conscripts who deserted from the national service and are now residing in different parts of the world do not speak with a single voice. The reason why there are multiple voices in spite of the conscripts' common or similar experience/s will be explained later. Here their narratives will be presented qualitatively and, to a limited extent, quantitatively.

Among the respondents who answered the question 72 per cent said that initially the national service built Eritrea's military manpower, but a considerable minority, 28 per cent, said that the national service did not contribute positively to Eritrea's military manpower. There were also some who expressed the view that the national service has substantially eroded Eritrea's military manpower. Many among those who said that the ENS had initially contributed to building the country's defence capability also said that it has become a liability and consequently eroded the country's defence capability after it became open-ended. Both those who think that the national service builds Eritrea's military manpower and those who think that the national service makes no contribution to the same were asked in an open-ended question to explain whether, in their opinion, the institution of the national service builds Eritrean's military manpower and fighting capability or not.

Although only those who answered the questions in the negative were expected to answer the follow-up open-ended question, two of those who thought that the national service builds Eritrea's military manpower and fighting capability also answered the question affirmatively without qualifications. One said, 'Without the national/military service, Eritrea's defence capability would have been very weak' (R #006). Another added, 'Indeed, the ENS has built Eritrea's fighting capability. Had it not been for the national service, Eritrea would have been re-colonised by Ethiopia [during the border war]' (R #068). These respondents, especially the latter, agree with the views of the defence minister and the president that not only does the institution of the national service contribute to defence and fighting capability, but its absence would sound the 'death knell' of the country as an independent political entity. Had it not been for the national service, Eritrea would have been re-colonised by its former occupier, Ethiopia. In the view of this respondent, the president and the defence minister, the survival of Eritrea as an independent state is inextricably linked to the institution of the national service. In these two respondents' views, the Eritrean army comprises the national service. Without the national service, Eritrea would be without an army, and its survival and security would be compromised.

Twenty-eight respondents either denied that the national service makes any positive contribution to the country's military manpower and fighting capability or said that after it became open-ended its positive contributions effectively ceased. Others said that the national service erodes the country's military manpower and hence undermines its fighting and defence capabilities. The following are some of the extracts from the narratives of the respondents and key informants. Abraham, with a post-graduate degree, for example, gave concrete examples to demonstrate the fact that the ENS did not boost Eritrea's defence capability. He narrated:

> During the thirty years' war of independence, the Eritrean People's army was invincible. This was notwithstanding the fact that the Ethiopian government had access to massive arsenal of weaponry and technical military assistance first from the US government and from 1977 onwards from the Soviet Union and its allies, especially East Germany and Cuba. The latter even had large number of ground troops fighting on the side of the Ethiopian military in the Ogaden

war between Ethiopia and Somalia. In spite of this, the Eritrean liberation army inflicted humiliating defeat on the large Ethiopian military. The victory of the EPLF over the Ethiopian military was considered as one of the most awesome and spectacular achievements of an African liberation movement. (Interview, Khartoum, 1 November 2010)

The accuracy of Abraham's account is consistent with the observations of many analysts. For example, Timothy Stapleton, in his book *A Military History of A*frica (2013: 98), writes:

In March 1988, the EPLF achieved its greatest victory by enveloping the Ethiopian 21 Division at the town of Afabet, where 18,000 Ethiopian troops were killed or captured and a massive amount of heavy equipment taken, including 50 tanks, 100 trucks, 60 artillery pieces, and 20 anti-aircraft guns. With retreat rendered impossible by burning tanks in Ashirum Pass, the Ethiopian 29th Mechanised Brigade was bombed by its own air force to prevent the capture of its armour. In what BBC journalist called the greatest triumph by any liberation movement since Dien Bien Phu.

Abraham continued:

In the light of its impressive formidable track record, the performance of the Eritrean Defence Forces in the Ethiopian Third Offensive (May 2000) was embarrassing. They were betrayed by the President and his inner circle in the PFDJ central office who in order to marginalise the heroes of the independence war were either completely excluded from command positions or relegated to the background. The outcome was shocking and humiliating. Ethiopia which used to suffer debilitating defeats during the war of independence, occupied large swathes of sovereign Eritrean territories during the border war. As if this were not enough, in March 2012, the Ethiopian army attacked inside Eritrea and the aggressors left unpunished. (See also BBC 2012)

According to *The Guardian*, the Eritrean Foreign Minister, Osman Salih, responded saying that Eritrea 'will not be entrapped by such deceitful ploys that are aimed at derailing and eclipsing the underlying fundamental issues' (Smith 2012). Abraham further stated,

To add insult to injury, the Tigray People's Democratic Movement (TPDM – Demhit) which was based in Eritrea as part of the two governments [Eritrean and Ethiopian] misguided policy of interference into each other's domestic affairs, on September 11, 2015 fled first to Sudan and later to Ethiopia without the EDF being able to stop them. Nothing can be more embarrassing than one's defence forces being unable to determine who exists and enters a country's sovereign territories. This is exacerbated by the fact that the TPDM were the running dogs of President Isaias. These incidents demonstrate the abject failure of the ENS to contribute to Eritrea's defence and fighting capability.

He also stated that the defence forces have been unable to stop the hundreds of thousands of conscripts that have fled the country to avoid the indefinite national service.

4

The Nature of the Eritrean National Service and its Effectiveness as a Fighting Force

> Your question regarding whether the ENS has built Eritrea's defence and fighting capability is misplaced. The President knows very well that a well organised and institutionalised military with a robust fighting and defence capability represents an imminent threat to his tyrannical rule. Rhetoric notwithstanding the tacit, but principal aim of the ENS is to control the youth and stifle their autonomy and ability to become agents of change.
>
> Abraham (Interview, Khartoum, 1 November 2010)

This chapter uses the perceptions of the respondents and key informants to examine the extent to which the Eritrean National Service (ENS) has contributed to the development of Eritrea's fighting and defence capability. The factors that have contributed to the failure of the ENS to build an efficient and capable defence and fighting capability are also discussed. We saw in Chapter 2 that participation in national service engenders a powerful sense of patriotism, inducing the affected not only to surrender their interests but also their lives in defence of the nation and the common good (Montesquieu 1989 [1748]; Hart 1994; Farar-Hockley cited in Board 2006). Contrary to these views, some of the respondents who served in the ENS before they fled believed that a country's military manpower and its fighting capability could not be built through coercion, blackmail and intimidation. The construction of a robust military manpower and an effective fighting capability, in their view, is a function of the readiness and wholehearted dedication of members of the armed forces or, in this case, of conscripts. The large majority said that although most of the conscripts were ready and willing to defend and die for their country, this initial powerful predisposition vanished after the ENS degenerated into forced labour. As one respondent put it succinctly, 'The ENS cannot build Eritrea's fighting capability as long as it remains compulsory' (R #106). Another respondent said, 'An armed force that is kept by force against its will for ten years or more cannot build the fighting capability of the country' (R #147). Not only are the conscripts forced to serve against their will indefinitely, but also noncompliance is punished by detention and torture. Human Rights Watch (HRW), for example, states, 'National service keeps most young Eritreans in perpetual bondage' and '[t]orture and other abuses during detention are routine. Punishments include mock drowning, being hung from trees by the arms, being tied up in the sun in contorted positions for hours or days, being doubled up inside a rolling tire, having handcuffs tightened to cut off circulation, as well as frequent beatings' (2013). The respondents reported that these types of punishments are routine in the ENS. As seen in Chapter 2, exactions of labour against the will of the persons concerned and the use or threat of punishment are the two critical elements in the definition of forced labour.

As we saw before, according to the proclamation on national service, the duration of the national service was limited to eighteen months, but as we shall see later, many of the respondents have been in the national service for more than ten years against their will. For example, a highly educated key informant, Yohannes, who served for seven years before fleeing the country, said, 'The hearts and minds of the *agelglot* (conscripts) are elsewhere not in Eritrea. The large majority spend their time either conspiring on how to escape or daydreaming. *Eritrea's defence or fighting capability cannot be built by relying on daydreamers*' (emphasis added). He further stated:

> A capable military manpower and a robust fighting capability are the function of advanced military skills, high level of concentration, passion, willpower, perseverance and powerful belief in the future. These critical traits are completely absent among the conscripts. In short, the ENS has deteriorated so much that it has willy-nilly defeated its own goals by creating and reproducing conditions of despondency, lethargy and obsession with life outside of Eritrea. The Eritrea we once dreamt of may not be dead but it is not insight.

A female deserter forthrightly noted, 'Building Eritrea's military man-power requires moral fortitude and openness on the part of the *tegadelti* (*yikealo* – ex-combatants) and the *agelglot* (*warsai* – conscripts). The commanders destroyed these values. 'The norm is "do it by force, if not, you will be detained or even killed"' (R #010). In her view, in the absence of moral fortitude, willpower and openness that enable conscripts to question the political system of which they are members and to evaluate their own role as citizens within that system in general, and the institution of the ENS in particular, their contribution to the building of the country's military manpower or fighting capability is likely to be limited or non-existent. This respondent thinks that building of fighting capability is a function of openness, willingness, moral fortitude and freedom of choice. In other words, Eritrea's military manpower cannot be built through coercion or intimidation. As one respondent put it; 'I can't say that the ENS has helped to build Eritrea's fighting capability, because it is not possible to build fighting capability on the basis of intimidation and blackmailing' (R #066). Another observed, 'The ENS has not built Eritrea's fighting capability because the *agelglot* are suffering morally and financially. Soldiers that serve against their will are demoralised' (R #070). A sizeable proportion of the interviewees saw the task of building the country's fighting capability or military manpower as inextricably linked to the morale and willingness of members of the armed forces, including the *agelglot*. The corollary is coercive military or national service inevitably saps servers' morale and stamina and consequently kills their self-esteem and willingness to fight. As one interviewee put it, 'Military power is measured by the morale and strength of mind of its personnel. In the Eritrean case, this has been abused by the compulsory military service policy. No ambition, no commitment within the military personnel. Hence I don't think the Eritrean military manpower has been built' (R #084).

This view was shared by a number of respondents whose conception of a country's strong military manpower and effective fighting capability can only be based on voluntary participation of citizens in military service. One respondent stated, 'A country's fighting capability cannot be built by forcing people against their will (R #160). Yohannes, a key informant, observed, 'The large majority of the fighters in the Eritrean war of independence were volunteers who joined the ELF and the EPLF to sacrifice their lives in order to liberate their country and people from foreign occupation. The circumstances were completely different from the ones under which the national service is implemented. It is stupid to see them as being analogous as Isaias [the president] does.' Adem stated, 'It is surprising that the incumbent as former leaders of the most formidable volunteer Eritrean People's Liberation Army have failed to draw a lesson from our historical experience. If the fighters were not volunteers who staunchly believed in the justice of the cause they volunteered to fight for, they would not have been able to defeat Ethiopia's huge military force.'

Contrary to Montesquieu's assertion (1989 [1748]), the data gathered from former conscripts who deserted, after serving on average six years, provide no evidence to show that attachment to the country and commitment to the ENS is an increasing function of suffering and hardship. Instead, the findings of this study show that the greater the hardship, the deeper becomes the resentment, as reflected in the decision to flee rather than stay in the country. Nearly all conscripts interviewed for this study cited the suffering they experienced at the hands of the government and its agents, the military commanders, as well as the indefinite nature of the obligation as the most important factors that drove them into exile. More importantly, as we shall see in the following chapters, unlike in Montesquieu's theorising regarding the positive relationship between hardship and attachment, data derived from the respondents show that the experience of hardship and affliction engender resentment and resistance rather than attachment.

Nevertheless, although the ex-conscripts of the ENS currently residing outside of the country, do not speak with a single voice, ironically, notwithstanding the suffering they endured as a result of the open-ended nature of the ENS, when the deserters were asked, 'Should the national service be discontinued?' Only 15 per cent said 'yes', 28 per cent said, 'it should be continued provided it is limited to eighteen months' and the majority – 55 per cent – said, 'it should be voluntary and be limited to eighteen months.' These data gathered from the former conscripts who had direct experience of the ENS clearly show that the deserters are not against the ENS per se. It is its compulsory nature they resent. However, the findings of this study show that hardship, instead of engendering feelings of attachment and commitment as Montesquieu hypothesises, has been causing deeply felt resentment and resistance among the conscripts of the ENS, reflected in the decision of tens of thousands to 'vote with their feet' instead of remaining attached and committed to a programme that has degenerated into forced labour.

INDEFINITE NATURE OF THE SERVICE

None of the prominent theorists and exponents of the philosophical foundation of national service, such as Edward Bellamy (1890 [1888], William James (1943 [1910]), Etzioni (1983), Janowitz (1983), Walzer (1983), Elberly (1988) and Moskos (1988), suggest that the duration of national/military service should be no more than a year or two, unless the country concerned is in a state of war or emergency. As noted previously, the ENS is open-ended and indefinite. Not only has this become the major cause of disaffection among the conscripts, but it has also become the cause of the government's inability to build robust military manpower and fighting capability. The ENS that was introduced for a maximum period of eighteen months has become an obligation for life. On average the respondents in the study have served 5.82 years instead of the 1.5 years required by the proclamation on national service. Those who have not fled are still in the service. HRW's observation that the 'National service keeps most young Eritreans in perpetual bondage' (2013) is accurate and is confirmed by the findings of this study. Although the duration is supposed to be eighteen months, 'in practice the government prolongs service indefinitely' (Human Rights Watch, 2013). Zerai, one of the key informants, said,

> I joined the ENS in 1995 voluntarily before receiving a call up paper. I was demobilised for a brief period after eighteen months, but I was called up when the border war broke out in May 1998. Although the border war came to an end after the signing of the peace agreement between Ethiopia and Eritrea in December 2000, my appeals to be released to support my aging parents fell on deaf ear.s Every time I raised the issue, I was subjected to threats and sometimes to severe corporal punishments. I was accused of being a malingerer and as a bad example. My commander said, 'People like you should be weeded out before they infect the rest.' Under those circumstances, there was only one choice, namely, flight abandoning the country I love and my family. I left my country after serving for sixteen years. Several of my friends are still there. (Interview, Pretoria 7 November 2013)

Among the respondents were those who had served for twenty years.[1] In a recent interview the famous Eritrean singer, Kiros Asfaha, who fled to Ethiopia after serving in the ENS for twenty years, said in a heartrending interview that he joined the national service in 1994.[2] His account of the suffering he experienced and witnessed during the years is distressing. He

---

[1]   For example, among the respondents, one served for 18 years, two for 17 years, two for 15 years, another two for 14 years, four for 13 years, five for 12 years, eleven for 6 years.
[2]   See Kiros Asfaha. Full Interview 'Life is prohibited in Eritrea', available at http://www.hamariweb.uk/watch?v=IeVjCa9QrXI (accessed 16 January 16).

said that he spent a substantial part of his time in prison where he sustained inhumane treatment. 'In other countries imprisonment may be considered abnormal. In Eritrea, it is normal. Prison was my home. Imprisonment was normal to me and to my parents.'[3] Kiros further said that what saddens him is not the requirement to serve in the ENS forever: 'I wouldn't mind serving my country even for a hundred years if I can contribute to its development and the wellbeing of our people. But nothing constructive is happening in the ENS. It only breeds and perpetuates idleness. I was in the national service for twenty years. If you ask me what contribution I have made to my country, the honest answer is nothing.'

As the service is still on going many of the conscripts are likely to serve for much longer than indicated here. A policy of demobilisation is not yet in sight. What two respondents who were interviewed independently of each other said can be roughly summarised as follows, 'It can be said that the ENS had built Eritrea's military manpower until 2000, but after that year, the country's military manpower hit rock bottom' (*mdri zebitu*) (R #024; R #066). The year 2000 is significant in Eritrea's post-war history for the following reasons: firstly, in May 2000, the 'third offensive' of the border war between Eritrea and Ethiopia was launched, in which Ethiopia gained control not only of the disputed territories but of large swathes of undisputed sovereign territories in south-western Eritrea. Fisher (2000), writing in *The New York Times,* for example, stated that Ethiopia 'pressed 65 miles into Eritrea, displacing 340,000 people.' Using UNHCR sources, Reuters (2000) also reported that about 18,000 Eritrean civilians and soldiers had fled to Sudan. In June 2000 the total number of internally displaced persons (IDPs) reached about 750,000. The displaced lived in different camps, caves, forests, and dry riverbeds inside Eritrea (Fisher 2000). On 17 June 2000 the two sides accepted and signed a ceasefire agreement, as proposed by President Abdelaziz Bouteflika of Algeria.

These swift developments and reversal of fortunes left the Eritrean armed forces, which during the war of independence were accustomed to constantly inflicting humiliating defeats on Ethiopia which had sub-Saharan Africa's largest army (see Welch 1991), frustrated and in a state of disarray. Not only did the loss of large territories to Ethiopia, which during the war of independence was perceived as no match for the invincible fighting capability of the Eritrean People's Liberation Army (EPLA), leave the conscripts disheartened, but it also indicated to them that the mobilisation of hundreds of thousands of youths into the national service forcibly and indefinitely did not in fact bolster the country's defence and fighting capability. Prominent historians of the region acknowledge the invincibility of the volunteer EPLF fighters during the war of independence. For example, the Ethiopian historian Gebru Tareke observes: 'The northern guerrillas became invincible. The EPLF repulsed a far-ranging, multi-faceted assault on its primary base, ensuring its survival and indeed that of the TPLF [Tigray People's Liberation Front]. Had Operation Red Star succeeded, there would not have been insurgent victories at Af Abet, Shire

---

[3]   *Ibid.*

and Massawa, the three battles that decisively tipped the scales. Af Abet, Shire and Massawa heralded the defining defeat of the Ethiopian military' (2009: 180–1). In view of this heroic history of the volunteer EPLF fighters, what befell the Eritrean army and the country in 2000 is, to say the least, bewildering, which is why the year 2000 marks an important watershed in the narratives of the respondents, as well as in Eritrea's modern history.

Secondly, in the immediate post-Algiers peace agreement the Eritrean government established a National Commission for the Demobilisation and Re-integration Programme (NCDRP) and a phased demobilisation programme of some 200,000 combatants was ostensibly formulated. In the first phase about 70,000 soldiers were to be demobilised. These were expected to be mostly women, individuals with limited skills, greater family needs or poor health. In the second phase 60,000 combatants expected to be demobilised by the end of July 2003. Due to uncertainties concerning funding availability, the government did not specify the exact time when the remaining 70,000 combatants would be demobilised (IMF 2003: 12). The main funder of the planned disarmament, demobilisation and reintegration (DDR) was the World Bank (see World Bank 2002b). None of these phased demobilisation programmes was implemented. The only exception was the pilot scheme under which about 5,000 soldiers, the large majority of whom were those who suffered disabilities during the border war, and a few members of the *yikealo* (individuals who fought in the war of independence) who were very old and those with long-term illnesses such as diabetics and asthmatics.

It was in desperate circumstances that the government recalled these individuals when the border war broke out in May 1998. When the peace agreement was signed and some funds were made available the government wanted, on the one hand, to appear to be doing something about demobilisation and, on the other, to get rid of the individuals who were, *de facto*, redundant due to injuries, old age and poor health. Although theoretically the pilot scheme was implemented to provide lessons of good practice for the planned large-scale phased programme of demobilisation, no such demobilisation has hitherto taken place (HRW 2009; Kibreab 2009b, 2013; UN Human Rights Commission on Eritrea 2015).

Human Rights Watch's report, appositely titled 'Service for Life: State Repression and Indefinite Conscription in Eritrea' (2009), clearly shows that there have been no demobilisations in the country. Five years earlier the UNHCR stated, '[i]n practice, it [ENS] has become indefinite as no meaningful demobilization has taken place so far. There is no right to conscientious objection' (2004; see also US Department of State 2002; AI 2003). After the border war broke out, alongside the introduction of the Warsai-Yikealo Development Campaign (WYDC) in May 2002, the Eritrean government, instead of demobilising the 200,000 ex-combatants and conscripts as agreed with donors, extended the ENS indefinitely in May 2002 under a new accronym known as the WYDC (see Isaias Afwerki 2002b).[4]

---

[4]   *Warsai* refers to the post-war young recruits. The term literally means one who inherits a legacy. *Yikealo* refers to the old freedom fighters. *Yikealo* in Tigrinya means someone who is able to do anything, including the impossible.

This was arbitrarily introduced by the head of state in the absence of an enabling law and without prior warning. It is, in addition, contrary to the terms of the ENS Proclamation No. 82/1995 that limits the duration of ENS conscription to eighteen months[5] except during periods of mobilisation and war.[6] When the hopes of the conscripts for demobilisation were dashed by the government's failure to respect its promise, the moral fortitude and sense of purpose of the conscripts seem to have dissipated and, as a result, tens of thousands began 'voting with their feet', fleeing from what had by then deteriorated into forced labour or a modern form of slavery (see HRW 2009; Kibreab 2009a, 2009b, 2013). This is consistent with expectation. The French general Maurice de Saxe must have had such a situation in mind when he insightfully observed nearly 260 years ago (in Hippler 2007 [1757]: 21):

> When recruits are raised by enlistment it is unjust and inhuman not to observe the engagement. These men were free when they contracted the enlistment which binds them, and *it is against all laws, human or divine, not to keep the promises made to them. What happens when promises are broken? The men desert. Can one with justice, proceed against them?* [...] *unless severe measures are taken, discipline is lost; and, if severe punishments are used, one commits odious and cruel acts.* (Emphasis added)

The unhappy scenarios that have been unfolding in Eritrea are identical to what General Maurice de Saxe predicted would prompt conscripts to 'vote with their feet' by deserting once the promise is betrayed. From the points of view of all the respondents interviewed in this study, the single most important reason that has prompted tens of thousands of conscripts to desert from the national service, and consequently undermine the country's defence or fighting capability, was the government's failure to abide by the eighteen months duration of the service stipulated in the proclamation on national service. One of the key informants, Amine, with a Masters' degree earned from the UK, who voluntarily joined the first cohorts of conscripts before receiving call up papers in 1994 stated:

> I was driven by an irresistible determination to rebuild my country in the immediate post-war situation. I could not wait for the call up papers to arrive. I joined the first cohorts that went to Sawa in 1994 voluntarily. The government and the Ministry of Defence that had an overall responsibility for the programme had made no preparations whatsoever to receive us. No shelter, water, or other essential amenities. Worse still, the area was infested with poisonous snakes. We had to start from zero. Most of us had never been to a rural area let alone to such wilderness before. Because of our resolve to make a difference, we faced the challenge without feeling daunted by the circumstances that initially seemed to be insurmountable. We had a burning desire to serve our country and people. This state of mind helped us to persevere in adversity and to tame the wilderness. After eighteen months, I was demobilised and I went back home. Unfortunately, I was re-called when the border war broke out in May 1998. I responded to the call without any hesitation and I was sent to the frontline where I sustained two minor injuries at the Tserona and Mereb fronts. (Interview, London, 17 November 2013)

---

[5]   According to Proclamation 11/1991, the minister (secretary at the time) of defence was given the discretion to determine the duration of the obligation of individual or groups of draftees within the range of twelve and eighteen months.
[6]   Art. 21 (1) Proclamation 82/1995

Table 4.1: Total number of Eritrean asylum-seekers and refugees in the EU+ countries 2008–2015

GEO/TIME	2008	2009	2010	2011	2012	2013	2014	2015
European Union (28 countries)	4,905	5,230	4,540	5,725	6,400	14,485	36,945	27,360
Belgium	40	75	110	70	80	70	820	360
Bulgaria	0	0	0	0	0	30	10	0
Czech Republic	0	0	0	10	0	0	0	:
Denmark	15	35	25	20	55	85	2,275	:
Germany (until 1990 former territory of the FRG)	280	380	660	650	670	3,640	13,255	10,990
Estonia	0	0	0	0	0	0	0	0
Ireland	80	45	15	10	5	0	5	:
Greece	45	45	60	35	140	155	260	:
Spain	45	35	10	10	20	5	10	:
France	120	425	730	935	495	430	725	:
Croatia	:	:	:	:	:	20	5	0
Italy	2,935	865	180	530	735	2,110	480	700
Cyprus	0	0	0	0	0	0	0	:
Latvia	0	0	0	0	0	0	0	:
Lithuania	0	0	0	0	0	0	0	0
Luxembourg	10	10	10	15	10	5	40	:
Hungary	0	0	0	5	5	90	120	550
Malta	175	270	15	315	435	475	60	:
Netherlands	250	485	410	500	480	920	3,910	7,455
Austria	20	20	15	25	15	60	110	:
Poland	0	0	0	10	5	5	10	5
Portugal	5	20	0	0	0	5	5	:
Romania	0	0	0	0	15	0	0	:
Slovenia	0	0	5	0	5	0	0	0
Slovakia	0	0	0	0	30	30	10	:
Finland	5	10	15	5	5	0	10	70
Sweden	885	1,035	1,465	1,705	2,405	4,880	11,530	7,230
United Kingdom	:	1,470	815	865	785	1,460	3,300	:
Iceland	0	0	0	0	0	5	0	0
Liechtenstein	0	110	0	0	0	0	0	:
Norway	1,800	2,665	1,710	1,255	1,185	3,250	2,880	2,950
Switzerland	2,850	1,725	1,800	3,450	4,410	2,560	6,920	:
Total	9,555	9,735	8,050	10,430	11,995	20,300	46,750	30,310

Source: http://ec.europa.eu/eurostat/web/asylum-and-managed-migration/data/database
(last accessed February 2016)

Amine continued:

> After the two governments signed the ceasefire agreement and the establishment of the National Commission for the Demobilisation and Re-integration Programme (NCDRP), the government promised to demobilise 200,000 combatants and conscripts. This promise gave us hope of returning to civilian life and I expected to be among the first to be demobilised. Contrary to our expectations, not only did the government betray its promise, but it also introduced a new programme that turned the national service into a never-ending modern form of slavery. When my repeated pleas for demobilisation produced no results, I had no alternative but to cross into Sudan defying the government's 'shoot to kill' policy at the border. I was one of the lucky ones who made it unharmed after serving for thirteen and a half years. My story is the 'tip of the iceberg'. There are people who have been in the national service for nearly twenty years.

He further pointed out:

> Eritrea is the only country in the world that forcibly and ruthlessly exploits its citizens indefinitely and without remuneration. Your question of whether the national service has built Eritrea's military manpower and fighting capability is a redundant one. *It is not possible to build a country's military power and fighting capability on the basis of slavery.* Given the adversity and suffering I experienced in the open-ended national service, I expected the feeling of relief to be exhilarating once I crossed the Sudanese border safely. To my surprise, I felt a sharp and an excruciating pain instead. I could not understand why, but after some reflection, I realised that my love for my country is so powerful that part of me did not want to be uprooted leaving the country to the hyenas (*nezabē*).[7] However, crossing the Rubicon meant reaching a point of no return, at least as long as my country remains in the grip of the tyrants. (Emphasis added)

Another key informant, Ahmed, said, 'Eritrea's military manpower and fighting capability can only result from the voluntary participation of citizens in accordance with the prescription of the law on the national service. Legally, no citizen is required to serve more than 18 months. But I served for twelve years before I got fed up and ran away.' In the views of the majority of those who answered the follow up open-ended question: had the duration of the national service been limited to the eighteen months as stipulated in Proclamation No 82/1995, *ceteris paribus*, the national service would have been able to build Eritrea's military manpower and fighting capability. The open-ended nature of the service seems to have undermined the goal of creating effective defence capability. According to R# 024, rather than building military fighting capability, '...the open-ended nature of the ENS has sapped the confidence and morale of the *agelglot* and therefore, the ENS has eroded Eritrea's military manpower and hence its fighting and defence capability was undermined.'

COERCION, INDEFINITE SERVICE AND FLIGHT PROPENSITY

One of the many consequences of the compulsory and the indefinite nature of the ENS is the high flight propensity amongst conscripts and people approaching the age of conscription. Not only are tens of thousands fleeing illegally (see Table 4.1), but also whoever gets a chance to leave the

---

[7] 'Hyenas' refers to the people who are misruling, mismanaging and exploiting the country's resources and citizens ruthlessly.

country legally is highly unlikely to return. For example, in 2009 the entire football team, which played in the regional tournament, disappeared after playing a match against Tanzania. Steve Bloomfield seems to capture the dilemma confronting Eritrean youth. When writing a book on African football, he watched the match and was asked by Renne Montagne of National Public Radio (NPR), 'When the national soccer team of Eritrea lost in a regional tournament in Kenya, its star players should have headed home. Instead, they defected – the entire team. All twelve players are now asking for asylum, say Kenyan officials' (Bloomfield in McConnell 2009). Montagne further wondered, '...the players did not show up at the plane that was waiting to take them back to Eritrea. And surely, it wasn't because they were taking their loss so hard' (Bloomfield 2009). Bloomfield said, 'No, it wasn't. Eritrea is not one of the greatest places in the world to live. I think it's fair to say. Many young people, in fact, all young people have to do military service. And this can last a very long time. I was actually in Eritrea about a month or so ago, and I met there in their late 20s, early 30s who are still doing their national service' (Bloomfield 2009). He further stated:

> Now, soccer is one of the few legal ways to get out of doing military service. All these players who are in the team would've been officially members of the army. So they'll be playing soccer for a few years, but unlike in most countries, if you have a career in soccer then, you know, when you retire, you can think about [:] do you want to go into coaching, do you want to become a commentator, do you want to set up a business?

Bloomfield 'hits the nail on the head' when he states, '*In Eritrea, once the soccer career ends, you go back to military service. So that would've been what they were hoping to escape from*' (Bloomfield 2009, emphasis added). No matter what kind of assignment one is given, as long as one is within the age of conscription, fifty-four for men and forty-seven for women (see HRW 2009; US Department of State 2012).

On 5 December 2012, a BBC Sport correspondent reported from Kampala stating, 'The seventeen Eritrean footballers and team doctor who vanished in Uganda on Tuesday have all applied for asylum in the country' (Oryada 2012). During the London Olympic games *The Guardian* reported, 'Eritrea's flag-carrying runner seeks asylum in UK to flee repressive regime Olympic athlete and middle-distance runner is one of four from country seeking escape from repressive regime' (Quinn 2012). The entire team and their doctor 'mysteriously' appeared in the picturesque small town of Gorinchem in the Netherlands on 21 May 2014 and sought asylum (Montague 2014). In October 2015 ten players who went to Botswana to play in a World Cup qualifying match refused to return to their country and sought asylum instead. The ten players were granted refugee status after initial threats of deportation (BBC News 2015). According to BBC News (2015), 'Six players claimed asylum in Angola in 2007, twelve in Kenya in 2009, and another eighteen in Uganda in 2012', and now another ten in Botswana.

It is not only the few, such as sportsmen and women, who obtain exit visas for different reasons to leave the country legally who seize every opportunity to seek asylum, but since the turn of the century hundreds of thousands of draft evaders and deserters have left the country illegally to seek asylum. Since 2004 hundreds of thousands of people have fled the country in search of freedom from the never-ending open service. Many of the respondents reported that the national service has neither built Eritrea's military manpower nor fighting capability because many have fled the country and those left behind are excessively pre-occupied plotting their illegal exit. A conscript who, subsequent to his military training in the first round, was assigned to become a trainer at the Sawa military camp said that the ENS has not built Eritrea's defence or fighting capability because 'I found the conscripts I trained at Sawa in Sudan. Not many are still in the armed forces' (R #055).

Some of the respondents also argued that building the country's defence or fighting capability was not in many of the conscripts' minds. As one put it, 'I was excessively pre-occupied with thinking about leaving Eritrea to help my family. I never thought about fighting or defending the country' (R #175). Zerai, a key informant, said, 'In the beginning, there was only one thing in our minds – making a difference to the shattered lives of our people. However, once the national service became indefinite with no end in sight, we became solely pre-occupied with the idea of flight. Nothing else mattered.' Another key informant, Berhane, surmised, 'The powerful sense of purpose and determination that permeated our attitudes when we joined the service evaporated into thin air once the ENS deteriorated into never-ending forced labour. After we realised that the government had betrayed its promise on demobilisation, not even its draconian and murderous "shoot to kill" policy could stop us from crossing the Sudanese or Ethiopian borders' (Interview, Khartoum, 2 November 2010). He further pointed out:

> Many of the forces that were trained to build the country's defence forces are: languishing in the squalid refugee camps in Ethiopia and Sudan – namely, Shagarab (eastern Sudan), Shimelba, Mai Aini and Adi Harush (northern Ethiopia). Many others are in detention centres in Libya, Egypt, Tunisia, Israel and many other transit and destination countries. There are also many who are held as hostages by members of the Rashaida tribe of eastern Sudan in collusion with some members of the Sudanese security and by members of the ruthless Egyptian Bedouin tribe of the Sinai for payment of prohibitive amount of ransom and organ harvesting. There are also many who have been perishing in the Sahara desert and the Mediterranean Sea, as well as the Red Sea. Many of our sisters are raped and sexually abused by military officers (in Eritrea, Ethiopia, Sudan, Libya and Egypt), smugglers, hostage-takers and middlemen throughout the migration cycle.

He continued that an unknown number have perished while trying to cross the Eritrean-Ethiopian and Sudanese borders. He concluded, 'The open-ended national service instead of building Eritrea's military manpower has become the single most important factor of displacement and erosion of Eritrea's military capability' (Berhane). A similar view was expressed by a female key informant, Hiriti, who said, 'Once the national service degenerated into slavery, every *agelglot* became obsessed with the idea of flight. The goal of building the country's defence competence has disappeared from the hierarchy of the *agelglot*'s list of priorities' (Interview, Stockholm, 10 September 2015). One respondent perceptively observed that the ENS has not built the county's fighting competence because,

'... everyone was thinking about their families and how to escape. People with such a state of mind cannot build a country's military manpower' (R# 57).

As previously noted those who joined the ENS before the border war and before the introduction of the WYDC were strongly motivated and were driven by a powerful resolve to rebuild the war-torn economy and defence capability of the country. For example, a respondent said, 'The youth were dedicated and hardworking, but over time, the pressure became too much to bear and they began grumbling and when their problems were not addressed, they began resorting to individualistic measures and the consequence was failure of the programme' (R #089). The 'individualistic measures' were reflected in high flight propensity instead of staying put in the country in pursuit of the ostensible 'common good'.

As we shall see later, a huge amount of pressure was brought to bear on conscripts from different angles. These include the indefinite nature of the service without remuneration; the economic hardship faced by their families and the helplessness they felt for not being able to bear the customarily prescribed responsibility of fending for them; the forgone educational and income-earning opportunities; the uncertainties precipitated by the state of no-war-no-peace permeating the tense relationship between the Ethiopian and Eritrean governments resulting, *inter alia*, from the unresolved border conflict and other issues. According to this respondent, when the pressure became 'too much,' some of the conscripts began to abandon the 'common good' in pursuit of self and familial interests (R #089). This view was eloquently expressed by a female key informant, Saba, who said, 'When the national service became open-ended, I was forced to stay in the army indefinitely. When I pleaded with my commander to release me to look after my ailing elderly mother, he said, "Your priority should be the interest of the nation. When our nation's problems are solved, so will your mother's. Our people's problems cannot be solved piecemeal."' She further stated, 'I thought what he said was gibberish. How could he tell me that I should prioritise service in the army when my mother cannot even help herself to get up from bed to go to toilet? It is utter hypocrisy.' She also said:

> It was rich coming from a man who left no stone unturned to make money at our expense [...] My priority was to help my mother, but if I fled to Asmara, I knew they could easily catch me and subject me to inhuman treatment. The only option I had was to flee the country, reach Western Europe, get a job and send money to my mother so that she could hire someone who could assist her. I have achieved that goal and I have been able to help my mother die a dignified death.

There were also others who argued that the commanders in the Eritrean armed forces were absorbed in self-interest promoting projects, as well as in sexually abusing female conscripts, and therefore unable to meet the defence needs of the country. One respondent said, 'The commanders of the Eritrean armed forces cannot be trusted. The majority think of their own personal interests and therefore cannot be the custodians of the nation's security' (R #172). One of the main escape routes has become flight across the border in search of freedom from forced labour. After the national service became a never-ending burdensome obligation, 'Everyone – old and young – dreams about leaving the country. *Indefinite service is incompatible with the goal of building fighting capability*' (R #176) (emphasis added). With time, the desire to leave the country to seek asylum elsewhere has become almost an obsession. In many of the respondents' views, the objective of building an effective defence force will remain unachievable as long as those who are supposed to be its backbone are 'voting with their feet'. A female key informant, Lydia, for example, said, 'The indefinite service is depleting the potential military manpower and therefore is responsible for the weak fighting capability which has left the country vulnerable to potential assault from any direction [...] *If people such as myself and others leave, how can Eritrea's defence capability be built?*' (Interview, Geneva, 26 June 2015) (emphasis added). An almost identical view was expressed by R #171.

INDEFINITE SERVICE WITHOUT REMUNERATION

The question of serving without remuneration was also a major pre-occupation for many respondents. As we shall see, conscripts do not earn anything during the first six months of their military training. During the remaining 12 months, they receive 150 Eritrean Nakfa (ERN), equivalent to US$10 per month at the official exchange rate and about $4 at the parallel market rate. After twelve months in the service, they receive 450 ERN (US $32 at the official rate and less than half of that at the black market rate). Instead of working without remuneration and, according to the respondents, under unbearable conditions indefinitely, many are 'voting with their feet' to disentangle themselves from forced labour. As key informant, Amine, put it, 'Thousands are fleeing the country because people do not want to work for ever without remuneration.' Another respondent stated, 'In the beginning, the national service had substantially built Eritrea's fighting capability. However, when the ENS became unrewarding and indefinite, the consequence was that valour and fighting capability of the armed forces dissipated' (R #152). The open-ended nature of the service without remuneration seems to be one of the major reasons the national service failed to build Eritrea's fighting capability, according to some of the respondents and most of the key informants. This respondent attributes the erosion of heroism in the Eritrean army to the unremunerated, open-ended and unfulfilling nature of the service.

A group of journalists in his ministry asked the Minister of Defence, Sebhat Ephrem, the following question: 'In the context of the prevailing circumstances in the country, is there no temporal limit to the ENS?' (Sebhat Ephrem 2008: 38). He said that the country was in a state of 'no-war no-peace.' In fact, he said, 'we are in a state of war' (Sebhat Ephrem 2008: 38). The *agelglot* are defending the frontline and at the same time, they are participating in productive activities. He said that if the multifaceted activities currently undertaken by the *agelglot* 'were to be performed by a private company, how long would it take it?' He further pointed out:

Even though each of the *agelglot* has between two and three children, they only receive 500 ERN per month. How do they do it? Their reward is not a salary because the amount they receive is insignificant. Instead patriotism (*hilina*) is the driving force. If a private firm were to take over, it would be solely driven by pecuniary interest rather than patriotism. In the beginning, the worker or the *agelglot* will be happy to receive 100 ERN, but soon after, he will demand more. If you raise the pay by 50 ERN, he will soon be dissatisfied and ask for more. In the end, money will dictate everything. Nothing can be accomplished in this way. However, the absence of remuneration should not have any negative impact on willingness to work hard, discipline and dedication. (Sebhat Ephrem 2008: 38–9)

The simple question that springs to mind in connection with such a brazen assertion is: who has asked the conscripts? At the same time, the Defence Minister admits that it is through 'imposition of force, morale and discipline that the *agelglot* have been performing the important activities' (Sebhat Ephrem 2008: 38–9). This clearly demonstrates that the ENS has degenerated into forced labour.

Not only are the views of the Defence Minister not shared by the *agelglot* (conscripts), but his view that introducing remuneration into the system would lead to incessant demand for higher wages which would defeat the purpose is groundless. In his view, if no wages are paid the *agelglot* will not demand to be paid and, oddly enough, he does not think that this would have any impact on their incentive to work and to defend the country. Not only does such reasoning defy any rational thinking but it is contradicted by his assertion that it is through imposition of force that the *agelglot* are made to work. If the requirement to work without remuneration does not kill the incentive to work, why would the government apply force to instil discipline? The fact that conscripts work without payment is even acknowledged by the president. According to HRW (2013) he stated that 'national service members and government employees are so poorly paid that they essentially "have been fulfilling their duties apparently without pay" for the past twenty years.'

As we shall see throughout this study, the indefinite ENS without remuneration and the severe punishment regime permeating it, as well as its damaging impact on the social fabric of Eritrean society, have been the most important drivers of forced migration in post-war Eritrea (Kibreab 2009a, 2009b, 2013). Although the exact number of deserters and draft evaders who have been fleeing the country is difficult to determine, since 2008 hundreds of thousands of Eritreans have been fleeing to seek asylum elsewhere (see Table 4.1). The large-scale displacement prompted by the indefinite ENS, which has degenerated into forced labour, has corroded the social capital developed prior to the erosion of the enthusiasm and resolve of the conscripts and this has had a damaging effect on the country's defence capability. A country's military power is not solely measured in terms of weapons and number of soldiers (conscripts in this case), but also by the quality of training provided and retention rates. As seen in the data in Table 4.1, a large number of conscripts and draft evaders have left the country since 2008 and the impact of this on the country's defence capability cannot be understated.

According to one of the respondents, the ENS has eroded the country's defence capability, and hence its net result has been counterproductive. One of the reasons he said the country's military manpower is eroded is because 'many of the *agelglot* have left the country' (R# 048). This respondent further said, 'Nearly half of Eritrea's army is in exile and therefore it is wrong to say that the ENS has built Eritrea's fighting capability' (R# 048). Zemheret, a key informant, said, 'You can force people to work for free, but you cannot force them to become good and committed soldiers. Absence of remuneration is a major disincentive.' He further stated, 'Forcing people to work without pay against their will indefinitely is pure slavery. That is precisely because we fled our country.' The corollary is that, as Lydia said, had it not been for the degeneration of the ENS into servitude, many of the youths would have stayed in the country, and consequently they would have been available to defend the country against external and internal threats. Another respondent said, 'Nearly half of Eritrea's army is in exile and therefore [...] who is to build the fighting capability? (R #048).

In the following the constraints that have reduced the ENS's potential to build the country's defence capability are discussed.

MISMANAGEMENT

Another reason the national service has failed to build Eritrea's military manpower and fighting capability is the mismanagement of the service by the government and by the commanders who are mandated to implement it. Many respondents repeatedly mentioned the problem of mismanagement: 'The ENS would have built Eritrea's military manpower had it been managed properly, but the way it is managed cannot foster trust and therefore the outcome has been abject failure' (R #094). Another opined, 'Only a properly managed and executed national/military service can build the fighting capability of a country.' The implication is that the ENS programme is mismanaged and hence cannot be expected to realise the goal of building the country's military manpower and fighting capability. Adem, with a university degree, who worked in one of the ministries within the framework of the national service for about eight years said:

> The original aim of the national service as stipulated in Proc. No 82/1995 was ground-breaking. In a country rising from the ashes of thirty years long of devastating war, the idea of re-building the economy and defence capability of the nation by mobilising the youth was excellent. However, after the end of the border war and the introduction of the WYDC in 2002, the national service became open-ended and its original aim of building the economy and defence capability were relegated to the background. Since 2000, the national service has been permeated by litany of mismanagement and neglect. Hence instead of building the country's defence power, the indefinite ENS has weakened it substantially. (Interview, London, 12 February 2014)

R #151 also said, 'Eritrea's national service programme is mismanaged and therefore it has not built the country's military manpower or fighting capability.' Another respondent admitted that, in the beginning, not only did the national service contribute to Eritrea's defence capability, but 'it also achieved spectacular success' which in his view was 'squandered' by the government (R #152). He did not state the reason why he thought the government squandered the actual and potential outcomes of the national service, but if we were to reflect on his remarks in the context of what the other respondents and key informants said, it was probably because of mismanagement, reflected not only in its degeneration into a never-ending duty without remuneration, but also, more importantly, in the country's single most important resource – manpower – with opportunity being wantonly wasted. The ENS according to the respondents and key informants is blighted with immense corruption and abuse resulting from its degeneration into forced labour. The International Covenant on Civil and Political Rights stipulates, 'no one shall be required to perform forced or compulsory labour' (Art. 8, para. 3 (a)). 'For this, the term "forced or compulsory labour" shall not include, "any service of a military character"' (Art. 8, para. 3 (c) [ii]). As will be evidenced, conscripts of the ENS are used for purposes that are completely different from those of 'a military character'. As well as being used in state and party-owned construction sites and agricultural projects, conscripts are also used for the personal enrichment of military commanders (see below). Abnet, a female key informant, even doubted whether building the country's defence capability is the priority of the commanders. She said, 'They are too busy exploiting the conscripts for personal gain and abusing female conscripts sexually under different pretexts.'

THE ENS: MECHANISM OF ENRICHMENT

In a series of discussions with key informants and respondents the question of the degeneration of the once noble project of national service into forced labour exacted in pursuit of the personal gain of military commanders and the firms of the ruling party, the PFDJ, was persistently raised. One key informant, Ahmed, for example, said, 'The single most important pre-occupation of the military commanders has become how to exploit the labour force of the *agelglot* for personal gain.' Zerabruk added, 'After 2000, the open-ended national service has become a mechanism of exaction of forced labour for personal enrichment. Building the country's fighting capability is not in the list of priorities of the commanders, as well as the government.'

Another respondent said, 'Yes, the ENS built Eritrea's fighting capability until 1999, but after that year, the PFDJ motives were exposed and since then, the ENS made no contribution to the growth of the country's fighting capability' (R# 050). One of the respondents stated, 'The national service besides serving those in power has not built Eritrea's fighting capability' (R #147). Since this concern was also raised by a number of key informants I asked three of them to elaborate by providing some examples. Their responses can be summarised as follows: they said, independently of each other, that the commanders exploit the unpaid labour power of the *agelglot* in a variety of ways under the pretext of the duty of national service. Firstly, they said that the commanders run small shops where they sell commodities, including alcoholic drinks to the *agelglot,* where most of the pocket money received by the *agelglot* is spent. Secondly, the people who work in the shops and for other business interests of the commanders are not paid. These activities are performed as part of their national service duties even though the sole beneficiaries are the commanders, rather than the state or the country, and therefore these activities are not even remotely linked to military duty or defence of the country. Suleiman said, 'Although it is not easy to say how much the commanders earn from such business activities, their profits are substantial. Many of the *agelglot* receive substantial amounts of remittances from relatives abroad and they spend it in the shops owned by the commanders.'

Thirdly, the three key informants and many others I interviewed said that most of the commanders use the *agelglots'* unpaid labour to clear large tracts of land for rain-fed agricultural production or for irrigated horticulture in which the irrigation canals are dug by free labour of the conscripts. The labour needed for land clearing, canal digging, irrigation, planting, weeding, protection against domestic and wild animal trespass, harvesting, transportation and post-harvest clearing of the plots is carried out by the *agelglot.* Commanders pocket the benefits, rather than those who do the work. Mehret, a female key informant, said, 'Working against one's will without remuneration for the personal gain of commanders was never part of the aim of the Eritrean national service. The fact that commanders are able to benefit from forcible and unpaid labour power of the *agelglot* and that there is nothing one can do about it because there is complete absence of any form of remedy or redress against such injustice, abuse and exploitation is an indication of the degeneration of the ENS into modern form of slavery' (Interview, London, 24 August 2014).

When asked whether the government is aware of such abuses she said, 'Without green light from the government, the commanders would have been unable to act with such high level of impunity' (Mehret). Aida, a female key informant, said, 'The president has given the commanders *carta bianca* (*carte blanche*) [free reign to act with impunity] without any fear of repercussions or accountability' (Interview, Stockhom, 10 September 2015). However, Asmerom disagreed and said, 'With regard to the ENS, corruption is only rife at the lower and middle rank of the chain of command. However, the fact that those in the middle and lower ranks are able to act with impunity without any regard to the human rights of the *agelglot* and fear of any consequences shows that the government does not care about the well being of the *agelglot*' (Interview, Pretoria, 8 November 2013).

Fourthly, the key informants, independently of each other, said that the commanders hire out the *agelglot* to commercial farmers and pocket their wages. The terms of payment and working conditions are negotiated by the commanders without consultation with or consent of the *agelglot.* Another key informant, Demsas, said, 'This is similar to what slave owners did when they sold the labour power of the human cargo under their possessions.' Fifthly, many of the commanders use unpaid conscripts' labour to build houses in their towns and villages of origin, as well as in the capital, Asmara. In fact, several of the key informants said that not only do military commanders build residential houses using the *agelglot's* free labour, but they also use the same unpaid labour to build houses for their relatives. Suleiman, for example, said, 'From our battalion in the Anseba Region, fifty of us were taken to Mendefera to work in a construction site belonging to a colonel who was not directly linked to our battalion.' Birikti, a female key informant, also said that she was sent by her commander to Asmara to be his wife's domestic servant. He kept on renewing her *menqasaqesi* (travel permit). She said, 'I was cleaning the house, washing and ironing the whole family's clothes, cooking their food, doing their food shopping, taking and collecting the children from school, and bathing the children' (Interview, Khartoum, 2 November 2010). She also said that sometimes, her commander's wife would ask her to go to her mother's house to wash clothes and clean. When asked how she felt about this she said, 'I felt degraded because I did not join the national service to become a domestic slave. However, in spite of this, staying in Asmara even as a domestic servant was preferable to life in the military.' Abraha, who worked as a driver within the ENS, said, 'I spent most of my time in Asmara running errands of my commander's wife, dropping and collecting their children from school under different pretexts concocted by my commander' (Interview, London, 12 June 2015).

The most damaging consequence of this abusive practice is, in the words of Samuel, a key informant, '*nyetna ketiluwo*' – 'it killed our stamina or stifled our drive' (Interview, Pretoria, 7 November 2013). The corollary is that an army without moral fortitude cannot build a country's fighting or defence capability. When probed further about the impact of this form of corruption and practice of forced labour, Samuel said, 'We were commodities readily available for exploitation and not only did this state of being sap our morale, but also our sense of identity'. The consequence of this on the *agelglots'* contribution to the country's fighting capability cannot be understated.

THE IMPACT OF THE CONFLICTS BETWEEN *YIKEALO* AND *WARSAI* ON DEFENCE CAPABILITY

The architects of the ENS perceive the *yikealo* (*tegadelti*) to be the embodiment of the national core values developed during the thirty years' war (1961–1991). They are also perceived as an effective conduit of these core values to the *warsai*. However, the government's assumption that the *yikealo* still embody the values of the revolution and are able to transmit these core values to the *warsai* is to some extent flawed. During the liberation struggle although some of the combatants exercised greater power than the rest due to the positions they held, there was no other distinction among them regardless of their positions. This was especially true in the early years when there were no base areas or privileges, largely because there were no privately possessed goods and privileges. Before the establishment of the base areas, those in top command positions even ate from the same pot regardless of their rank. The combatants were a homogenous group and the relationship among them was marked with a high level of equality.

This has changed dramatically in the post-independence period, especially since 1995, when formal ranks, insignia and salaries were introduced. In the post-independence period, not only were the ex-combatants faced with multifarious competing demands, but they have also become highly stratified, in the sense that some enjoy greater privileges and greater income and amenities and others have become destitute and impoverished. Some enjoy enormous privileges by virtue of their connections with the president and the lucrative positions they hold which give them leverage to gain access to resources through corruption and other means. These differentiations, changes and transformations the *yikealo* have undergone in the post-independence period have eroded the integrity and weakened commitment to public causes among some members of the *yikealo*. The majority of the military commanders in the ENS undoubtedly fall into this degenerate category. Given the high degree of differentiation and corruption that characterise the ex-combatants in the post-independence period, the term *yikealo* has become a misnomer. In view of the fact that there are, on the one hand, disenfranchised former combatants and, on the other, highly privileged, corrupt and well-off *yikealo*, the general use of the term is meaningless. This caveat should also be borne in mind when reading any critical remarks made in this study on the *yikealo*. The criticism is directed against the privileged and corrupt members of the *yikealo*, including the military commanders associated with the ENS.

The government's assumption that all the *yikealo* are bearers of the core values of the liberation struggle is deeply flawed. Even if we assume, for analytical purposes, that the *yikealo* are still the incarnation of the lofty values of the liberation struggle, whether or not they can be effective mechanisms of transmission of these values to the *warsai* is to a large extent dependent on their relationship with each other. In the following the relationship between the *warsai* and the *yikealo* is briefly discussed.

The Eritrean government assumes that the *warsai* would disseminate the treasured revolutionary core values they inherit from the *yikealo* to the rest of society through different means, including through the military, families, communities, schools, workplaces, theatres, music, sports, a variety of activities undertaken in pursuit of the common good and through dense social networks developed in the course of training, learning, working and living together at Sawa and after. Consequently, the country, the state, government, society, families and the *warsai* themselves are expected to benefit not only from increased security, industrial, agricultural and service production, as well as development of infrastructure, but more importantly from the transformative effect of the national service and the WYDC.

Whether the *yikealo* would be an effective mechanism for transmitting the primary values and legacies of the revolution to the *warsai* and the extent to which the latter would embrace or take on the said values, characters and norms is to a large extent dependent on four critical factors.

These are, firstly, the extent to which the *warsai* perceive the *yikealo* not only as the repository and embodiment of the values, characters and norms of the revolution, but more importantly as positive role models from whom they would want to learn through emulation. Secondly, the extent to which the *warsai* are willing and able to embrace or take on the values, characters and norms developed during the violent war in peacetime. This is crucial not only because the conditions of war which engendered these values, characters and commitments and impelled the EPLF fighters to accept their moral and patriotic duty to fight and die for their country had changed in the post-independence period, but also it cannot be taken for granted that the *warsai* consider these values and norms as being prized and worth emulating. Unless the *warsai* admire, venerate and look up to the *yikealo* as role models, instead of emulating them they may reject and resent the values and traits associated with them. Therefore, the question of transmission of the values of the revolution and the characters and moral fortitude of the revolutionaries cannot be considered in isolation from the *warsai's* opinion or perception of the *yikealo*.

Thirdly, whether the *yikealo* would be able to transmit the values and the legacy of the revolution is dependent on the extent to which they have been able to preserve these values in the post-independence situation, notwithstanding the multiplicity of individual and familial demands and pressures that may substantially erode the values and virtues developed and internalised in a state of war wherein the ex-combatants had no competing or conflicting interests. During the war of independence, the combatants dedicated their lives to the revolution and were ready and willing to sacrifice their lives (Alemeseged Tesfai 2005; Kibreab 2008). Independence and fighting for the primary values of the polity was the single most important, if not the only, goal the combatants lived and fought for and everything else was subordinated to this. It may not be safe to assume, therefore, that the *yikealo's* level of dedication, commitment, resilience and moral obligation to fight for and serve the country and society in the post-independence period is the same as during the war years. If the primary values produced during the war are diluted by the changed circumstances and by the temptations and conflicting interests and demands that permeate civilian life, the so-called prized and core values the *yikealo* are said to embody and transmit may be a myth rather than reality. Fourthly, the ability or inability of the *yikealo* to transmit the primary values of the revolution to the *warsai* is also dependent on the nature of the relationship between the two. If the relationship between the *yikealo* and *warsai* is marked by inequality and conflict rather than harmony, equality and cooperation, the *warsai* may resent rather than embrace the values the *yikealo* represent.

Drawing on data elicited from key informants and respondents who completed the questionnaires, an attempt is made to shed light on these complex and inextricably intertwined factors. A number of the respondents said that the contribution of the national service to the building of Eritrea's military manpower or fighting capability was limited or, in the worst case scenario, undermined by the cacophony that marked the relationship between the *yikealo* commanders (former combatants) and the *warsai* (conscripts). For example, R #051 said that one of the reasons why the ENS failed to augment Eritrea's fighting capability was because of the conflict between the *yikealo* and the *warsai*. He said, 'At the beginning, we had a great sense of determination, but the conflict between the *warsai* and the *yikealo* was very damaging.' Zere said, 'As complementary forces, the *yikealo* and the *warsai* should treat each other with trust and respect on the basis of equality. Unfortunately, the *yikealo* treated us as their inferiors and in the worst-case scenario as their slaves. Many of them also abused sexually female conscripts. It is not possible to build Eritrea's defence capability based on mistrust and subservience' (Interview, London, 26 January 2013).

When R #051 was asked to describe the method of his conscription, he said, 'I received call up papers and went voluntarily.' It was the strong sense of determination to serve a country that was recovering from a devastating thirty years' war that enthused most of the pre-1998 cohorts interviewed in this study to participate voluntarily in the ENS. Those I interviewed from the cohorts conscripted before 1998 said that they had felt elated by the opportunity the national service provided them to serve their country. The strong sense of purpose interviewees felt at the launch of the ENS programme was shared by the majority of those who belonged to the first cohorts in spite of the daunting challenges they faced due to the government's lack of preparedness. A respondent who belonged to the first cohort in 1994 described Sawa, the military training centre, as an 'unmitigated wilderness' (R # 051). That the government was ill prepared to receive the first cohorts at Sawa was even admitted by General Teklay Habteselassie (2004), the military commander. Besides a dearth of infrastructural development, the areas, as some key informants put it, were ridden with poisonous snakes. However, the first and second cohorts' sense of purpose and resolve were not affected negatively by the hardship they faced.

When answering the question of whether the national service had contributed to Eritrea's defence capability, one respondent said, 'Not at all. On the contrary, it has depleted the country's fighting capability because of the tense and hostile relationship between the *warsai* and the *yikealo*' (R #054). The respondent further said, 'The level of mistrust between us and the *yikealo* was so severe that it was impossible to work together'. When asked to elaborate on the bearing of the unfriendly relationship between the *yikealo* and the *warsai* on building Eritrea's defence capability, R #153 said, 'The *agelglot* are disrespected and made subservient to ex-combatants (*yikealo*) and unlike in the beginning when they were enthusiastic, later they were only there physically, demoralised and without any sense of purpose and commitment.' The consequence of this on Eritrea's manpower and fighting capability is obvious. A country's defence or fighting capability cannot be built by using conscripts who are demoralised and lack a sense of purpose.

Data elicited from ex-EPLF fighters show that the single most important factor that determined the successful outcome of the war of independence was that the combatants devotedly believed in the justice of the cause they fought for and did not hesitate to sacrifice their lives to achieve it because the struggle was prioritised over all other considerations. A respondent among the *warsai,* for example, said that the ENS, '...was not based on just principles of national service' (R #094). Andom said a national service based on judicious principles is one 'which is not open-ended and the rights of conscripts are protected by law as well as the relationships between its members regardless of ranks are defined and regulated by law or rules. At present, the ENS is governed by the arbitrary caprice of the commanders. We were at their complete mercy. An aggrieved conscript has nowhere to turn to in order to seek remedy against injustice and abuse' (Interview, London, 10 March 2014). Andom probed, 'Do you think such an environment is conducive for building a country's military manpower?' Many of the *warsai* (conscripts) I interviewed considered the majority of the *yikealo* (ex-combatants) to be part of the oppressive machinery of the government and the party that ruthlessly exploited their labour power, deprived their families of breadwinners and subjected them to an unforgiving punishment regime intended to break their agency and instil fear and blind obedience, as well as to engender docility and sycophancy.

In view of the overarching scale of the ENS, measured, on the one hand, in terms of the number of people affected and, on the other, in terms of its devastating impact on the social fabric of Eritrean society (see Chapters 8 and 9), it is comparable to the feudal institution of *posse comitatus* (see Chapter 2) in which the government has unconstrained power to force its able-bodied citizens to serve in the military and in different ministries and departments, not only to defend the country against internal and external enemies, but also to build prisons, roads, water supply systems and so on indefinitely and without remuneration. The Eritrean *posse* members are required to surrender their freedom to dispose of their labour power, careers and their way of life in order to serve the government and the incumbents. This, besides being unprecedented in modern history, is inauspicious for building a country's defence capability.

Another interesting conclusion that emerges from the data is that the former EPLF combatants, the *yikealo* commanders, who were selfless and dedicated to the common good of the Eritrean people have undergone changes reflected in excessive preoccupation with self-interest maximising tendencies which are incompatible with the behaviour of people endowed with social capital as was the case during the liberation struggle. Two decades after the end of the war, the former paragons of virtue have become corrupt and self-interested, according to my respondents and key informants. What this may suggest is that, unless nurtured, there is no guarantee that social capital once developed will not be eroded. It is also unrealistic to expect the same level of selflessness and dedication to public causes in the post-independence period where the reality is completely different from that during the liberation struggle, where, among other things, there was no cash or any form of private ownership or possession. The other interesting consideration emerging from this chapter is that the social capital the conscripts developed and internalised in the course of performing national service may have dissipated when they deserted and became scattered across the globe. However, this is an empirical question, which cannot be determined *a priori*.

5

The Eritrean National Service as a Mechanism of Preserving and Transmitting the Core Values of the Liberation Struggle

One of the aims of the Eritrean National Service (ENS) is to preserve and transmit the core values engendered during the liberation struggle to the present generation. This chapter examines the extent to which the ENS is an effective mechanism of preserving and transmitting these values to the present generation. It also discusses the impact of a war fought against an external enemy on internal solidarity and on citizens' willingness to serve and sacrifice their lives in defence of these values, as well as in the service of the nation. As discussed in Chapter 4, the relationship between the *warsai* and the *yikealo* is hostile, and understandably these inauspicious relationships between those who are supposed to transmit the values of the liberation struggle and the recipients is likely to impact upon the effectiveness of the ENS as a mechanism of transmission. This chapter also identifies the virtues and vices the conscripts developed and internalised in the process of participating in the national service. Some abuses unrelated to the aims and objectives of the ENS, such as exploitation of conscripts' labour power for commanders' personal gain and how these corrupt activities and practices reduce the effectiveness of the ENS to function as a mechanism of preservation and transmission of the values and culture of the liberation struggle are also discussed.

As evidenced in Chapter 2, national/military service is perceived as a civic duty and as an expression of political and civic rights; this is said to create and reproduce core values that are amenable to greater cross-cultural understanding, mutual respect, national unity and greater commitment to the common good. More often than not, these values are developed and reproduced in conditions of war fought against a common enemy. As set out in Chapter 2, war fought against a common enemy produces social capital, which is the glue that holds a society together, including those marked by 'super diversity' (on the latter concept see Vertovek 2007). The gluing effect of war on solidarity and social cohesion is well documented (see Chapter 2). This is due to war's ability to engender a set of values and a sense of common purpose among citizens that are necessary conditions for solidarity and unity. Edward E. Carr (1942: 115) observed that war engenders meaning and purpose otherwise absent in modern societies. War, he argues, sets the political and economic machine in motion, engendering a powerful sense of moral purpose and obligation, as well as cohesion (Carr 1942: 124).

Not only do wars, in spite of their destructive effects, promote social cohesion and solidarity, they also create and reproduce values such as steadfastness, sacrificial patriotism, camaraderie and perseverance in adversity (Chapter 2). This is because of the intrinsic polarising effect of war in terms of creating mutually antagonistic 'insiders and outsiders'. Differences, including pre-existing animosities between the 'insider groups' may be forgotten or relegated to the background until the common enemy is defeated. One of the objectives of the ENS is therefore to transmit the values produced during the liberation struggle when the Eritrean people were engaged in a life and death war against an external enemy.

The preamble of the Eritrean Proclamation on the ENS No 82/1995, for example, states, 'The present and future generations have the historical responsibility of preserving a free and sovereign Eritrea as a legacy of thousands of martyrs. For the realization of this noble objective it has become necessary to proclaim and issue this proclamation on national Service'. This indicates that preservation of a 'free and sovereign Eritrea' and honouring the legacy of the martyrs by preserving, continuing and transmitting the core values they laid down their lives for is the second major aim of the national service. Article 5 (Proc. No. 82/1995) stipulates that one of the aims of the ENS is to: 'preserve and entrust future generations the courage and resoluteness, heroic episodes shown by the people in the past thirty years.' Therefore, at least in theory, one of the most important national core values the government claims it wants to foster and transmit to present and future generations of Eritreans is sacrificial nationalism, devotion to the cause of the nation, as well as the glue that held Eritrean society together during the adverse war years (see Chapters 1 and 2).

It is important to underscore, however, that the meanings of concepts such as 'cause of the nation', 'national interest' and national core values are highly contested. Often the in-group exercising political power may deliberately present its own cause or interest as constituting the public cause or national interest. It may also present its culture and way of life as constituting national core values and impose these on the rest of society. The important question that arises is what if a government is unable to 'pursue successfully' the 'public cause' or the 'interest of the nation'? What if the ruling élites pursue their own agenda to serve their own sub-national interest in the name of public cause and national interest? Given the ambiguity of the meanings of the concepts of 'public cause' or 'national interest', such concepts can be high-minded slogans lending legitimacy to policies that may have been arrived at in tyrannical ways, in pursuit of self-interest to the detriment of general societal interest. Such policies may have little or nothing to do with what are in fact the real needs or interests of most Eritreans. Concepts such as 'public cause' or 'national interest' can be used as a cover for policies designed by particular sub-national groups to pursue their own interest to the detriment of the whole nation's real interest.

The core national values fostered during the thirty years' war (1961–1991), which the Eritrean state and the EPLF (and its successor, the PFDJ), wish to preserve, develop and transmit to present and future generations through the all-embracing ENS and WYDC are articulated in the preamble of the country's would be supreme law, the constitution, which was ratified in 1997. However, after awaiting implementation for seventeen years, this has now been abandoned through a simple utterance of the president on 24 May 2014.[1] The constitution, ratified, but unimplemented and now about to be ditched by the president's whimsical will, states:

> We the people of Eritrea united in a common struggle for our rights and common destiny, standing on the solid ground of unity and justice bequeathed by our martyrs and combatants:
>
> With Eternal Gratitude to the scores of thousands of our martyrs who sacrificed their lives for the causes of our rights and independence, during the long and heroic revolutionary struggle for liberation, and to the courage and steadfastness of our Eritrean patriots; Aware that it is the sacred duty of all Eritreans to build a strong and developed Eritrea on the bases of freedom, unity, peace, stability and security achieved through the long struggle of all Eritreans, which tradition we must cherish, preserve and develop; Realising that in order to build a developed country, it is necessary that the unity, equality, love for truth and justice, self-reliance, and hard work, which we nurtured during our revolutionary struggle for independence and which helped us to triumph, must become the core of our national values.

The single most important overarching core national value accentuated throughout the preambles of the ratified constitution and the Proclamation on the ENS is martyrdom: perceived in the 'master-narrative' as a treasured national core value which every worthy Eritrean should embrace and emulate in his or her everyday life. Not only did the leaders of the EPLF and the government consider the substantial stock of social capital based on mutual obligations, respect, solidarity, reciprocity and trust (Kibreab 2008), as well as the readiness to sacrifice one's life for the common good of the nation and the powerful sense of selflessness and patriotism (see Alemseged Tesfai 2002) fostered during the thirty years' war fought against a more populous and stronger enemy, to be indispensable for the triumphant outcome of the liberation struggle (see

---

[1]   After the Eritrean head of state, in connection with his speech on the 23rd anniversary of Independence Day (24 May 2014), stated that his government has decided to draft a new constitution, the status of the 1997 ratified constitution is unclear. The decision by the president to draft a new constitution rather than implementing the already ratified constitution is dumbfounding and caught Eritreans and international observers by surprise. According to official discourse, the major obstacle that has prevented the implementation of the 1997 constitution is Ethiopian threat. If it is now decided to draft a new constitution, the so-called Ethiopian threat was not the real reason why the country has been ruled unconstitutionally. This is because if there were an Ethiopian threat, where is it now? The government representatives have also told the Eritrean people that the constitution is being implemented in stages. How can a constitution, which has been allegedly implemented gradually, suddenly be abandoned? There are clearly more questions to be asked.

Isaias Afwerki 1995, 2003a, 2004; Sebhat Ephrem 1995, 2008), but also as constituting the edifice of the foundation on which a united and viable Eritrean state should rest. The powerful sense of sacrificial patriotism, formation and consolidation of national Eritrean identity, engrained norms of solidarity, unity and mutual trust transcending the social cleavages of religion, region, ethnicity, class, sex and political opinion were partly the result of the need to stand together against a 'mightier' enemy and partly due to the development of social capital. This was engendered, on the one hand, by the war fought against an external enemy and, on the other, resulting from the intensive and deep social interactions stemming from working, living and fighting together under conditions of severe adversity.

Nevertheless, although there is a common agreement that war fought against a common enemy engenders a powerful sense of solidarity, internal cohesion and common purpose, there is no guarantee that the powerful feelings of camaraderie, social cohesion, unity of purpose and mutual trust engendered under conditions of war would necessarily endure *ipso facto* in peace time (James 1963 [1910]; Carr 1942). As we shall see, Isaias Afwerki, the prime architect of the ENS, feared that after the common enemy's removal from the country, not only might the stock of social capital, the glue that held Eritrean society together during the war, corrode or dissipate, but in the worst case scenario, the society might disintegrate or implode (in Kaplan 2003). The Eritrean national service is therefore conceptualised and implemented by its architects as a substitute for war in order to *regenerate, preserve* and to *transmit* the national core values reflected in the characteristics, commitments, social solidarity, unity, sacrificial nationalism, heroism and dedication developed during the war to present and future generations (see Isaias Afwerki 1994, 1995, 2003b, 2004; Proclamation No. 82/1995 on National Service; Kibreab 2009b).

The president's preoccupation with the risk of post-war disintegration or implosion of the social capital that permeated Eritrean society during the war is clear from a number of interviews he held with local and international journalists. For example, on 18 April 2003 he was asked by a journalist on state radio to comment on the following critical observation:[2]

> One of our most treasured core values of our society is our cultural heritage based on mutual respect and trust. However, currently, there is no shortage of people who say that these positive attributes of cultural treasure and heritage based on mutual respect, trust, social solidarity and sense of feeling of gratitude or societal indebtedness (*zeymrsesaè*) are not as powerful as they were in the past. They are being diluted [eroded]. (Isaias Afwerki 2003a)

In Eritrea, where there is an absolute dearth of freedom of speech and where the media is fully controlled by the government and the ruling party, it is reasonable to assume that, more often than not, the president is asked to comment on issues that he worries about. The fact that he was asked

---

[2]   This is my own translation from Tigrinya into English.

to comment on the allegedly rapidly changing public attitude toward social solidarity, co-operation, mutual trust and public-spiritedness was an indication of the extent to which the president was apprehensive about the potentially detrimental consequences of the changes that were taking place in the post-war period. These worrying signs were allegedly reflected in the rapid erosion of social capital, which was the major discerning feature of the thirty years' war and Eritrean society in general (see Kibreab 2008). In response, the president said:

> [c]ulture can be defined in different ways. In my view, of all the distinguishing features of our culture, devotion or dedication is the single most important. However, at the present, there seems to be a fundamental contradiction between dedication and greed. On one side, there is greed and voracious gluttony and on the other, boundless dedication. (Isaias Afwerki 2003a)

The attitudinal polarity the President is referring to is a representation, on the one hand, of wartime and the combatants who were socialised into the values of the EPLF and, on the other, of the post-war period and the '*gabar*' (those who did not take part in the war), who the president alleges are in the grip of boundless greed. In the interview, he states that the main contradiction in post-war Eritrea is between devotion and greed and he describes the so-called alleged new 'culture of greed' in highly poignant terms such as '*gnam gnam ...tebajajel...shama shama*' (Isaias Afwerki 2003a). Although a full translation of these highly emotive lamentations into English is unfeasible, to get a gist of his ostensible 'angst,' just imagine a group of hungry hyenas devouring a deer in a game without a gamekeeper, in which each is egoistically engrossed in grabbing as much meat as possible before the other hyenas finish off the carcass. None of the hyenas is concerned about the welfare of the animal, the victim (read Eritrea), it is devouring or of the other hyenas taking part. Its own selfish ends drive each hyena. Each is trying to maximise self-interest to the detriment of the other and the 'common good'. In the president's view the new culture of greed that allegedly permeates post-war Eritrean civilian society represents an imminent danger to the country's present and future interests. In his view, if these greedy and 'regressive' proclivities are not completely removed they could erode the core values reflected in the powerful sense of sacrifice, solidarity and social cohesion produced and consolidated during the thirty years' war. This erosion, in his view, may ultimately threaten Eritrea's very existence as an independent entity. The ENS seems to have been developed and implemented as a means of counteracting these alleged dangerous developments. The surest way to avert these alleged dangers, in the view of the president and the Eritrean government, is by shielding the youth from being contaminated by these corrupted values. The best way to achieve this, in their view, is by transmitting the core values of the war of liberation to present and the future generations of Eritrean society through a grand scheme of social and cultural engineering: the ENS.

During the war of independence most Eritreans displayed unlimited dedication, as reflected in their readiness and willingness to sacrifice their families' interests, careers, education, professions, occupations, material possessions, time, and, for many, their lives, in pursuit of what was regarded as the ultimate common good, *Summum bonum* (national independence). As previously discussed, one of the factors that influenced the successful outcome of the war was social capital that engendered mutual trust, cooperation and dedication, as reflected in a powerful sense of common purpose.

The question, however, is whether these values are desirable in a post-war situation. Post-war Eritrea requires different values that transcend the endless celebrations of the glorious past. The challenges facing post-independence Eritrea are qualitatively different. The Eritrean government and the ruling party are dominated by people who are stuck in the glorious past, which to a large extent is irrelevant or even detrimental to the challenges of present day Eritrea. Bruce Springsteen's edifying lyric of 'glory days'[3] is instructive in this regard. Instead of turning over a new leaf the former leaders of the liberation struggle are obsessively pre-occupied with the achievements of the past without realising, or by deliberately ignoring, the fact that building and running successful state institutions is completely different from leading and managing a successful liberation struggle, without superpower patronage and against all odds. Richard Reid's observation, in a different but similar context, that '...the EPLF is frozen by its perception and interpretation of the past...' (2005: 469) is very accurate. He further states, '...the EPLF was actually obsessed with the past [...] History was everything; and in particular, Eritrea was to be governed by a series of what we can call "liberation legacies"' (Reid 2005: 471).

What the ruling party and the state want to transmit to the *agelglot* is, among other things, what Alemseged Tesfai refers to as the 'spiririt of *tegadelti*' (combatants) (2002: 44). He was himself *tegadalai* (a freedom fighter), and in his poignant essay, 'Two Weeks in the Trenches', he states that the 'spirit of the *tegadalai*, especially in the face of a challenge is difficult to describe, much less to explain' (2002: 44). He further states: 'Death and adversity are expected and accepted as ordinary happenings in the normal course of things. So, the call to active duty, regardless of its nature, always creates such excitement that reluctance is rarely encountered. The sick try to hide their ailment and the lazy are suddenly motivated. This is the norm' (Alemseged Tesfai 2002: 44).

To demonstrate the level of dedication of the *tegadelti* and their undaunted willingness to sacrifice their lives for the good of the nation, he offers the example of Beshir, who was told to stay behind because of the leg wounds he had suffered during an earlier battle. Beshir refused to listen and joined the queue to march to the frontline, defying the order of his commander, in order to lay down his life for the cause. When he was told to leave the queue, '[h]e raised hell, refused to move from the line and had to be given a final military command to submit to authority' (Alemseged Tesfai 2002: 44).

In comparison to this breed of youth, those who grew up in the parts of Eritrea controlled by the Ethiopian government during the thirty years'

---

[3] Available at http://www.azlyrics.com/lyrics/brucespringsteen/glorydays.html (last accessed 24 May 2014).

war were not seen as having the same degree of love of country and work ethic. One of the aims of the ENS and the WYDC is, therefore, to instil in them the values and experiences of the *gedli* (liberation struggle) so that they undergo fundamental transformative change in terms of their attitude towards their own lives, work and country, as was the case with the street boys and others who grew up in Sudan and joined the struggle to lay down their lives in pursuit of the 'grand cause' and in the process underwent fundamental change and transformation.

This is often wrongly attributed to the EPLF's programme of alleged political education. However, contrary to this widely held assumption, the EPLF never had a programme of political education. What it had instead was a far-reaching programme of political socialisation – indoctrination – designed to transmit the values of the liberation struggle and to instil fear and discipline, ensure compliance by stifling quizzical and critical thinking, and suppress participants' ability to engage in discursive analysis and conversation. In fact, the central *raison d'être* of the EPLF's programme of political socialisation, which included the obnoxious practice of 'criticism and self-criticism', was to force people to toe the line. Whoever questioned the EPLF version of the truth was considered a 'deviant' and, in the worst-case scenario, a traitor, and subjected to torture and inhuman treatment at the hands of the infamous *halewa sowra* (guards of the revolution) or to the excruciating ritual of 'criticism and self-criticism' (humiliation) to make them toe the line (Kibreab 2008).

This is precisely what the architects of the Eritrean national service want to transmit to present and future generations, by mobilising the whole of Eritrean youth into the all-embracing national service and the WYDC. The architects of the ENS were not the first to emphasise the importance of national core values for nation building, national unity and youth disciplining. Long before such a high level of devotion to a cause was referred to by the ideologues of the French Revolution as '[t]he fullest embodiment of the norms of the nation,' which was said to be achieved when an individual voluntarily sacrifices his or her life for the good of the nation. The vitality of this point was demonstrated by the cult of the martyrs (Hippler 2007 [1757]: 78). The terminologies the leadership of the EPLF and the government use to celebrate the martyrs, but not necessarily to honour the causes they gave their lives for, are identical to those used by the ideologues of the French Revolution. '[t]hose who died for the nation are truly incarnations of this unitary conception of equality, that stressed relinquishing all personal interest in order to promote the effacement of the particular in the face of the civil and universal, where the individual should "count his interest for nothing compared to that of the fatherland"'(Chemin year II :5 in Hippler 2007 [1757]: 78). In spite of the two centuries in between, the core values the French revolutionaries cherished and tried to foster among the Revolutionary Guards were similar to those core values the Eritrean *tegadelti* sacrificed their lives for, which the post-independence government considers vital for nation building, national unity and future sustainability. These values are central to the national service.

In a speech to the National Guards in Valenciennes, Briez stated that republican death would be followed by resurrection: 'the man who dies in service for his fatherland falls and gets up. His irons are broken. *He is free; he is the King; he seizes heaven*' (Briez 1792, cited in Hippler 2007 [1757]: 78, emphasis in original). Likewise, Robespierre stated that the French army was 'the glory of the nation and of humanity; our virtuous warriors are shouting Vive la République when marching towards victory; falling by the enemy sword, their scream is Vive la République. Their last words are hymns to liberty; their last sighs are vows to the fatherland' (cited in Hippler 2007 [1757]: 79). Similar slogans reverberated in the Eritrean liberation struggle. Common slogans the EPLF used to motivate the *tegadelti* to lay down their lives for the nation included '*harbegna aynebrnyu tariku iyu zwres*' (A revolutionary does not live long, but her/his legacy is eternal), 'To sacrifice one's life for the good of the nation is the ultimate dignity'. I asked several former EPLF fighters currently living in London the extent to which such slogans made sense to them. All of them independently said effectively that sacrificing one's life to save a comrade's life or the valuable possession of the Front, such as tanks, kalashinikovs, AK 47s, etc. was the ultimate honour every *tegadalai* aspired for. For example, Samuel, a former combatant, currently residing in London, said, 'We genuinely believed we owed our lives to the revolution. Our lives had no other meaning' (Interview, London, 13 January 2014).

The core values the Eritrean authorities try to inculcate into the *agelglot* through transmission of the values of the revolution are thus similar to those the French revolutionaries tried to instil in the National Guards. When Alemseged Tesfai wrote his diary on 5 August 1985, there was no indication to suggest that either he or the leadership of the EPLF had any knowledge of the ENS and WYDC, to be introduced nine and seventeen years later, respectively. But his emphasis on the need to transmit to future generations the boundless degree of dedication, strong sense of work ethic and love of country, reflected not only in the willingness to serve, but also to die for the good of the nation was accurate. But the question is whether the values engendered in the context of extreme conditions of war and via a merciless punishment regime that tolerated no questioning or nonconformity can be replicated after the cessation of hostilities. The appeal of such values in peacetime is questionable.

Although the *tegadelti*'s illimitable devotion and heroism are recognised by those who visited the areas controlled by the EPLF during the 1980s (Connell 1997), in the minds of the builders of the post-war Eritrean state, unless nurtured, the values engendered during the war of independence would inevitably be eroded following defeat of the external enemy. This is consistent with rational expectation. The fact that external conflict engenders internal cohesion is amply documented in the literature, as already discussed. William Graham Sumner, for example, states:

> A differentiation arises between we-group, the in-group, or ourselves and everybody else, or the others-groups, out-groups [...] The relation of comradeship and peace in the we-group and that of hostility and war towards others-groups are correlative to each other. The exigencies of war with outsiders are what make peace inside [...] Loyalty to the group, sacrifice for it, hatred and contempt for

outsiders, brotherhood within, war-likeness without – all grow together, common products of the same situation. (Cited in Putnam 2000: 267)

Although the mobilising power of war and shared adversity is recognised by different analysts (see Putnam 2000) there is no guarantee that the social changes, solidarity, unity of purpose and esprit de corps engendered by war will persist in peacetime. For example, Robert Putnam states, '[t]he powerful explosion of solidarity and self-sacrifice triggered by the attack on Pearl Harbor [as well as by WWII] did not continue ...' (2000: 271). Although, in light of the dominant discourse, this may sound offensive, it cannot be denied that at the heart of the Eritrean president's ceaseless creation and reproduction of external enemies is an intention not only to divert public opinion so that the people overlook the follies of the government, but also to mobilise people against the purported external threat. The Eritrean national service is conceptualised and implemented by its architects as a 'substitute for war', so not only as a means of ensuring national unity and social harmony in the multi-faith and multi-ethnic Eritrean polity after the end of the war, but also as a means of keeping the flame of nationalism and patriotism permanently ablaze (see Afwerki 1994, 1995, 2003, 2004; Proclamation No. 82/1995 on National Service; Kibreab 2009a, 2009b, 2013).

In the president's view, the post-independence situation was so fragile that any attempt of competition for power and ideas, including through peaceful means, could destabilise the post-war political landscape. For example, when he was asked by a journalist from one of the ruling party's magazines, *Hidri*, whether groups other than the ruling party and the PFDJ, the successor of the EPLF, would be allowed to form political parties, he said that these organisations were based on a politics of division and consequently if allowed would organise themselves on the basis of clan, tribe, religion and ethnicity. He said if that was allowed, 'We will create another Rwanda, Yugoslavia, Somalia and Liberia. There will never be political parties based on clan, tribe, religion and ethnicity in the country' (1996). The banning of organisations that allegedly espouse sectarianism and parochialism from the public sphere, and the transmission of the values of the EPLF to present and future generations through the national service and the WYDC, would, in the view of the president and the government, not only enable the creation and reproduction of citizens imbued with the same values, attitudes and determination as the former EPLF combatants, but more importantly, over time engender values that foster cultural homogeneity, national unity and solidarity. The corollary of allowing the other groups to form political parties and vie for power in a democratic process, would undermine the president's and the government's project of cultural standardisation and political homogenisation. By privileging the EPLF's notion of nationhood and by depriving any form of political space to others, the sectarian and regressive values allegedly espoused by the latter political organisations are expected to die out. Hence its architects perceive the ENS as an instrument for fostering cultural homogeneity and standardisation in a society marked by immense heterogeneity.

CONSCRIPTION AS A VEHICLE OF HOMOGENISATION AND NATIONAL INTEGRATION

The Eritrean authorities consider homogenised nationalism to be *sine qua non* for nationhood. The military and the *de facto* official choice of the Tigrinya language as the dominant means of communication play a vital part not only in homogenising the society, but also in the process of nation building. The outcomes of the ENS, as perceived by the Eritrean government, are consistent with most governments' conceptions of national service worldwide. Most governments, both in developed and developing societies, emphasise the social virtues of military service (see Lerner and Robinson 1960; Jones 1985). For example, President Roosevelt and his contemporaries expected that military training would 'Americanise' immigrants (Krebs 2006: 1). Brezhnev also believed, 'service in the Red Army would forge a unified Soviet citizenry committed to the Socialist Motherland...' (cited in Rakowska-Harmstone 1979: 139). Ellen Jones argues that in the on going debate on the advantages and disadvantages of manpower systems based on conscription, those in favour of conscription in Western democracies perceive it as a 'socialising experience'. She states that in the US, military service has been perceived as a vehicle for 'inculcating spiritual and moral ideals in support of American democracy' (1985: 148). She further states, 'The Israeli defence forces have been regarded since their inception as "the workshop of the new Israeli culture," instilling civic spirit and patriotism' (Azaria, in Jones 1985: 148). The same was said to be true in West Germany. Many states believed, '...the experience of service has a measurable impact on social and political attitudes' (Jones 1985: 148). Governments see conscription as a vehicle of homogenisation and national integration (Enloe 1980). Morris Janowitz, amongst others, argues:

> ...the military also serves as an agent of social change. At a minimum, this implies that the army becomes a device for developing a sense of identity – a social psychological element of national unity – which is especially crucial for a nation which has suffered because of colonialism and which is struggling to incorporate diverse ethnic and tribal groups. At a maximum, this implies that experience in the military gives the officer and enlisted man a perspective which is compatible with, or essential for, economic development. (1964: 80–1)

In his view, unlike with other institutions of a new nation, in the military, 'the probability of equal treatment is greater. The result is a sense of cohesion and social solidarity, because men of various regional and ethnic backgrounds are given a common experience and come to think of themselves as Indians, Egyptians, or Nigerians' (Janowitz 1964: 81). John Johnson (1962), amongst others, argues that in developing societies the military was assumed to be an institution of modernisation, nation building, development and socialisation (see also Lerner and Robinson 1960; Janowitz 1964; Dietz, Elkin and Roumani 1991; McCann 2004). The Brazilian poet Olavo Bilac argued that universal military service is '... the complete triumph of democracy; the levelling of social classes; the school of order, discipline, and cohesion; the laboratory of self-dignity and patriotism [...] The barracks are an admirable filter in which men cleanse and purify themselves: they emerge conscientious and dignified Brazilians...' (cited in Beattie 2001: 230).

Although the Eritrean conscripts sometimes take part in indoctrination sessions in their own vernaculars and receive information on the same, the military training and all forms of communication in the Sawa military camp and after are conducted in Tigrinya. Serving in the national service meant that even those who had never heard of the Tigrinya language previously become fluent in it. For example, when I conducted the survey in this study, the Arabic and other translations of the questionnaire and interview schedules were abandoned after my research assistants found out that all the potential respondents, regardless of their ethnicity, were able to read and write in Tigrinya. Although this is likely to be contested or even resented by those who may feel their languages and particular identities are unrecognised, and in the worst case scenario eroded, the ENS has elevated the Tigrinya language to a core value that directly or indirectly fosters trans-ethnic and trans-faith communication and understanding. However, although the key informants and respondents included members of the different ethno-linguistic and faith groups, none of the respondents articulated such a concern. This is notwithstanding the fact that the research assistants comprised members of the different ethno-linguistic and faith groups. Hirt and Mohammad (2013) state, 'In Sawa, ...[T]he use of minority languages is not tolerated... Students who use languages other than Tigrinya or Tigre ... are intimidated, because they are suspected of planning illicit activities such as flight.' This is inconsistent with the findings of my study. None of the 190 respondents comprising, as we saw earlier, members of the two religions and different ethnic groups reported that they were discouraged from using their own languages at Sawa. Nor did any of the key informants that included ten non-Tigrinya-speakers report any kind of language restriction.

Supposedly, the EPLF, and later its successor, the PFDJ, as well as the post-independence government, have been trying relentlessly, *inter alia*, through the institution of the national service, to effect social and cultural changes resulting from the development and internalisation of shared patriotic nationalist values that transcend allegiance to 'sub-national parochial projects' of clan, tribe, ethnicity, religion and region (Isaias Afwerki 2003c; Sebhat Ephrem 1995, 2008). One of the central aims of the national service has therefore been to create a prototype of an ideal and committed citizen inimical to clan, tribal, ethnic, religious and regional loyalties, as was presumably the case during the war of independence among EPLF fighters and members of its mass organisations. The *warsai* are expected to undergo fundamental transformation and consequently relinquish their sub-national clan, tribal, ethnic and regional identities in favour of a secular Eritrean national identity. The discipline they learn in the course of performing national service is also expected to make them non-questioning and compliant citizens committed to the 'national project'.

After Ethiopian rule was successfully overthrown, the major sources of threats to national security, unity, social cohesion, mutual trust and solidarity were, in the president's view, the politics of ethnicity, religion, tribalism and regionalism. In his view, at the heart of such threats lay the heterogeneity of Eritrean society. Throughout the thirty years' war of independence, the EPLF leadership systematically suppressed any manifestation of ethnic, religious or regional identity by overstating an all-encompassing secular Eritrean national identity based on unity. All EPLF combatants were, for example, discouraged or even prohibited from stating their religion, ethnicity or region even amongst themselves. It was due to such a policy that the EPLF leadership thinks they were able to create a highly centralised and disciplined formidable army single-mindedly devoted to the goal of national independence. The dividend of this carefully and meticulously engineered and enforced approach was remarkable indeed. The EPLF had an intensive programme of political socialisation (discussed below) designed to inculcate among the volunteer fighters common secular and nationalist core values that over time erased markers of distinct social identities. The institution of national service is therefore designed as a mechanism of institutionalising common national identity formation and as a tool of political socialisation. The aim of the latter is to transmit to hundreds of thousands of young men and women – the conscripts – the values, character traits, loyalty and norms of solidarity developed during the thirty years' war so that they reject any form of sub-national identities and loyalties in favour of embracing national Eritrean identity and allegiance to the Eritrean nation state.

As already discussed, this is clear from the many interviews the president has held with the government-controlled mass media and with foreign journalists (see, for example, Isaias Afwerki 1990, 1996, 2001, 2002a, 2003a, 2003b). During the liberation struggle political socialisation played a critical role, on the one hand, in forging unity among the fighters and members of the mass organisations hailing from heterogeneous religious, ethnic and regional backgrounds and, on the other, in fostering sacrificial nationalism, heroism and commitment to the common good of national independence. Drawing on previous positive experience, the EPLF and the PGE made political socialisation of the youth through the institution of national service the centrepiece of their project of nation building and post-conflict (re)construction. This is briefly discussed below.

POLITICAL SOCIALISATION AS OPPOSED TO POLITICAL EDUCATION

In the ENS conscripts receive rigorous political socialisation and indoctrination in their respective mother tongue, except the Blin who join either the Tigre or Tigrinya speakers. The aim of this is to socialise the conscripts into the values of the liberation struggle, such as commitment to public causes, patriotism, sacrificial nationalism and, more importantly, unquestioning obedience to authority. The government's rhetoric notwithstanding, this should not be mistaken for political education. The two are completely different. Political socialisation refers, on the one hand, to the means by which societies or governments transmit basic political and social orientations to their members and, on the other, to the processes through which individuals learn to behave appropriately in political and social contexts. The main focus of political socialisation is on transmission rather than education (Gorhman 1992). Eric Gorham rightly states that the emphasis of political socialisation is 'less on developmental processes, or psychological mechanisms of political learning...' (1992: 15). The latter, Gorham argues, are '...aspects of political education' rather than political socialisation (1992: 15).

As opposed to political socialisation, political education refers to the processes that nurture learners' capacity to think critically and creatively concerning politics and power relations in society, as well as to reason about the purposes of the political community:

> This model of political and social learning emphasises the critical assessment of a polity, on the behavioural norms of that polity. Democratic education engages individuals in a critical dialogue with their society, and encourages people to learn about their society by participating in it. Democratic political education then is not a process of transmission, it is a two-way exchange between the individual and his or her society – one in which the individual learns from others but in which others also learn from him or her. (Gorham 1992: 15)

The Eritrean government's decision to focus on political socialisation, rather than political education, is therefore strategic. The aim of political education is to empower and enable the subjects concerned to question and interrogate the status quo, not only in order to understand it but also to critique it and transform it. Given the autocratic and paternalistic nature of the Eritrean government and the ruling party, provision of political education that develops conscripts' critical thinking and questioning ability would defeat the whole scheme of transmission of the values engendered during the liberation struggle to the conscripts.

Promotion of political education is inconceivable in societies such as Eritrea that are ruled by autocratic rulers. Such regimes are an anathema to freedom of expression, open dialogue and questioning of official discourse. As mentioned earlier, Eritrean polity is supremely plural-istic or heterogeneous, hailing from diverse ethno-linguistic and faith backgrounds. One of the key goals the EPLF/PFDJ want to achieve by implementing an all-embracing national service is homogenisation of the polity by relegating the differences that permeate the social landscape to the background. This goal is best served by political socialisation rather than political education. This is because at the heart of political education lies questioning and freedom of choice rather than mechanical transmission and imposition of values.

Burton Zwiebach distinguishes between political socialisation and political education. The former, he argues, is the means by which citizens are trained to accept civic responsibilities imposed upon them by social institutions and authorities, whilst the latter is '...the education of free citizens in the practice of making independent political judgements' (cited in Gorham 1992: 213, endnote 23). Amy Gutmann (1987: 43) defines political socialisation as 'unconscious social reproduction' in which learners are not trained to think critically or to make correct moral choices, whilst in political education, learners '...are not socialised to their communities, but are learning how to reason about their communities and how to come to a thoughtful decision about joining them.' This is only possible in democratic societies where citizens are free, not only to engage in free dialogue but to question and interrogate the status quo freely.

That the ENS is an institution of political socialisation designed to transmit the values and norms of the EPLF that would guide participants' behaviour is evident from the way the goals and objectives are defined. In view of the fact that there are no democratic rights in the country, such as freedom of association, speech and expression (see AI 2004; HRW 2009, 2015; UN Commission of Inquiry on Human Rights in Eritrea 2015; UN Rapporteur on Human Rights in Eritrea 2014), the ENS can only be an institution of political socialisation and indoctrination rather than political education. For example, the proclamation on national service is prefaced by the following statement: 'The present and future generations have the historical responsibility of preserving a free and sovereign Eritrea as a legacy of thousands of martyrs.' It is further stated, '[f]or the realization of this noble objective it has become necessary to proclaim [promulgate] and issue this proclamation on National Service.' The preamble of the ratified constitution, which the president of the country has refused to implement since 23 May 1997, states: 'Realising that in order to build an advanced country, it is necessary that the unity, equality, love for truth and justice, self-reliance, and hard work, which we nurtured during our revolutionary struggle for independence and which helped us to triumph, must become the core of our national values' (Preamble of the ratified Constitution of Eritrea 1997).[4] One of the main purposes of the ENS therefore is to preserve and transmit to present and future generations these national core values.

THE ENS AS A MECHANISM OF TRANSMISSION AND PRESERVATION OF CORE VALUES: DESERTERS' NARRATIVES

One way of finding out the extent to which the ENS and the WYDC 'preserve and entrust future generations the courage and resoluteness, heroic episodes shown by the people in the past thirty years' is from the *warsai* themselves. The respondents and key informants from whom the data have been elicited have, on average, served in the national service for about six years, and are therefore the best judges of the effect of the national service in regard to its transformative effect. It is important to emphasise that the *warsai*, in spite of their common experiences in the ENS and WYDC, do not speak with the same voice. However, in spite of the multiple and contested voices, it is still possible to evaluate the extent to which their consciousness, their values, hierarchy of priorities and dedication to public causes are shaped by the ENS. The respondents were asked to rank in order their responses to the

---

[4]   The Constitution of Eritrea, ratified by the Constituent Assembly on 23 May 1997.

following generalisation: 'The national service preserves and transmits to present and future generations the courage, resoluteness, dedication and heroism shown during the 30 years' war', by stating (1) strongly agree; (2) agree; (3) disagree; (4) strongly disagree; (5) other. The results show that about 17 per cent and 30 per cent respectively, stated that they 'strongly agree' and 'agree' with the generalisation, so a total of 47 per cent think that the national service functions as an effective mechanism of preserving and transmitting to present and future generations the courage, resoluteness and heroic episodes of the thirty years' war.

A slight majority, 53 per cent, think that the national service does not preserve and transmit the values of the thirty years' war. Although opinions on this were divided the fact that about 47 per cent believe the national service is an effective mechanism for preserving and transmitting the values and characteristics produced during the thirty years' war to present and future generations is an indication of its usefulness in achieving the goal it was designed to accomplish. Nevertheless, the fact that a slight majority of the respondents did not think that the national service preserves and transmits such values may indicate that there are problems associated with the assumption underpinning the ENS and the manner in which it is implemented and managed. As we shall see herein very few of the respondents are in principle negatively predisposed to the idea of national service, and therefore its weaknesses cannot be attributed to opposition to the notion of national service per se.

It is interesting to note that the opinion of the respondents concerning whether the national service transmits the primary values of the liberation struggle to the *agelglot* is a function of the method of conscription. There is a clear relationship between the method of conscription, the *agelglots'* opinions and the transformative effect of the ENS. The majority (62 per cent) of respondents who joined the national service voluntarily before receiving call up papers, or before it became open-ended, said that the ENS shapes the *agelglots'* sense of public service. The converse was the case with those who were rounded up and forced to join the national service. The majority (71 per cent) in this category said that the ENS does not shape the *agelglots'* sense of public service. There is also a clear relationship between the year of conscription and the respondents' opinion concerning whether the ENS shapes the *agelglots'* sense of public service. Those who were conscripted during the border war and in the immediate post-border war (1999–2003) period said that the ENS does not in any way shape the *agelglots'* sense of public service.

The respondents were asked a similar, but more specific, question concerning the extent to which the national service shapes the *agelgolots'* commitment to the common good. A majority – 55 per cent – said that the ENS had shaped their attitude towards the common good, as well as fostered their commitment to the same. A slight minority, 44 per cent, said that the national service had no influence on fostering commitment to the common good. This may not necessarily suggest that they lack commitment to the common good as such. It only means that the national service did not inculcate and foster such values among those who denied the national service fosters commitment to the common good. This was the case regardless of the method and year of conscription.

The key informants were also asked to express their view concerning whether the ENS constitutes an effective mechanism of preserving and transmitting the values of the thirty years' war. One key informant, Abraham, said, 'Yes, the national service was an indispensable instrument of connecting the second generation of nationals – the *warsai* – with the first generation of fighters – the *yikealo*. Before we went to Sawa, our knowledge and understanding of the significance of the thirty years' war was superficial. At Sawa and after, not only did we gain greater insights and understandings of the liberation struggle but we also embraced the primary values and norms that lay at the heart of its success.' Zere, who was generally positive about the effectiveness of the ENS in preserving and transmitting the culture of the thirty years' war, said, 'Although the ENS and the WYDC have helped us to undergo considerable transformation in our attitudes, values and sense of patriotism, we were equally put off by the high level of heavy-handedness and inequality that characterized our relationship with the *yikealo*.'

Another pointed out, 'The *yikealo* were privileged. The quality of the food they ate was far better and they could order us to cook their food, wash their clothes, clean their houses and could even demand sexual service from our female cohorts. These practices engendered among us a general feeling of resentment and consequently the *yikealo* failed to play a positive role model' (R #024). Others rejected the notion that the national service could preserve and transmit the values, such as courage, resoluteness, dedication and heroism, produced during the war. However, as stated by Ahmed:

> For the national service to be able to preserve and transmit to us and to the next generation the positive characteristics that were dominant during the thirty years' war, the *Yikealo* who are supposed to be our role models ought to represent those values. Although there is no doubt that during the thirty years' war, the *yikealo* were heroes, judging from the way they behaved and interacted with us and the society at large in Sawa and elsewhere, there was nothing that indicated that they were still in possession of the values and traits they had internalized during the thirty years' war. In fact, the behaviour of the commanders was so disgraceful that they discredited the legitimacy not only of the values of the revolution but also of the national service. The tendency among some of us was to dissociate from the values and norms that regulated the behaviour of the *yikealo*. (Interview, London, 1 October 2014)

When the defence minister was asked, in a marathon interview by journalists working for the ministry of defence, '[w]hat measures have we taken to preserve the prized core values we gained from our experience and have we been able to preserve them effectively?', he said, '[o]f course. That is why we are talking about them. Not only have we been able to preserve them, but we are also transforming them to suit the present situation' (cited in *Te'ateq* 2004: 46). He continued, '[w]hen we talk about the WYDC, if we talk about war, we are willy-nilly talking about preservation (continuity) and change, but if you want to understand how we preserve the core values, go and ask our soldiers. We have institutionalized the experiences and the core values of the liberation struggle' (2004: 48). He identifies what he refers to as the twelve 'institutionalized core values, namely, initiative, courage, speedy decision-making, self-esteem, flexibility, perseverance, creativity, maturity, skill, self-discipline, trustworthiness, humility and responsibility' (2004: 47).

In the absence of any other means of measuring the effectiveness of the ENS in preserving and transmitting the values of the thirty years' war, the views of the *warsai* interviewees who had served in the national service and the WYDC for about six years on average is a good measure of the extent to which the ENS can serve as an instrument of preservation and transmission of the values of the liberation struggle. After all, one of the major purposes of the ENS and the WYDC is to transmit the prized values fostered during the thirty years' war to the *warsai*. Another way of measuring the effectiveness of the national service as an instrument of preserving and transmitting the main core values fostered during the war of independence has been to ask the respondents to state the virtues and vices they learned in the course of performing national service.

The respondents were provided with a list of eight 'virtues' and seven 'vices' and were asked to identify the ones they learned in the national service and the WYDC. Of the 190 total numbers of respondents, 65 per cent said that the main virtue they acquired in the ENS and the WYDC was hard work. Among the total, 53 per cent, 52 per cent, 47 per cent, 36 per cent, 35 per cent, 33 per cent and 24 per cent, respectively reported that the main virtuous values they learned/internalised in the ENS and WYDC were dedication to public causes, solidarity, cooperation, patriotism, reliability, respect for others and honesty. The values the *agelglot* said they acquired in the process of performing national service and participating in the WYDC clearly indicate the transformative effects of the ENS, which is consistent with the aims, and objectives of the programme.

However, ironically, a minority of the respondents also said that they learned some vices that are incompatible with the values the ENS is intended to inculcate the *agelglot* with, namely, the core values of the liberation struggle. The vices they said they learned are briefly discussed below.

VICES LEARNED IN THE ENS AND THE WYDC

The findings show that not only did the *agelglot* learn some of the virtuous core values fostered during the thirty years' war, but they also learned some vices which seem to be incompatible not only with the declared *raison d'être* of the ENS, but also with some of the core values that were said to be fostered during the thirty years' war. As mentioned previously, the single most important goal of the ENS is to transmit the values of the liberation struggle, such as sacrificial nationalism, selflessness, heroism, relinquishment of self and familial interests, and dedication of one's life to the common good of the nation and the Eritrean people. Although not explicitly stated, by transmitting these primary values the Eritrean government intends to foster citizenship, or to create and reproduce good citizens who serve the country and people honestly, full-heartedly and enthusiastically, as well as nurturing a strong sense of common purpose.

Although the meaning of good citizenship is contested, as it means different things to different people, some of the character traits a minority among the *agelglot* said they acquired in the ENS and the WYDC are inconsistent with the meaning of citizenship no matter how it is defined, as well as with the declared goals and aims of the ENS. A good citizen, among many other things, is someone who is trustworthy, ingenuous and respectful of the rights of others, is law abiding, upholds high moral standards and has a strong sense of right and wrong, integrity and patriotic fervour, in the positive rather than the jingoistic sense. Someone who cheats, deceives, acts dishonestly or fraudulently and exhibits sycophantic compliance is far from being a good citizen. Fraudulence, conformism and submissiveness are indeed the antithesis of good citizenship.

Although, as seen earlier, the *agelglot* said that they learned some invaluable virtues and values in the ENS, a minority also said that they learned some vices that may defeat the purpose of the ENS. The data show that among the respondents, 11 per cent, 38 per cent, 15 per cent, 14 per cent, 11 per cent, 34 per cent and 2 per cent, respectively, reported that they had learned how to defraud, cheat, deceive, lie, to be opportunistic, docile and lazy. The interview was conducted in Tigrinya, save the few that were conducted in English, Tigre and Blin. The meanings of the terminologies used to describe the learned vices in the ENS are not substantially different when translated into English. If we put together those who reported that they have learned fraudulence, cheating, deception, dishonesty, opportunism, docility and laziness in the ENS and the WYDC under one category, the proportion of the *agelglot* who have learned vices is surprisingly high.

In view of the fact that these findings seem to represent the antithesis of the core values that were said to be developed during the thirty years' war, the question that springs to mind is: where do these vices emanate from? Social values are not immutable and static. They are subject to erosion and transformation over time, especially when the conditions under which they were fostered and maintained change fundamentally. The conditions under which the holders of the core values of the thirty years' war, the *tegadelti*, lived during the liberation struggle are completely different from those prevailing in the post-independence period. It may be unrealistic therefore to expect that the core values developed during the thirty years' war would remain intact in the post-independence period and that the *tegadelti* would be able to transmit them to present and future generations straightforwardly despite the profoundly changed circumstances.

In an attempt to understand and explain the underlying reasons for such behaviour, I interviewed some key informants in detail. One of the questions I asked was: 'In view of the fact that the *tegadelti* had an unblemished reputation of being honestly devoted to the cause of their organisation or the revolution, but not necessarily in terms of upholding universally-accepted and prized values, it is worthwhile to understand and explain why some of the *agelglot* failed to inherit this character trait?'

When I asked this question to a key informant, Habtom, who fled Eritrea after serving in the ENS for thirteen years, he laughed derisively and said, 'So you think the *tegadelti* (combatants) during the thirty years' war and the *yikealo* (ex-combatants in post-independence Eritrea) are the same?' He added:

> Although it is necessary to guard against unwarranted generalization, the large majority of the *yikealo* have nothing in common with what they used to be, i.e. when they were *tegadelti*. The world the *tegadelti* inhabited was radically different from the world the *yikealo* currently inhabit. As a result, the interests, priorities, attitudes, hopes and aspirations of the *yikealo* have changed dramatically in the post-independence period. For the rank and file *tegadelti*, the common good of the Eritrean people and the Eritrean nation was the single most important goal they fought for. Every *tegadalai* was ready and willing to die for the revolution and many did so honourably, God bless them. None of the *yikealo* I met in the ENS and under whose command I served exhibited any sense of commitment to the core values the thirty years' war fostered. Instead, self-preservation and wealth accumulation seemed to be the guiding principles of their lives. Many of the *yikealo* I met in the ENS and the WYDC were corrupt, vile, excessively self-interested and cruel. (Interview, Geneva, 22 November 2013)

Kemal said, 'Some of the *yikealo* are engaged in a cutthroat competition to make up for lost time not only in terms of wealth accumulation, but also in terms of sexually abusing as many female conscripts as possible. They have no moral or legal boundaries when they cheat, punish, insult, steal and abuse their power' (Interview, Geneva, 23 November 2013). The views expressed by most of the key informants were similar. Although the immorality of the commanders cannot justify the fraudulent behaviour of the *agelglot*, the probability of copycat actions is perhaps unavoidable. Abeba, a female key informant, for example, said, 'When the commanders resort to all sorts of immoral actions to enrich themselves by exploiting the conscripts and to violate the sexual autonomy of female conscripts, why would any of us be expected to act honourably in an environment polluted by corruption and immorality? In a situation like this, dishonest behaviour becomes normal.'

Although the aim of the ENS is to generate values that promote national cohesion and nation building, some of the activities the conscripts are forced to undertake have nothing to do with such objectives, because they are undertaken in pursuit of the private gains of the military commanders and the ruling party, the PFDJ. Ironically, the findings of the study show that, contrary to the goals of the ENS, not only did the conscripts learn and internalise virtuous values that contribute to nation building and post-conflict (re)construction, but they also developed vices that are potentially detrimental to its aims.

In the following chapter the extent to which the ENS functions as a vehicle for national unity and social cohesion is examined.

6

The Eritrean National Service:
A Vehicle for National Unity and Cohesion

The primary achievement of the EPLF was to bring about a level of bonding, in opposition to the Ethiopian 'other', that was sufficient to sustain the long and extremely costly conflict that eventually resulted in victory. Even if this bonding never reached the level of unanimity that official discourse suggests, and some Eritreans maintained alternative viewpoints – in favour either of the Moslem ELF, or of continued union with Ethiopia – it was still an extraordinarily successful project.

Christopher Clapham (2001: 8)

Military training brings a man into contact with his fellows solely upon the basis of fellow-citizenship. For the time, at least, the differences of wealth, education, locality, taste, occupation, and social rank, which divide Americans as effectively as though they lived on different continents or in different centuries, are lost sight of. Men are brought face to face with the elemental fact of nationality.

Perry (1921: 260)

We have nine languages. But we are all from the same ethnic group and the same background. We have been living in this region for centuries. This is what distinguishes us in addition to the maturity of the people that they gained from their experience during the period of struggle. They triumphed because they were united; they lived in harmony; and they had one goal despite the differences in the cultural and denominational structure and other matters. This is one of God's gifts to this land.

Isaias Afwerki (2009)

This chapter examines the extent to which the Eritrean National Service (ENS) functions as a vehicle for national unity and social cohesion. It examines whether national service functions as a 'sociological mixer', enabling conscripts hailing from disparate ethno-linguistic, geographical, religious and cultural backgrounds to bond and forge a secular Eritrean national identity at the expense of their sub-national identities and allegiances. The chapter also discusses the factors that enhance national unity and greater trans-cultural understanding through enhanced knowledge of different places and communities in the course of performing national service. The chapter also discusses whether trans-ethnic, trans-religious and trans-regional friendships have developed among the conscripts. It also devotes some space to the dissenting opinions of a few respondents concerning whether the ENS promotes national unity and social cohesion.

The assumption that universal national/military service promotes national unity and social cohesion among ethnically and religiously diverse, or divided, societies is an old one. As seen in Chapter 2, the values reflected in the sense of common purpose and commitments to national causes that promote national unity and social cohesion by interconnecting people across the social cleavages of particular identities and by eroding the values that reinforce sub-national loyalties and belongings are said to be created and reproduced as a result of the meeting, working, interacting and training together of servers (conscripts) from disparate classes, ethno-linguistic and faith groups, as well as geographical regions and political opinions (Bellamy 1890 [1888]; James 1943 [1910]; Etzioni 1983; Janowitz 1983; Walzer 1983; Moscos 1988; Montesquieu 1989 [1748]). For example, one of the great proponents of national service, Amitai Etzioni, describes the functions of national service as follows:

> The most obvious function of national service...is to unify, energise, and mobilise people – a coming together that is otherwise only accomplished by wars. In the most optimistic of dreams, national service programmes will turn swords into ploughshares; young people [...] will become part of one [...] community, working shoulder to shoulder [...] A new kind of [...] excitement and dedication generated by such a drive against poverty, pollution, and other social ills would replace that incited in the past by wars. (Etzioni 1990: ix)

In another work, he observes, '... *one of the most promising payoffs of a year of national service for young Americans is that the programme could serve as the "great sociological mixer"* America needs if a stronger national consensus on fundamental values is to evolve ...' (1983: 160, emphasis added). National service that brings young men and women from different geographical areas, religions, languages, ethnic and class backgrounds to live and work together leads to them knowing each other, learning from each other and sharing common experiences. This is said to create a powerful bond and mutual understanding, which are auspicious in en-gendering the values that foster national unity and social cohesion. Many other historians and analysts share this view. Eugen Weber, for example, stated:

> One appeal of universal military training and national service rests in the supposed ability of such programmes to foster national unity by mixing together young men (and in some versions, women) from all parts of the country. Military service has been supported in developing countries just on such grounds. National unity was one aim of conscription in France during the early years of the Third Republic, and as one French historian observes, 'By the 1890s there is persuasive evidence that the army was no longer "theirs" but "ours". The army becomes "as potent an agency for acculturation and civilisation as the schools"'. (Cited in Cohen 1985: 128)

There is common agreement among the exponents of compulsory national service that it fosters national unity and trans-ethnic and trans-faith cohesion in multi-ethnic and multi-faith societies lacking common history and ancestry (James 1943 [1910]; Walzer 1983; Moskos 1989). In such societies, national unity is achieved when individual citizens identify with the national community. This is because national service is supposed to create and reproduce the values and norms that make the participant identify in this way. Accordingly, the values, the interconnecting threads, the glue that holds society together, and the sense of patriotism national service produces, are substitutes for the values that prompt loyalty to a national community in societies that lack, as Moskos argues, 'common ancestry and some divine foundation myth' (1989: 9).

In the process of performing national service together with many others hailing from disparate cultures, faiths and places, exponents of national service argue that participants develop and internalise the values and norms that prompt them to subordinate their particular interests to the national interest. Advocates of compulsory national service during the French Revolution considered all forms of egoism and individual interests as 'contrary to patriotic unity.' They argued, 'Amour-propre (literally "love of oneself," which may be translated as self-respect or pride) and amour de lapatrie (love of the fatherland) become synonyms: the individual is to see him-or herself primarily as a part of the national community' (Hippler 2007 [1757]: 78).

Multi-ethnic and multi-faith nations use the institution of national service as a means of producing a set of civic values and virtues that promote trans-ethnic and trans-faith cooperation and cohesion, on which viable nation states are built. This set of civic virtues and values is also critical in the process of healing wounds and reconstructing fractured social norms of cooperation and trust resulting from the toxic effects of intra-state wars. For example, as seen before, one of the main reasons the Federal Military Government in Nigeria introduced the National Youth Service Corps (NYSC) programme in the aftermath of the defeat of the Biafra civil war, in 1973, was to foster national unity and trans-ethnic and trans-faith cohesion in a country where there are over 374 ethnic groups. As Ebenezer Obadare (2010: 20) states: 'Faced with a total breakdown of social harmony following Nigeria's thirty-month Civil War (1967–70) [...] the then Federal Military Government realised that having won the war, it was imperative that the peace – of solid and voluntary national unity – be won [...] true feelings of loyalty and solidarity that produce national cohesion and unity [...] could only be an outcome of a deliberate social process.'

One of the central aims of the ENS is to 'foster national unity among our people [Eritreans] by eliminating sub-national feelings' (Art. 5 Proc. 82/95). In spite of its small population and physical size, Eritrea is home to nine disparate ethno-linguistic groups with a limited pre-existing affinity for one another in the remote rural areas. The population is also equally divided between the two religions: Christianity and Islam. Although Eritrea's political, economic and social history by no means began with the advent of colonialism (see Reid 2011), as in the rest of Africa, these diverse ethno-linguistic and faith groups were brought together under the same colonial reign during the 'scramble for Africa' in the 1880s. Although the common experience of suffering experienced under the consecutive colonial powers and the thirty years' war of independence (1961–1991) against an external enemy have brought Eritreans closer to each other, the process of nation building remains incomplete and is still in progress. Its architects perceive the ENS as a key catalyst in fostering the development and consolidation of common Eritrean national identity, as well as in nation building.

Before the 1998–2000 border war, in a series of interviews, the architects of the ENS, President Isaias Afwerki, and the former defence minister, Sebhat Ephrem, presented the ENS as a vital mechanism for nation building and forging national unity in the disparate Eritrean polity. However, the emphasis of the narrative shifted substantially thereafter. During and after the border war the ENS has been presented not only as the lifeblood of the process of nation building, unity and consolidation, but also, and more importantly, as an existential matter, as if the present and future survival of the country and its citizens were dependent on its success. In 1994, when the first cohorts of the ENS were about to be sent to the Sawa Military Camp, the Eritrean president, after pointing out that different states in the world have used the institution of national service to achieve different goals, stated that the ENS, owing to the country's specific history, has a different meaning and significance:

> Because we need to rebuild what has been destroyed [...] unlike in other countries, our national service programme is not limited to military ends [and consequently], it should be perceived as an integral part of a broad programme of national reconstruction. *The national service has both economic and moral significance.* (Cited in Interview with President Isaias Afwerki 2004: 3, emphasis added)

Soon after the enactment of the second proclamation on the ENS (Proc. No 82/1995), the former defence minister stated, 'The pillars on which the very existence of this country stands is the ENS' (Sebhat Ephrem 1995). He further observed, 'Our country is small and so is its population.' The main aim of the national service therefore is, he said, 'to ensure the survival and continuity of the country.' In October 2002, the head of state was asked to spell out the objectives of the ENS and the rationales underlying it. He said that one of the central aims was to 'promote national unity (*hadinet*) and to create a new society (*hadish hibreteseb nmimsrat*)'. The Eritrean People's Liberation Front (EPLF), and later its successor, the People's Front for Democracy and Justice (PFDJ), as well as the post-independence government, seem to believe strongly that the institution of the ENS could affect social and cultural change, due to the development and internalisation of shared patriotic nationalist values that supersede allegiance to sub-national 'parochial projects' of clan, tribe, ethnicity, religion and region (Sebhat Ephrem 1995, 2008; Isaias Afwerki 2003b, 2004). During the Fifth Youth Festival, held at Sawa in July 2012, the president identified three key roles the ENS plays, namely, honouring the trust of the martyrs, safeguarding the nation's sovereignty, and laying a firm foundation for the process of nation-building (Isaias Afwerki 2012).

The central aim of the national service has therefore been to create a prototype of an ideal and committed citizen inimical to clan, tribal, ethnic, religious and regional loyalties, as well as one who subordinates his personal and familial interests to the common good of Eritrea and its citizenry. The *agelglot* (conscripts) are expected to undergo fundamental changes and consequently relinquish their sub-national loyalties and identities in favour of a common Eritrean national identity. During the Second Youth Festival, held in the military training camp in July 2006, the president, said, 'Sawa training centre was founded not for military purpose [...] the aim was to ensure the nation's continuity and pass over generational responsibility' (Isaias Afwerki 2006). Inasmuch as

Eritrean youth played a vital role in the making of the Eritrean state its continuity and reproduction are unthinkable without their commitment and participation. In the opening ceremony of the Festival he said, 'Sawa represents a permanent symbol for our continued existence as a people and nation' (Isaias Afwerki 2006).

'Nationalism,' he said, 'is not a matter of automatic phenomenon [that occurs naturally] but one that needs to be deliberately nurtured [fostered]' (Isaias Afwerki 2006). This is not just any sort of nationalism, but, as Victoria Bernal (2014) argues, 'sacrificial nationalism'. The ENS is therefore meant to foster nationalism and a powerful sense of belonging to the same national community. In the president's view, Sawa is the school of the nation where unity based on shared values, sense of common purpose, identity, loyalty, national cohesion and commitment to the common good are forged and consolidated. The ultimate goal of the ENS is to produce citizens who count their interests as inconsequential compared to the interests of the nation, as was the case with the combatants during the thirty years' war of independence. However, as seen before, in the post-independence period, the interest of the regime or of the personal ruler, Isaias Afwerki, has supplanted the interest of the state. During the thirty years' war of independence, fought against a more populous enemy, Ethiopia, the need to fight against a ferocious external enemy without military or political support from either of the then superpowers relegated internal differences to the background. What makes the successful outcome of the liberation struggle meaningful is the fact that disparate ethno-linguistic and multi-faith communities fought together, relegating their differences to the background in pursuit of a common goal.

NATIONAL SERVICE: A FORM OF MASS MOBILISATION AGAINST IMAGINED FOREIGN THREAT

After the war of independence ended with victory in 1991, the government, especially the president, feared that the cause that rallied all Eritreans to stand together in pursuit of a common purpose against a foreign enemy disregarding their religious, ethnic, class, political and regional differences would be lost if not nurtured persistently and with unrelenting vigour. It was thought that this loss would represent an imminent threat not only to Eritrea's unity, sovereignty, territorial integrity and social cohesion, but that this might threaten the very survival of the country (Isaias Afwerki 1996). In his view, unless there was permanent vigilance and action plans were in place to countervail the corrosive effects of the activities of political organisations based on tribalism, ethnicity, religion and region in the post conflict situation, not only might the achievements of the thirty years' war risk being wantonly squandered, the society itself might disintegrate.

This is clear from the many interviews he holds with the government-controlled mass media and with foreign journalists. As we saw before, he told Kaplan of *The Atlantic Monthly*, '*But we have not yet institutionalised social discipline, so the possibility of chaos is still here. Remember, we have nine language groups and two religions* [...] Therefore we will have to manage the creation of political parties, so that they don't become means of religious and ethnic division, like in Ivory Coast or Nigeria' (cited in Kaplan 2003, emphasis added). The ENS is therefore conceived as a means of wearing down the conditions that may pave the way for the emergence of sectarian political organisations. By controlling and indoctrinating the youth the regime also stifles the development and consolidation of pluralistic and democratic values that threaten to challenge the hegemonic discourse.

The president and the former defence minister identified different enemies at different stages that had to be defeated by the success of the national service. The nature and the identities of the so-called enemies were shifting depending on the specific goals the incumbents wanted to achieve, or the potential or actual danger they wanted to avoid. At the early stage of state building, in the immediate post-independence period, the enemies against which the government tried to mobilise the Eritrean people were the Islamist State of Sudan and the Eritrean Islamic Jihad (EIJ) (see Kibreab 2009c). Towards the end of 1995 Eritrea and Yemen clashed over the Hanish Islands in the southern Red Sea (see Dzurek 1996) and the focus of the conflict temporarily shifted there. In May 1998 a border war broke out between Eritrea and Ethiopia that devastated the affected areas. Although a peace agreement was reached in December 2000, Ethiopia failed to abide by the award of the Eritrea-Ethiopia Border Commission and a state of 'no-peace-no-war' has prevailed between the two countries ever since. The Eritrean authorities use this as a pretext to keep the whole nation armed in anticipation of an alleged Ethiopian invasion. In June 2008 fighting broke out between Eritrean and Djiboutian forces over Eritrea's incursion into the Ras Doumeira area in Djibouti (Ira and Lantier 2008). The Eritrean government uses the imagined threat of foreign invasion as an instrument of mobilisation and, more importantly, as a means of engendering a state of unremitting fear and anxiety. If such enemies don't exist readily, they are invented.

THE ENS: INSTRUMENT OF NATIONAL INTEGRATION

According to the former defence minister, Sawa provides youngsters who come from different corners of the country the opportunity to know each other and to live in harmony. This 'helps in getting rid of feelings of suspicion [...] caused by lack of interaction, and in creating instead a new dynamic Eritrean generation' (Sebhat Ephrem 1995). This is consistent with Cynthia Enloe's description of governments' attitudes towards conscription. She states, '...conscription in the nation-state period was considered an integrative process. Conscription was a form of mass mobilisation that would increase each citizen's (or, at least, each male citizen's) sense of affiliation with the political system and his stake in the maintenance of that system' (1980: 53).

The Eritrean president states that the country's youth are a force that can homogenise the multi-ethnic and multi-faith Eritrean polity. For the new generation to serve as agents of continuity and change he said that youth should mix with each other, know one another and become aware of their responsibilities (Isaias Afwerki 2004: 3). It is only then, in his view, that the youth would be fit for purpose from all perspectives (Isaias Afwerki 2004: 3). The national service brings together youth from both sexes and from different ethnic, religious, regional and class backgrounds, to learn to know each other, gain common experiences and consequently develop shared values which will contribute to character formation and inculcate a powerful moral fibre of solidarity and mutuality and a sense of common purpose (Isaias Afwerki 1994, 2004).

This is consistent with how some philosophers writing on national service conceptualise its impact on national unity, social cohesion, character building, public spiritedness and commitment to public causes (see James 1943 [1910]; Walzer 1980, 1983; Etzioni 1983; Moskos 1988). Etzioni, for example, states, '[a]t present America has few of the structural opportunities for shared experience to develop shared values that are essential if the polity is to reach agreement on courses of action with sufficient speed and without disruptive conflict' (1983: 160). He further observes:

> A year of national service, especially if it were designed to enable people from different geographical and sociological backgrounds to work and live together, could be an effective way for boys and girls, whites and non-whites, people from parochial and public schools, North and South, big city and country, to get to know one another on an equal footing while working together at a common task. The 'total' nature of the situation – being away from home, peers, and 'background' communities, and spending time together around the clock – is what promises the sociological impact. It is the reason such a year may be more effective than several years of casual contact in high school or college, cafeterias, pool halls, or bowling alleys. (Etzioni 1983: 161)

Margaret Mead (1967: 99), an exponent of national service, states, '[a] nationwide draft helps to underline a sense of national commitment and the urgency of total national involvement in the maintenance of an orderly world.' She further observes, 'The poor and rich, the highly technologically gifted and those with obsolescent skills, the white collar and the blue collar, are each reared in almost total ignorance of one another.' She suggested that a universal national service would compensate for the increasing 'fragmentation, ignorance, and lack of knowledge of their fellow citizens.' In her view, this constitutes one of the justifications for compulsory national service.

In the following, using data elicited from respondents who deserted from the ENS after serving six years on average, an attempt is made to appraise the impact of the ENS on their attitudes toward national unity and cohesion.

THE ENS: MECHANISM OF NATIONAL UNITY AND COHESION: RESPONDENTS' AND INFORMANTS' PERCEPTIONS

Given the large number of nationals affected by the ENS, and assuming the values, attitudes and habits the conscripts develop and internalise in the course of participating in the ENS and the WYDC are propitious to national unity and cohesion, they can be effective agents of transmission of these prized values and consequently contribute to national unity and cohesion, as well as to attitudinal changes and transformations in terms of allegiance to the national community at the expense of self-interest, primordial loyalties and ethnic and religious allegiances.

In light of the long (currently indefinite) duration of the ENS and subjecting servers to 'rigorous' political socialisation aimed at imbuing them with the values of the liberation struggle and a strong sense of patriotism, as well as commitment to public causes, that permeated the liberation struggle, the architects of the programme assume that the institution of the ENS will play a key role in fostering national unity and cohesion and in transmitting these values to the rest of the population. This is more likely to be the case in view of the government's policy and practice of assigning all conscripts to any part of the country, including to areas and communities previously unknown to them, potentially with a different faith, ethnicity, culture and way of life. Since one of the central aims of the ENS is to promote national unity and integration, the respondents interviewed in the study were asked the following question: 'Since the fourth aim of the ENS is to promote national unity and social cohesion, the Eritrean government strongly believes that the national service would unite and integrate Eritreans from the different ethnic, religious, class and regional backgrounds into one nation with a sense of common citizenship – as a means of unifying Eritrean society. Based on your experience in the ENS, do you think the national service unifies Eritrean society?' They were further asked: 'If your answer is "no", please explain why you don't think the national service contributes to national unity and cohesion. Or: If your answer is that the national service contributes to national unity and cohesion, please explain how this has happened by giving examples based on your own experience and observation.'

Among the respondents, the overwhelming majority, 90.5 per cent, said that the ENS fosters national unity and cohesion, with only 9.5 per cent disagreeing. This finding is highly significant in light of the fact that the respondents were deserters; as a consequence, one would expect their evaluation of the impact of the ENS on national unity and cohesion to be negative. Because the interviewees fled from the ENS one might expect them to have an incentive not to acknowledge its positive contribution, but the converse was true. The qualitative data produced by the second part of the question are more important than the quantitative data produced by the first. In the following the reasons for the respondents thinking that the ENS promotes national unity and cohesion are presented.

In order to do justice to the voices of the respondents the stated reasons are presented verbatim in what follows. Asked whether the ENS promotes national unity and cohesion and why, R #003 said, 'Yes, I strongly believe that bringing together in one place of nationals from diverse regions, ethnic, religious and cultural backgrounds promotes mutual love, understanding, unity and cohesion.' R #041 expressed similar views, stating:

> National service brings together Eritreans from all corners of the country. This provides an opportunity for those who come from the Eritrean highlands and

lowlands to learn about their cultures and traditions. This enables participants to learn about how the different groups throughout the country live. Living and working together brings them closer and this creates common national purpose.

R #010 observed, 'sharing of common experiences with different people from different ethnic groups helped me to know more about Eritrean society, history, geography, etc.' Another observed, 'Eritrea has different ethnic groups and different cultures and traditions and the national service provides an opportunity to the youth to get together and exchange experiences. This is good for national unity and social cohesion' (R #017).

Not only does the opportunity of meeting people from different faith and ethno-linguistic groups and visiting areas inhabited by people who are different from one's own, enhance mutual knowledge and under- standing about each other, as well as producing shared experiences which interconnect people across differences of religion, ethnicity, gender, class and region, but also, as R #020 insightfully observes, these experiences engender attitudinal changes about each other and about society at large. R #032 and R #035 reiterated similar views. It is these changes and transformations that produce the glue that holds servers hailing from different socio-linguistic and cultural backgrounds together and fosters unity and cohesion. 'Because you meet people from different ethnic groups, your views about them change. For example, before going to the national service, I never thought that the Kunama interacted with other groups' (R #020). R #065 also said, 'before I went to the ENS, I never met an Eritrean Kunama or Nara. I did not also know there were Christian Blin.' In a similar vein, R #022 observed, 'Yes, in the process of working and living together, we developed a culture of cooperation, mutual respect, harmony and unity.' In R #021's view, the ENS has built bridges that eliminate cross-cultural misunderstanding and mutual ignorance. They stated, 'The lowlanders were running away when they saw us, but now they welcome us with water and food when we visit their villages.' R #130 observed, 'Muslims, Christians, highlanders and lowlanders work together without any distinction and this promotes cohesion and unity.' In R #146's view, 'the mixing of people from different nationalities, regions and religions in one place brings [prompts] people to develop a common national purpose and the process of mutual interaction and living together is highly educational.' R #022 pointed out, 'I know more about Eritrean society now than before because we teach each other about the history, cultures, geography and religions and way of life of our particular societies.' Another respondent said, 'the distribution of the ethnic groups is scattered throughout the country. The national service brings all into a single location and this creates suitable environment for knowing each other and this engenders unity and common understanding' (R #024).

R #026 bears witness to the educational value of the ENS by stating, 'before I joined the national service, I had no clue about the other Eritrean ethnic groups but thanks to the national service, I gained knowledge and this engendered a sense of commonality and harmony.' A similar view was expressed by R #042 who stated,

In national service, one meets people from different ethnic groups and builds friendships and learns about their traditions and cultures, including the types of food they eat which one can enjoy. The reason why the ENS promotes national unity and social harmony is because one meets, lives and works with people from different ethnic groups and builds life based on common experience and learns about the varieties of cultural backgrounds of the different ethnic groups in the country.

It is interesting to note that the universal nature of the ENS has both an integrative and a transformative effect on the views of some respondents. For example, R #167 observes that not only has the ENS integrated the previously excluded and marginalised groups in the country, such as the Kunama and the Hedareb, but it has also influenced the society at large. This respondent observes, 'Yes, there was real unity. Inside the country, the youth learned about and mixed with all Eritreans, such as the Kunama and the Hedareb and also learned about their national duty and have applied this knowledge to influence their societies as well as to bring about change and renewal.' Some respondents perceived the ENS as an effective mechanism of 'cultural exchange', which is *sine qua non* for unity and cohesion (R #171). R #175 summarised the effect of the ENS on national unity and cohesion as follows: 'Living and working with people from different backgrounds creates auspicious conditions for friendship, social harmony and for learning many things from each other.'

R #122 stated, 'instead of learning about Eritrean ethnic groups and their cultures from books, one learns through direct experience regarding their physical appearance and their cultures. In the ENS one learns about the country's religions, ethnic groups, places and in short one gains knowledge about the social resources in one's country' (R #025). There is also some evidence to suggest that the practice of bringing together people of diverse religious and socio-cultural backgrounds in one place is in the beginning marked with misunderstanding, but that this changes over time. For example, R #028 observed, 'In the beginning, there is misunderstanding resulting from the wide gap in the level of awareness, outlook and traditions of the people who are brought to Sawa from the different ethnic groups and regions. However, after living and working together for a long time, you don't only know and get used to each other but you develop relations [that are] characteristic of a family based on mutual respect and empathy.' It is interesting to observe that this was reported by a respondent who characterised the type of 'political education' provided at Sawa and in the overall ENS as 'superficial or nominal'. This indicates that it is the living and working together over a long period of time, rather than the so-called political socialisation provided at Sawa and after, that functions as a 'sociological mixer'. In R #050's and R #051's views, bringing people with different occupational, educational and ethnic backgrounds provides convivial environment for bonding and national unity. R #098 states, 'when many people with different backgrounds get together, they exchange experiences and [this] brings integration.'

One of the respondents stated that the desire to bond with conscripts originating from different ethnic and faith groups was so powerful that the youth competed with each other to befriend themselves with the 'Others'.

R #068, for example, observed, 'the youth mixes easily to form a cohesive entity. At the time I was there (1999–2006), there was competition among the youth to excel each other in terms of getting along with the "others."' In the same vein, R #089 stated, 'From my own experience, after I joined the ENS, I worked together with others who had different backgrounds and behaviours for the same cause – the nation – as well as with people I had no knowledge about before, such as the Afar where in spite of my lack of knowledge of their language was able to bond with them.' After their assignment to different locations in different capacities, the servers participate in different forms of ceremonies and events and these contribute to the development of harmonious relationships with the population in the areas where they are assigned. As stated by R #090, 'wherever one goes, it is easy to get on with the people. It is common to participate in weddings, *ngdet* (annual religious ceremonies in villages) and funerals in the areas where one is assigned to and these positively contribute to greater understanding, social interaction, national unity and cohesion. There are even some who intermarry.' Zere, a key informant, said, 'The national service enabled us to mix like milk and water.'

Enhanced Knowledge of Places and Communities, and National Unity

A high proportion of the respondents reported that participation in the ENS has substantially augmented their knowledge of the country and its population, including its disparate cultures. The narratives recounted by the respondents in this regard clearly show that in the process of visiting and working in different places inhabited by different ethnic, faith and occupational groups, the *agelglot* and their hosts are able to establish social networks that interconnect them with each other irrespective of their language, faith, culture, sex, way of life and place of abode. Over time, the mutual familiarities and intimacies produce the glue that holds people stemming from diverse geographical locations and cultural backgrounds together. Before participating in the ENS, the overwhelming majority of the servers said that they had never travelled beyond where they lived, with this being more pronounced among those who had been born and grew up in urban areas. Some of those who grew up and lived in rural areas often moved from place to place to graze and water their animals and that provided them with opportunities to bond with people inhabiting different places in the country.

For example, R #003 stated, 'In the ENS I have come to know lots of places I did not know before. I also learned a great deal about the various ethnic groups and their cultures.' R #009 said, 'National service takes you to different places and the common experience we gain [...] enables us to learn about Eritrean societies, history, cultures, geography and religions.' The same respondent further observed, 'because of the ENS, I have visited different places in the country. I have also learned about the different cultures, traditions of Eritrean society.' The same was reiterated by R #023, who in addition noted, 'I visited most parts of Eritrea and this helped me to see the places that I had learned about at school. I would have been unable to do this had it not been for the ENS.' After the six months military training one is assigned to a region different from one's own, and as one lives among the people in such regions, he/she learns about their cultures and their ways of life. R #143 stated that the ENS promotes national unity and cohesion, 'because the youth are assigned to different areas than their own places of origin and work with the people they did not know before. For example, the youth from the highlands are assigned to work in farms in the lowlands and work with the people there.'

A key informant, Saleh, who grew up in a village in the Anseba region, for example, said that he used to accompany his family's livestock when they migrated seasonally to Barka and Gash Setit where he acquainted himself with different groups from the Tigrinya, Nara and Kunama ethno-linguistic groups. He also said that he frequently visited the cities of Keren, Barentu, Tessenei and Agordat to sell animals, ghee and hides, as well as to buy commodities, such as salt, clothes, pepper, salt, kerosene and medicine. He said that this gave him the opportunity to make friends in the marketplace. For those who grew up and lived in the cities, the school, neighbourhoods and playgrounds were the only venues that provided them with opportunities to meet and connect with others. The national service provided those from both urban and rural areas with an exceptional opportunity to know, mix and bond with tens of thousands of Eritreans hailing from diverse geographical areas and backgrounds. It is in this sense that Amitai Etzioni characterises national service as 'a great sociological mixer' (2001: 114).

R #026 recounted, 'before I joined the national service, I only knew Asmara and my village, but the ENS has enabled me to gain extensive knowledge about the different places.' R #032 reported, 'before I joined the ENS, I did not know any place except Barentu. In NS, I knew lots of other places.' R #036 also noted, 'I only knew Keren and my village. My knowledge of Eritrea expanded in the ENS.' Another reported, 'the ENS helps one to see and work in different places and this provides one an opportunity to learn about other regions, religions, ethnic groups and sharing of common experiences and views with them' (R #043). R #019 also recounted, 'when I was in the ENS, I visited different areas and learned about the cultures, traditions and ways of life of the people inhabiting the places I visited and worked in.' This view was reiterated by Respondents # 152, 153, 166, 167, 174, and many others. Another respondent reinforced this view, stating 'participation in the ENS has enlarged my geographical knowledge of Eritrea' (R #046). This may indicate that not only does the ENS enlarge servers' minds but also their hearts. In a similar vein, R #089 observed, 'I gained knowledge of Eritrea's geography, history, culture, society and religions because I visited places outside where I grew up and met different people from whom I learned some knowledge from all.' Assignment to different places and working in places inhabited by different socio-cultural groups allows interaction and mutual understanding, which is auspicious to national unity and cohesion. R #091, for example, stated, 'When one interacts with the youth that comes from all parts of Eritrea [...] one's knowledge and understanding about Eritrea expands considerably. *This is because there is no comparison between the knowledge one acquires at school and through direct personal experiences*' (emphasis added). A number of respondents stated that there is a massive difference between the knowledge one acquires from books at school and that gained through direct experience. This is because by meeting Eritreans from all places and from different walks of life they are able to build friendships with them and to visit different places throughout the country. Many said that they felt at home wherever they went.

Some respondents also stated that working in different places beyond their region of origin and interacting with people living in those places, besides expanding their knowledge of the populations and cultures, had the effect of enlarging their hearts and minds, as reflected in their respect for Eritreans belonging to other regions. This experience has also made them tolerant of diversity. R #021, for example, stated, 'The reason why national service has increased my tolerance and respect for people from other religions is because my placement in different regions other than my own has enabled me to understand and appreciate that the others are human beings like me and their needs are the same as mine *and more importantly, I realise that unless I respect them, they will not respect me*' (emphasis added). In a highly pluralist society, such as Eritrea, respect for the 'Other', as opposed to mere tolerance, is a prized value that cements unity and social cohesion.

Trans-Ethnic, Trans-Faith and Trans-Regional Friendships among the *Agelglot*

According to the respondents, who had served on average about six years before deserting to seek asylum, the ENS was an effective 'sociological mixer' and hence was a critical instrument of fostering national unity and cohesion. This is consistent with the ideas expounded by the philosophers and political theorists presented in Chapter 2 and in the introduction to this chapter. This is also consistent with the central tenets of the theory of social capital. As seen in Chapter 2, the theory of social capital postulates that where people of different ethnic, geographical, religious and occupational backgrounds interact repeatedly with each other, over time they come to know and trust one another, interconnect with each other and share experiences, values and norms that encourage cooperation, openness, compromise and bonding (Coleman 1990; Putnam 2000; Kibreab 2008). In the process, a series of webs of social networks and friendships based on mutual trust are developed which people can draw upon in pursuit of goals of mutual and national interest.

In view of the fact that the respondents said that serving, living, studying, working and interacting with each other produces values that promote unity, it is reasonable to assume that the ENS is an effective instrument that fosters bonds of friendship and mutual trust across the social markers of religion, ethnicity and region. In order to understand the extent to which the ENS has been instrumental in fostering friendships among the *agelglot* originating from the different regions, ethnic and faith groups, the respondents interviewed in the study which included members

Table 6.1 Ethnicity of the interviewees' friends

	Region	Afar	Bilen	Hedareb	Kunama	Nara	Saho	Tigre	Tigrigna	Rashaida
	Afar	0	0	0	1	0	1	1	2	0
	Bilen	7	13	5	5	10	12	20	30	0
	Nara	0	1	0	0	0	0	1	1	0
	Saho	0	2	0	1	1	3	4	8	0
	Tigre	7	15	3	13	7	16	21	28	0
	Tigrigna	25	51	16	35	21	43	74	153	1

(Ethnicity of the interviewees)

of the different ethnic and religious groups were asked the following question: 'Did you make new friends in the ENS?' Those who reported having made new friends in the course of performing the ENS were further asked to state their new friends' 'ethnicity, religion, region ...' About 95 per cent of the respondents said that they had made new friends in the ENS. It is not the establishment of friendships per se that is interesting, but rather the diversity of the backgrounds of the new friendships in terms of ethnicity, religion and region.

Table 6.2 Religion of the interviewees' friends

	Region	Christianity	Islam
	Afar	2	3
	Bilen	45	55
	Nara	1	2
	Saho	11	8
	Tigre	45	65
	Tigrigna	208	203

(Religion of the interviewees)

The data in Table 6.2 show that trans-faith friendships have been flourishing in the ENS. The Afar, Saho and the Tigre are exclusively Muslims, but they have been able to build friendships across the two dominant religions in the country. The Blin are both Christians and Muslims and so, to some extent, are the Tigrinya-speakers, although the vast majority are Christians. It is equally interesting to note that the respondents have made friends originating from different regions of the country. All the respondents, especially the Blin, Saho, Tigre and Tigrinya, said they had made friendships with people from the different regions of the country. These data clearly show that the ENS has, by bringing citizens from the different ethnic and faith groups, as well regions of the country, together, provided a convivial environment in which trans-regional, trans-

Table 6.3: Regions of origin of the friends of the interviewees

Region of interviewees	Anseba	Central	South	Gash B	N. Red Sea	S. Red Sea
Afar	0	1	1	2	1	0
Bilen	26	16	19	29	5	6
Nara	1	1	0	1	0	0
Saho	3	6	4	5	1	0
Tigre	23	18	19	35	8	7
Tigrigna	86	81	84	100	32	28

ethnic and trans-faith friendships and harmony have flourished. This can only contribute to greater national unity and inter-regional, inter-faith and inter-ethnic understanding and mutual respect. These data show that the ENS functions, as Amitai Etzioni insightfully hypothesised, as a 'great sociological-mixer' (2001: 114).

In order to assess the transformative effects of the ENS the respondents were asked to state the extent to which they would do things which they would never have considered doing had it not been for their participation in the ENS. The large majority said that some of the things they now consider normal would have been inconceivable had it not been for their participation in the ENS. When asked to state what these 'things' are, many mentioned, for example, such events as falling in love and marrying someone from a different religion. Some of the respondents also said that they would fall in love and inter-marry outside of their ethnicity. A considerable proportion said that they would happily enter into a business partnership with people they have met in the ENS regardless of their place of origin, ethnicity, religion and sex. These phenomena were by no means unheard of in Eritrean society, but inter-faith marriages were rare except in the province of Senhit, in the present day Anseba region. At least hypothetically, many of the conscripts seem now to consider marrying outside of one's faith, ethnicity and region to be normal.

Although only a few of the respondents said that they were married to someone outside of their faith, a considerable number were married to someone outside of their ethnicity. However, a number of respondents stated that they were in relationships outside of their own faith. All the respondents said that participation in the ENS has made them more respectful and tolerant of Eritreans who are from other religious and ethnic groups as well as regions. Asked to explain why this is the case, the respondents gave two main reasons for this, namely, sharing of common experience and meeting of people from all regions, classes, sexes, religions, occupations and ethnicities resulting from training, studying, working, suffering and so on together. As one key informant, Mustafa, put it, 'In the ENS, we were a big family who cared for each other.' Abnet, a female conscript said, 'living and working together erases all prejudices'. The use of the concept erasure is significant. She stated that 'The commanders victimised all of us regardless of our geographic origin, religion and ethnicity,' and added, 'Not only did this engender mutual empathy, respect and solidarity, but also emitted the glue that held us together regardless of our pre-existing religious, ethnic and regional identities and prejudices.' Mehret, a female conscript, added, 'mistreatment at the hands of abusive commanders engendered powerful yearning to form a united front against common oppression and whatever differences existed between us were corroded (*lahlihom*)' (Interview, London, 24 August 2015).

DISSENTING OPINIONS

Although the overwhelming majority of the *agelglot* perceive the ENS as a 'great sociological mixer' (Etzioni 2001: 114), in terms of being an effective mechanism of national integration, unity and cohesion, there were three dissenting voices among the respondents. One respondent in particular warned against exaggerating the positive effect of the ENS on national unity and cohesion. The respondent argued that Eritrean society has historically been marked by a great sense of unity, solidarity and common purpose, as reflected in the absence of violent conflicts based on ethnic or religious identity (R #160). This respondent further observed, 'The Eritrean people have always been united and always lived peacefully and respectfully [of each other].' To emphasise this point of view, the respondent stated, 'the Eritrean people have never fought against each other on the grounds of ethnicity and religion. *This has always been the hallmark of Eritrean society. I reject the postulation that the national service has created previously unknown sense of harmony and unity. This has always been there*' (emphasis added). In this respondent's view, the harmony and cohesion that marks Eritrean society has nothing to do with the ENS.

Another respondent also argued that although, initially, the impact of the ENS on national unity, integration and cohesion was positive, this critical social resource was squandered when the programme, contrary to the limited duration stipulated in the proclamation on national service (Proc. No 82/1995), became indefinite and consequently degenerated into forced labour. This development represented a huge deviation from the initial aims of the programme and, as a consequence, the ENS could no longer foster national unity and cohesion (R #112). The respondent further stated, 'Initially, the trend was towards unifying the Eritrean society. However, when the whole programme failed, the objectives of unifying the society were defeated.' The significance of this insightful observation will be discussed later in connection to the issue of the flight of tens of thousands of conscripts from the ENS to seek asylum.

A third respondent (R #069) narrated that the failure of the government to demobilise those who complete the eighteen months as stipulated in the proclamation has rendered the programme ineffective in terms of promoting national unity and cohesion. The respondent observed, 'in the early years when conscripts were demobilised after serving the statutory obligation of eighteen months, the effect on social cohesion and national unity was clear and obvious.' The corollary of this argument is that because the ENS has become open-ended it has lost its potency in relation to being an agent for fostering national unity and cohesion, as well as social change and transformation. The respondent said, 'because the ENS has degenerated into modern form of slavery, tens of thousands are fleeing the country daily putting their lives at imminent risk of being taken hostage for ransom en route to Israel, dying in the deserts and/or drowning in the sea *en route* to Western Europe.' The respondent further observed, 'it was the process of living, working and enduring hardship together that engendered the glue and the values that interconnected the *agelglot*'.

The *agelglot* are now scattered all over the world (see Table 4.1, Chapter 4), such that it is difficult to see how the values they developed and internalised in the ENS can be of any benefit to Eritrean society in terms of promoting national unity and cohesion. There is evidence to suggest that although the deserters from the ENS currently residing in the West have spurned the identity-based opposition groups, they have not been able to create an effective and united political movement underpinned by the social capital they internalised in the national service. This may indicate, albeit inconclusively, that the core values they developed and internalised either remain dormant or are lost in exile. Recently, however, there has been a concerted action that may counter such a narrative. For example, on 26 June 2015 over 6,000 youths, the large majority of whom were draft evaders and deserters, assembled in Geneva in support of the publication of findings of the UN Commission of Inquiry on Human Rights in Eritrea. This was unprecedented and the future will show the extent to which the action will set a discernible pattern of resistance for change. There are a few political and civil society organisations, such as the Eritrean Solidarity Movement for National Salvation (ESMNS), which according to one of the activists, Isaac, has ninety-six chapters worldwide, and the Eritrean Youth Solidarity for Change (EYSC). All members of the two organisations are former conscripts.

The ENS, due to its never-ending nature, has become the single most important driver for forced migration (Kibreab 2009b, 2013). Consequently, the values and attitudes that would have been instrumental in promoting national unity and cohesion are lost to the country, which may reduce the potency of the ENS to function as an agent of unity and cohesion. It is important to note that although tens of thousands have fled the country those who have stayed put, either because they don't want to flee or because they are unable to do so, are likely to exist in greater numbers than those who 'voted with their feet', and therefore they may still be playing an important role in promoting national unity and cohesion. On the other hand, it is important to recognise that if those who are still serving in the ENS are demoralised by its endless duration and the reason they remain put in the service is not due to commitment, rather because of lack of an alternative, their contribution to the project of national unity may be either limited or even counterproductive.

It is also worth noting that among those who deserted from the ENS the glue that previously held them together has to some extent worn out. When the respondents were asked, 'Do you still keep in touch with any of the new friends you made in the ENS?' some said that they still maintain contacts with their friends from national service, but only with those who are in the same country as themselves. However, the majority said that they are no longer in touch with many of the friends they met in ENS service. This may suggest that the degeneration of the ENS into open-ended forced labour, in prompting tens of thousands to flee the country, has weakened the social capital produced in the ENS.

In conclusion, it is important to underscore the fact that although the Eritrean government's objective of using the ENS as an instrument of promoting national unity and cohesion is innovative and consistent with policies and practices of other governments world-wide, it is vital to recognise the contested nature of 'unity'. What Michael Walzer said of America is equally true of Eritrea. In his article, 'What does it mean to be "American"?' he argues that to define American citizenship invites controversy, because the American people are too diverse: 'America has no singular national destiny – and to be an "American" is, finally, to know that and to be more or less content with it' (1990: 614). In pluralist societies, such as Eritrea, unity based on diversity is more sustainable than that based on national homogeneity. The corollary is instead of aiming at homogenising the heterogeneous and multiple identities of the Eritrean polity, the outcome of the ENS would have been far greater had the focus been on encouraging the conscripts to embrace difference and be comfortable with diversity.

7

The Eritrean National Service and Forced Equality

Each citizen should be accustomed in good time...to considering the fortune of the state as his particular fortune. This perfect equality and this kind of civil fraternity, that makes...all citizens like a single family, makes all equally interested in the good and evil of their fatherland...Love of the fatherland is becoming a kind of amour-propre. Loving the fatherland, one loves oneself, and finally grows to love it more than oneself.

Briez cited in Hippler (2007: 78)

The government may do almost whatever it pleases, provided it appeals to the whole community at once; it is the unequal distribution of the weight, not the weight itself, that commonly occasions resistance.

de Tocqueville, *Democracy in America* (1945: 286)

The Eritrean National Service (ENS) is both compulsory and universal, with all citizens between the ages of eighteen and forty required to take part without exception, except for the veterans of the liberation struggle and those who are physically disabled and mentally infirm. The former are only exempted from the military training component of the service, and are still required to perform national service commensurate with their physical and mental capabilities. The aim of this chapter is therefore to examine the extent to which the national service is equally enforced, notwithstanding class, religion, sex, ethnicity, wealth, power, region and family connections. The chapter also examines the prevalence of corruption and the extent to which it is possible to buy oneself out from the service and/or to influence the decision regarding the place of assignment subsequent to the six-month military training at Sawa.

In light of the compulsory and universal nature of the ENS, every Eritrean citizen is supposed to be treated equally, regardless of class, gender, religion, region and ethnicity, based on the principle of forced equality. The principle of forced equality or equal sacrifice in bearing the burden of serving in the national service is in theory absolute. Although the ENS, as stipulated in Proclamation No 82/1995, is marked by the principle of absolute equality, there are a few exceptions and exemptions, as well as deferments. For example, Eritrean citizens who performed national service before the promulgation of Proc. No. 82/1995 and all the fighters and armed peasants who 'spent all their time in the liberation struggle' are exempted from performing national service. Citizens who are declared unfit for military service by the board, comprising the ministry of regional administration under the directives given by the ministry of defence, 'will undertake eighteen months of national service in any public or government organ according to their capacity and profession.' Contrary to widespread misunderstandings, including among immigration authorities in Western countries, those who are unable to perform military service either due to physical disability or mental infirmity are not exempted or excepted from national service. They are only not required to take six months military training as part of the national service. Not only are they required to perform eighteen months non-military national service, but 'they have the compulsory duty of serving according to their capacity until the expiry of fifty years of age under mobilisation or emergency situation directives given by the government.'

It is worth noting that the exemption of those who are declared unfit on health grounds is not permanent. It is temporary in the sense that although they may be declared unfit upon examination by the board for active national service due to diminished health, they 'may be called for national service if before the exemption period expires their health is improved'. Students in regular daily courses may be deferred from active national service for a limited period, which deferment is only valid as long as the student concerned is not dismissed from school either due to poor academic performance or any other reason.[1] No student can be awarded a certificate, diploma or degree until they have completed active national service. There are no other exemptions, exceptions or deferments. Even conscientious objectors, such as the Jehovah's Witnesses, are forcibly recruited against the canons of their faith, and non-compliance leads to indefinite incarceration (AI 2004).

Before the border war broke out between Eritrea and Ethiopia in May 1998 the Eritrean government adhered to the eighteen months duration stipulated in the proclamation on national service and, accordingly, the first four cohorts were demobilised after serving the required period. However, when the border war broke out, not only did the Eritrean government recall those who were demobilised from the national service, but it also embarked on large-scale mobilisation to defend the country. None of those who were recalled at the onset of the border war, were mobilised during the border war or joined the ENS after May 1998 have been demobilised, on the grounds of what the Eritrean government calls a 'no-peace-no-war' situation prevailing in the country.

In May 2002 the government also introduced the Warsai-Yikealo Development Campaign (WYDC) that required all the *agelglot* (conscripts) to participate in defence of the country and in national (re)construction programmes in different capacities within the framework of the ENS under the auspices of the Ministry of Defence. Since the border war and the introduction of the WYDC, the ENS has degenerated into open-ended forced labour or a modern form of slavery (Human Rights Watch 2009, 2013; Kibreab 2009a, 2009b, 2013; Tronvoll and Mekonnen 2014; UN Rapporteur on Human Rights 2014). The above-presented data clearly

[1]   Proc. 82/1995 articles 12 (1), 12 (2); 13; 13 (2); 14 (1); 14 (2); 14 (3).

demonstrate that the principle of forced equality, in terms of bearing the burden of performing the open-ended national service with one exception, the case of ex-combatants, is universal and absolute.

As we saw in Chapter 2, Eritrea is not the first country in the world to introduce such a wide-ranging, compulsory and universal national service based on the notion of forced equality. In the twentieth century, France, Britain and the USA made use of compulsory military service, mainly to build their defence and fighting capabilities. In France universal conscription was adopted to sustain the revolution of 1789. The revolutionary government embarked on a large-scale mobilisation of conscripts in which the concept of *egalité* was to mean equality in relation to the obligation to serve in the army: 'every able-bodied man [was] liable' (Flynn 2002; Hippler 2007). The ideology of the revolution emphasised, on the one hand, the rights of man and, on the other, the threats foreign enemies posed. As a consequence the leaders defined military service as *sine qua non* for full citizenship (Flynn 2002: 15). In the USA (Dawson 1982), conscription was introduced during the civil war, and in Britain during WWI (see Barnett 1979; Board 2006).

There were many philosophers and political thinkers who advocated for the compulsory and universal conscription of youth in national service (see Chapters 2 and 5). At the heart of contemporary philosophers' support for compulsory and universal national/military service lies the principle of 'equality in bearing the burden', which is said to have a transformative and unifying effect, *inter alia*, through production of cohesive societies and citizens committed to public causes or the common good. Montesquieu, for example, states that the establishment of a collective desire requires a strict application of a uniform rule, which applies to everybody equally. He observes:

> Love of the republic in a democracy is love of democracy; love of democracy is love of equality. [...] As each one there should have the same happiness and the same advantages, each should taste the same pleasures and form the same expectations; this is something that can be anticipated only from the common frugality. Love of equality in a democracy limits ambition to the single desire, the single happiness, of rendering greater services to one's homeland... (1989 [1748]: 43)

Margaret Mead also states:

> [a] nationwide draft helps to underline a sense of national commitment and the urgency of total national involvement in the maintenance of an orderly world. A draft potentially touches every household in the nation, no matter how small the number who are actually drafted, and where it is conducted on any sort of lottery basis, it selects men of all types of temperament and character, and many kinds of social economic background and training. (1967: 99)

Equality in bearing the burden of serving is the central thrust of her support of national service. Michael Walzer, one of the eminent exponents of national service, also stated, 'all dirty, disagreeable, dangerous, menial and humiliating work in any society should be shared equally by every member of that society without any regard to distinction of sex, class, ethnicity, religion and race' (1983: 175). Walzer justifies national service on the grounds of equality in the sense that such an activity may break the link between dirty work and disrespect. Eric Gorham (1992: 9) states that national service requires an ethic of egalitarianism and participation.

In pluralist societies such as Eritrea, where people adhere to different religions, ethnicities, classes and political allegiances, and where power is perceived to be concentrated in the hands of the Tigrinya-speaking group from which the autocratic president hails, public perception regarding the equitable distribution of the burden, or the sacrifice citizens are required to make through participation in the indefinite and open-ended national service, is of profound importance. If the burden of bearing the cost of performing national service were to fall heavily upon the numerically inferior and politically and socially marginalised groups, they may rightly perceive the ENS to be an instrument of discrimination, domination and oppression.

In light of the absence of freedom of press, expression and speech that permeates the Eritrean political landscape, and in view of the fact that the government publishes no information about the ENS, there are no readily available data to enable analysts to evaluate the extent to which the principle of forced equality is enforced equitably without any discrimination or favouritism. The question of whether every Eritrean is equally likely to bear the burden is critical, not only for the sustainability of the ENS/WYDC, but also for its legitimacy. In the absence of reliable data, however, it is difficult to determine the fairness of the mechanism of enforcement and its impact on the different classes, religions, regions and ethnicities. In terms of the dearth of freedom of press, a journalism group based in New York, for example, found that Eritrea was the most severe violator of press freedom in the world. The group stated, 'Eritrea leads the world in imposing censorship on the media, followed closely by North Korea, Syria and Iran...' (Journalism Group 2012). Reporters without Borders, in their World Press Freedom Index (2014), which '...is a reference tool that is based on seven criteria: the level of abuses, the extent of pluralism, media independence, the environment and self-censorship, the legislative framework, transparency and infrastructure' describe Eritrea, together with Turkmenistan and North Korea, as 'the biggest information black holes' (Reporters without Borders 2014). All privately owned newspapers have been banned since September 2001 and most of the journalists have been held in incommunicado detention since then. All print and non-print media, such as newspapers, magazines, radio and television are monopolised by the state, such that there is no independent reporting in the country either by domestic or foreign journalists. In view of these severe restrictions and lack of freedom and liberty, it is difficult to establish the extent to which the burden of the indefinite ENS/WYDC lays equally on all citizens regardless of ethnicity, faith, class, gender and occupation.

One of the series of questions the Country of Origin Information Service of the United Kingdom Border Agency (UKBA) asked the officials at the British Embassy in Asmara, Eritrea about national service and exit from Eritrea in March 2015 was:

> Is it possible for wealthy individuals to bribe military officials to avoid undergoing military or national service? If so, have there been actual cases of this happening?

> Can individuals close to the political ruling class avoid military or national service? If so, have there been actual cases of this happening?

In response, the officials at the British Embassy in Asmara replied:

> Wealthy conscripts and individuals who are close to the political ruling class may be able to influence the decision as to where they will be located (e.g. Asmara, living at home but working for military/ministry) *but cannot avoid military/national service altogether*. Individuals who can afford it, and do not want their children to undergo military/national service, may try to send their children overseas to study. *But it is notable that even respected and senior government officials send their children to military/national service assignments*. (UK Home Office 2010, emphasis added)

To their credit, the British Embassy officials in Asmara rightly premised their answers to the series of questions they were asked by the Country of Origin Information Service of the United Kingdom Border Agency (UKBA) with an important caveat stating:

> Embassy officials wish to make it clear that it is virtually impossible to be categorically certain about military/national service practice and exit procedures in Eritrea. *The official rules/regulations are mostly obscure, liable to subjective interpretation, and can be changed without notice, consultation or public information campaigns*. The information contained in this note, provided by local sources and contacts in Eritrea, is what embassy officials believe to be true. (Emphasis added)

In light of the absence of freedom of press and expression, the quality of information provided by local sources is likely to be compromised by fear, rumour or even lack of access to accurate information. However, what is clear from this and from the data gathered from a variety of sources, including from the respondents and key informants interviewed for this study, is that no transparently enforced rules govern the administration of the ENS. Nor are there effective mechanisms of accountability and responsibility. Everything can be changed at the whim of the autocratic leader and the military commanders. Notwithstanding the widespread arbitrariness that permeates the ENS, the obligation to perform the service equally applies to all citizens at least theoretically, with the exception of those who are excepted by Proc. No 82/1995. As indicated in the response from the officials of the British Embassy in Asmara, wealthy families may be able to influence decisions concerning the location of assignment after the six months military training at Sawa, but it may not be possible to bribe their way out of it altogether. However, as will be seen later, the children of the 'haves' resort to different means to avoid or minimise hardship in the ENS, but not necessarily to escape from it.

RESPONDENTS' PERCEPTIONS AS TO WHETHER THE ENS ENSURED EQUALITY AMONG CONSCRIPTS

The respondents and key informants were asked the following question: 'One of the direct and indirect aims of the national service is to ensure equality by conscripting all eligible nationals irrespective of class, sex, religion, ethnicity and region so that they share the duties and burden of the ENS on equal basis. Do you think that the national service has been achieving this goal? If you don't think so, please state your reasons.'

As stated earlier, the respondents do not speak with a single voice. R #017, for example, stated, 'All Eritreans without any regard to their ethnicity or religion participate in the national service.' Some respondents think that the ENS is enforced on the basis of equality but they argue that it is important to recognise the prevalence of self-interest, which may distort the principle of equality and impartiality. R #021 stated, 'Yes, all sexes, ethnic and religious groups take part in the national service and in that sense the national service can be said is an equaliser but nevertheless, it cannot be denied that there are pursuits of self-interest by some.' The people who use the ENS in pursuit of self-interest are those who are in positions of power and influence. If power and influence are factors that determine who serves and who doesn't, and in what capacity, the ENS/WYDC, instead of becoming a leveller, may become an instrument of inequality and distinction. Some respondents, however, think that the ENS is enforced on the basis of equality and impartiality. R #051, for example, observed, 'The national service applies to all regardless of religion, race, ethnicity, class and gender on the basis of equality.' This view was shared by R #053, who stated unequivocally that 'There was no distinction. All Muslims and Christians, women and men were in the national service. It is a leveller.' R #065 expressed a similar view: 'The ENS affects all Eritreans equally because the Eritrean government makes sure that every citizen regardless of religion, ethnicity, gender or class participates.' This opinion was also expressed by R #152, who observed, 'Yes, the proof of this is that the youth hailing from all the Eritrean national groups were with me in the ENS.'

Notwithstanding these observations, many respondents argued that the ENS, and later the WYDC, affect the different classes, ethnic and religious groups differently and that, inadvertently, the government has been presiding over the inequitable distribution of bearing the burden. Given the alleged imbalance of power pervading the political landscape in the country, one would be forgiven for thinking that it is the politically marginalised and underrepresented ethnic groups in the power structure of the country who bear a greater burden than those which allegedly dominate the spheres of political power, policy-making and implementation. The findings of the survey, based on the experiences and perceptions of the deserters from the national service, however, show that, ironically and contrary to expectation, it is the allegedly dominant Christians and Tigrinya-speaking nationals who bear the greater burden of serving in the ENS than the rest of the ethnic and religious groups that are allegedly underrepresented in the exercise of political power.

Regarding this apparent anomaly, Zemheret said that in the context of the government's limited administrative and implementation capacity, which is made worse by the underdeveloped infrastructure, the scale of the programme is too complex and hence permeated with fundamental problems from the outset. One of the consequences of this, according to key informants, has been that some of the ethnic and religious groups who inhabit the less accessible and hard to reach areas have been able to avoid bearing the burden on different grounds. Firstly, the areas they inhabit are often remote and the infrastructure is either absent or extremely underdeveloped, such that the transaction cost involved in searching, reaching and rounding up those who deliberately refuse to comply with the requirements stipulated in Proclamation 82/1995 is too high. Hence, the government has been unable to enforce its own law equitably throughout the country. Instead, its mobilisation approach has been far more aggressive and heavy-handed in the easily reachable and accessible areas of the country, where the political and transaction costs are less than in the hard to reach areas and populations.

The Tigrinya-speaking Christian section of the population predominantly inhabits most of the easy to reach areas. For example, when asked whether all the ethnic groups are equally affected by the ENS, R #119 said, 'No. Well, the Tigrinya ethnic group is over-conscripted largely...'. A similar view was expressed by R #009, who stated, '...you cannot achieve such a goal by forcing people from all national groups. For example, let me give you a proof [...] one of the ethnic groups – the Rashaida – do not participate and the government failed to force a single individual from the Rashaida. Therefore this is enough evidence of the failure.' A similar view was expressed by R #165, who stated, 'Generally, all citizens participate, but not on equal footing. For example, the Tigrinya ethnic group are over-conscripted and the Afar are under-conscripted.' R #166 thinks that the burden of bearing the cost of the ENS is so inequitably distributed among the disparate ethnic groups in the country that 'it should be eased on the Tigrinya' speaking citizens. Abeba, a female key informant, observed, 'It has to be admitted that the Eritrean government seems to take for granted the Tigrinya-speaking citizens. That is why they bear the unbearable burden of shouldering the duty at the expense of their own and their families' wellbeing.'

EQUALITY, RELIGION AND WOMEN'S PARTICIPATION IN THE ENS

The degree of inequality is far worse in the case of women. There is a common understanding among the respondents that the burden weighs much more heavily on Christian women than on their Muslim compatriots. Had there been breakdown of the annual intakes at the Warsai-Yikealo School at Sawa in year 12 based on gender, ethnicity and religion of the students, it would have been possible to countercheck the information gathered from the respondents and key informants. Although the authorities publish statistics based on gender distribution, it is against their policy to distinguish students at Sawa or elsewhere on the basis of their religion and ethnicity. For example, in the 2012/2013 academic years, there were 17,417 12th grade students at the Sawa military camp of which 7,422 were female (Ministry of Education 2013). Women are underrepresented in secondary schools in the country (see Dawit Teclemariam Bahta 2016, Table 1). During the 29th round national service members' graduation, the commander of the Sawa Military Camp, Colonel

Debesai Gide said that there were 14,000 graduates, of whom 48 per cent were female (2016).

The data gathered from the respondents and key informants indicate that the burden of bearing the cost of performing national service is not shared equally among female conscripts. R #122, for example, stated, 'the legislation on the ENS is supposed to affect all citizens equally, but in practice, the proportion of women from the Hedareb, Afar, Rashaida and Saho is very low...' R #020 reiterated this view, 'Women from certain ethnic groups are not in the national service.' This implicit reference is to Muslim women in general, and to the minority ethnic groups, which are predominantly Muslims. A similar view was expressed by R #066, who stated, 'Generally, yes. However, when I look at the situation in depth, I wouldn't dare to claim that all ethnic groups and classes are equally affected.' Andom noted, 'the government is reluctant to force some sections of the Eritrean society, especially the conservative and traditional groups, such as the Afar, the Rashaida and the Hedareb for fear of provoking revolt and open resistance.'

The majority of the respondents do not think that the principle of equality in terms of bearing the burden of the ENS is consistently applied. Abraham, who has a post-graduate degree, insightfully observed:

> The authorities' hands are tied by political expediency in the sense that they turn a blind eye to the failure of female Muslims to participate in the ENS. They fear mobilisation of Muslim women would provoke resistance and in the worst-case scenario an uprising as was the case in the area among the Afar.

Zere also noted, 'the government is reluctant to force some sections of the Eritrean society, especially the conservative and traditional groups, such as the Afar, the Rashaida and the Hedareb for fear of provoking revolt and open resistance.' An additional explanation as to why there are fewer female Muslim women in the ENS is also because of the widespread practice among Muslims of 'early arranged underage marriages'.[2]

In Eritrea, where it is believed that Muslims and Christians each represent 50 per cent of the population and where the social landscape is marked by inter-faith harmony, people are exceedingly cautious when expressing opinions, and particularly negative ones about each other's religions or faith-based practices. This also became clear in the interviews. Although it was obvious that the respondents were referring to Muslim women, very few openly used the word 'Muslim'. Instead, the common terminologies they use are 'women from other religions' or 'from other ethnic groups' rather than directly referring to them as 'Muslims', 'Christians', and so on. R #067, for example, stated, 'The ENS is not based on equal participation. There are less women participating from one of the religions in the country. Women from one of the religions are dominant.' Such a way of speaking, even among the youth in the ENS, is deemed politically correct. Eritreans are highly sensitive when expressing views regarding the cultures and faiths of their compatriots.

---

[2]   Thanks are due to Abdul Saleh Mohammad, one of the reviewers of the manuscript, for pointing this out to me.

In the words of R #068, 'All including the Rashaida participate in ENS, but it cannot be said that the level of participation is the same among all the religions and ethnicities.' Sometimes, political correctness may stand in the way of telling the truth about others, but in Eritrean society the subjects of religion and ethnicity are regarded with utmost sensitivity and consideration. R #068, for example, was one of the few who reported that the Rashaida participate in the ENS. This observation is not backed by other sources, but when looked at in the context of the general impression Eritreans try to give about the high degree of unity that characterise their society and commitment to the national project, singling out the Rashaida ethnic group as being draft dodgers is considered politically incorrect and damaging to the notion of national unity and commitment to the common project of nation-building.

When I asked Zenab, a Muslim woman, why many of the respondents might be reluctant to straightforwardly identify the religious and ethnic categories that fail to participate in the ENS/WYDC under different pretexts, she stated, 'That information serves no purpose. It only engenders resentment and hence bad for national unity and social cohesion.' I asked her, 'Does this mean then people don't mind if a certain religious or ethnic group refuses to participate in the ENS and the burden is borne by the other ethnic and religious groups?' She said:

> [t]he notion of freeriding or living at the expense of others is considered a loathsome behaviour in Eritrea. Of course people resent those who do not share the common burden, but they don't loudly talk about it. This may be is because the number of those groups who do not participate in the ENS is insignificant in comparison to those who do so and most people think overstating the problem may have unforeseen divisive consequences.

In spite of the reluctance of many respondents to reveal the religious identity of those who do not participate in the ENS, there are some who openly state that Christian women are over-represented in the ENS and, thereby, bear a greater burden. R #069, for example, states, 'The government turns a blind eye to those who object on the basis of religion – Islam.' R #077 reiterated this view by stating, 'All citizens participate without any distinction of religion and sex, but this does not apply to women from the Saho, Nara and Afar ethnic groups.' These are all Muslim communities. R #102 was frank about the fact that the Rashaida ethnic group do not participate in the ENS, simply stating, the 'Rashaida are not in national service.' To the question of whether all religious and ethnic groups participate in the ENS equally, R #119 unequivocally stated, 'No. Well, the Tigrinya ethnic group was [is] over-burdened …'

THE ENS, WEALTH, CLASS, POWER AND CORRUPTION

In socially and economically differentiated societies, especially where corruption is rife, the assumption that every citizen will be treated equally regardless of class, gender, religion, sex and ethnicity, based on the principle of forced equality or equal sacrifice in bearing the burden of national obligation, such as the performance of national service, is spurious. In the immediate post-independence period, Eritrea had a reputation for being free of corruption. For example, in an extensive and well-documented report on Eritrea, the World Bank (2002) stated that financial corruption was almost absent in the country. Under a sub-heading 'Corruption and Crime,' the World Bank stated:

> Not surprisingly, for anyone familiar with Eritrea, corruption and crime/theft/disorder are considered virtually non-existent. The majority of respondents (84 per cent) in this ranking exercise answered that corruption is not a problem. This was corroborated by other questions throughout the survey. One asked specifically about the 'total value of gifts or bribes required' during inspection visits by government officials from the Health Ministry, Fire Inspector, or Labour and Social Security Ministry. The universal answer was zero. When asked in general what percentage of revenue is used for informal payments to 'get things done,' the answers averaged 0.2 per cent. By comparison, in a global private sector survey conducted in 1997 by the World Bank, results for sub-Saharan Africa showed that on average 50 per cent of entrepreneurs were frequently asked for these types of payments. The difficulty in assessing the presence of corruption lies in the fact that a more complete definition of corruption includes more than simply the payment of bribes. Preferential treatment given through discretionary power in the awarding of contracts or allocation of land or foreign exchange is also considered corruption and can have quite distortionary effects on the growth of the private sector. *There are hearsay, but frequently heard, complaints that party-owned firms, being closely linked to the government, have occasionally used their 'pull' to get things done.* (World Bank 2002, emphasis added)

Until 2003 Eritrea was a relatively corruption-free country and this is confirmed by Transparency International's statistics (2015, see Table 7.1). However, there is evidence to show that this situation of absence of corruption changed for the worse from 2004 onwards, according to the Transparency International Corruption Perception Index. When a dramatic change was reported in the Transparency International Corruption Perception Index in 2004 someone who previously worked in Eritrea was surprised and asked Transparency International to explain. The person concerned stated:

> Corruption in Eritrea: According to Transparency International's Corruption Perception Index (CPI), Eritrea is a rather corrupt country. I find this puzzling. When I was stationed there in 1997-98 petty corruption (and petty crime) was not accepted in society and bribing was not practiced in public administration. I would like to know what has changed. I know, of course, that the situation for civil servants and citizens has changed dramatically since then but I still find it difficult to imagine that people have changed that much. (Transparency International 2015)

In a five-page carefully authored response, Dr Victoria Jennet, Transparency International Secretariat, in Part 3 of the Report under the sub-heading 'Eritrea in the TI (Transparency International Corruption Perception Index' stated:

> Eritrea has long maintained a reputation for a relatively low level of corruption in comparison to its neighbours. However, the changing situation since 1998 has seemed to affect the expert perception of corruption in Eritrea in the CPI (as well as other indicators). *Eritrea entered TI's CPI for the first time in 2004 when*

Table 7.1 Prevalence of corruption in Eritrea, 2004–2015

Year	Score	Rank out of
2004	2.6	102 out of 145 countries
2005	2.6	107 out of 158 countries
2006	2.8	111 out of 179 countries
2007	2.8	111 out of 179 countries
2008	2.6	126 out of 180 countries
2009	2.6	126 out of 180 countries
2010	2.6	123 out of 178 countries
2011	2.5	134 out of 182 countries
2012	25.0	150 out of 175 countries
2013	20.0	160 out of 175 countries
2014	18.0	166 out of 174 countries
2015	18.0	154 out of 168 countries

Source: https://www.transparency.org/research/cpi/cpi_1998/0/ (last accessed January 2016)

it scored 2.6 from a best score of 10. It maintained this score the following year, then marginally improved in 2006 with a score of 2.9 (by way of comparison Eritrea's neighbour, Ethiopia, scored 2.4 in this year's CPI). *This improvement is not considered to be significant. Indeed scores below three indicate that corruption is perceived as rampant. Eritrea is ranked at number 93, with the same score as Argentina, Armenia, Bosnia and Herzegovina, Syria and Tanzania.* (U4 Expert Answer, emphasis added)

The data in Table 7.1 clearly shows that corruption has seen a rapid progression in post-independence Eritrea. In 2004 Eritrea was ranked 102 out of 145 countries in the world. In 2012 and 2013 Eritrea was one of the most corrupt countries in the world, according to data from Transparency International. Its rank in 2012 was 150 out of 175 countries and the corresponding figure for 2013 was 160 out of 175 countries. These data, based on the perceptions of respondents, show the progressive acceleration of corruption. In 2013, only fifteen countries were perceived to be more corrupt than Eritrea. Literature on corruption in the country has been burgeoning in recent years. The available evidence shows that, over time, the country's score and rank have deteriorated dramatically.

Yemane Desta conducted a survey on the extent, causes and remedies of corruption in Eritrea. The questionnaire was given to sixty-two public officials from thirteen ministries of the government. The study concludes,

'The survey responses indicate that while on the whole Eritrean officials perceive that there are relatively low levels of corruption in the country they believe *the top five leading causes of corruption are: the low salary of public officials, lack of accountable/transparent political process, lack of meritocratic personnel policy, lack of effective corruption reporting system and the self-serving attitudes of public officials'* (Desta 2006) (emphasis added). This finding should be read with the proviso that the study was conducted in 2006, at a time when the problem of corruption was not yet widespread, and that the interviewees were public officials in a country where there is dearth of freedom of expression and a lack of protection against expressing critical views about the government or its policies and practices, including the prevailing reality on the ground. The fact that they identified the causes of the so-called 'low level of corruption' in spite of such constraints is edifying.

Whether or not the burden of serving in the ENS comes to bear equally on all citizens, regardless of their own or their families' wealth, class and power is largely dependent on the extent to which the Eritrean Defence Forces (EDF) are free of corruption. If corruption is rife among the EDF, as discussed above, it is inevitable that the principle of forced equality or equal sacrifice in bearing the burden would be illusory. Those who have relatives in positions of power within or outside the EDF may, under different pretexts, avoid fully or partially bearing the burden of becoming part of the ENS/WYDC. Those who have wealthy parents or relatives may be in a position to bribe army officers and commanders to obtain frequent travel permits (*menkasaqesi*) for home leave, to extend the duration of home leave permissions indefinitely, or to gain bogus 'assignments' or 'positions' in Asmara where they are indirectly able to pursue income-generating economic activities under the pretence that they are participating in the ENS. The International Crisis Group (ICG), for example, states:

> Worse still, corruption and misuse of resources is rife in the EDF [Eritrean Defence Forces]. Isaias has reportedly had to detain and reprimand senior officers for allowing this, although he is reluctant to do so publicly. It is widely suspected that some senior officers themselves are involved in illicit activities. Would-be deserters can pay agents – some of whom are officers – to facilitate their escape across the border; fees vary, but up to $10,000 can ensure that at least part of the trip is in a land cruiser, while smaller sums may cause an officer to turn his back at the decisive moment. (ICG 2010: 10)

The 2011 Index of Economic Freedom states that '[c]orruption is perceived as pervasive' in Eritrea. In its 2014 Index of Economic Freedom, The Heritage Foundation states, '[c]orruption is a major problem. The President and his small circle of senior advisers and military commanders exercise almost complete political control' (Eritrea Index 2014). Recently I asked a friend and former classmate, who still lives in Asmara and is considered to be close to the government, about the extent to which it is possible either to buy oneself out of national service or to avoid conscription fully or partially due to being a relative of wealthy or high-ranking military officers. He told me, 'Sometimes it happens. These days if one has money, the sky is the limit as to what one would be able to do'

(Negassi, Interview, London, 13 May 2014). He further stated, 'Corruption is rife among the middle and high-ranking officers in the armed forces and these being the next most powerful men in the country, after the president, anything is possible.' However, he qualified his answer by stating, 'In spite of the widespread corruption, it is very unlikely that one would be able to buy him/herself out from national service fully, but if one is loaded with money, it is possible to influence the decision concerning assignment subsequent to the six months military training at Sawa.' Some key informants also reported that there were conscripts who disappeared a few weeks or months after induction.

The ICG states that '[t]he army has for some time been the key stabilising force in Eritrea, indeed the focal point of the EPLF's social engineering project, but it is becoming less stable, riddled with corruption and increasingly weak in terms of trained men, adequate equipment and morale' (ICG 2010: 270. The Bertelsmann Stiftung's Transformation Index (BTI) (2014) states:

> [d]uring the period under review, the [Eritrean] leadership seems to have de facto abandoned the official policy of fighting corruption. Corruption in the civil administration and especially in the military increased sharply. High-ranking officers engaged in illegal activities such as smuggling goods, and increasingly in human trafficking. They facilitated the flight of Eritreans willing to leave the country, only to hand them over to criminal gangs of human traffickers in Sudan, who in turn sold them to Bedouins on the Egyptian Sinai Peninsula who tortured them to extract ransom from relatives abroad.

The author interviewed Andom, a graduate from the defunct University of Asmara, in June 2015 in Geneva. After receiving military training at Sawa he was assigned to work in the Ministry of Education within the framework of the ENS. He fled after eleven years. I asked him about the extent of corruption in the EDF and whether those who have wealthy families can avoid conscription. He said, 'It is not possible to avoid national service completely, but there are different ways by which those who come from wealthy and powerful family backgrounds can be in the national service and elsewhere simultaneously.' When asked to explain, he said, 'They go to Sawa as everyone else. Some disappear soon after. Others complete the six months military training and then are assigned to the cities, mainly Asmara where their families live. Others may be assigned elsewhere, but pay bribes to obtain *menqasaqesi* (travel permits) and extend the duration against payment of bribes almost indefinitely.' He added, 'There are even some who are formally in the ENS, but engage in different forms of income-generating activities' (see Chapter 4).

The corollary of the data presented in the first part of the chapter, on corruption in Eritrea in general, and in the army in particular, is that it is illusory to assume that the duty of participating in the ENS would be governed by the principle of forced equality or equal sacrifice in bearing the burden regardless of class, political clout, wealth or family connections. We will examine what the respondents who experienced directly the pitfalls of corruption in the ENS say about the extent to which participation in the ostensibly universal and compulsory ENS is affected by sleaze, favouritism and partiality. The respondents interviewed in this study, for example, were asked whether or not they agree, strongly agree, disagree or strongly disagree with the following generalisation 'the ENS has become so corrupt that it delivers favours rather than equal service and obligation to all'. Among the respondents 47 per cent and 25 per cent respectively strongly agreed or agreed with the generalisation. Only 7 per cent disagreed and 2 per cent did not answer the question. In view of the fact that 72 per cent think that the ENS is corrupt and delivers favours rather than equal service and obligation to all, as well as being damning this suggests that the principle of equality is either non-existent or illusory.

R #010, for example, stated, 'Some commanders were partial and even sold papers for leave and those without money could not go on leave. As a result, the best soldiers [conscripts] left the country. Unequal treatment of different groups caused disunity and disharmony.' Given the hardship permeating life in the ENS the single most important respite from the grind and privation intrinsic to the service is access to *menqasaqesi* (permission to go on home leave). This document is highly prized as it legitimises absence from one's assignment and provides protection against being rounded up in the periodic *giffas*. It is one of the key instruments military commanders use in pursuit of personal gain, including sexual favours from female conscripts. R #024 stated that participation in the ENS is a function of connections with those who exercise political power or hold a position in the military. Abraham, for example, said, 'The commanders' integrity is so low that their favours can be purchased in the corruption market.' When asked whether the principle of equality governed participation in the ENS R #024 stated, 'Yes, in the beginning there was equality, but later the level of participation of children [sons and daughters] of those in power or people connected to them is nominal. They go to Sawa and then disappear after a while.' A similar view was reiterated by Kidane, a key informant, who stated, 'In the beginning, every national except the Rashaida ethnic group and Muslim women from some ethnic groups, such as the Afar, rural Beni Amer, Saho and Hedareb participated in the ENS, but this changed dramatically after the service degenerated into open-ended slavery-like compulsion in the aftermath of the 1998–2000 Eritrea-Ethiopia border war and after the government introduced the WYDC in May 2002.' When asked to explain what happened, the informant said, 'When the endless service wrecked education opportunities and future careers of the *agelglot* (conscripts), although it was not possible to buy oneself out of the service, those with financial means and links with people in power managed to get extended leave of absence through different means, including through assignment in Asmara where they live comfortably at home.' Those who have money and connections can also easily secure access to *menqasaqesi* and indefinite renewal (see Chapter 4).

Although R #049 said that all citizens are required to serve in the national service and didn't believe that there is distinction based on class, ethnicity or gender, they nevertheless admitted that, '...in a few occasions, wealth and influence can exonerate a person from participating in national service.' R #060 stated, 'Undoubtedly, there is a distinction between the rest and the children [sons and daughters] of people in power and of rich families, but overall, the ENS applies to all on the basis of relative equality.' The corollary is that among those who are without wealth and family members in positions of power, the ENS is enforced impartially and equitably, but not among the offspring of the 'haves' and the powerful. R #071 observed, 'There are distinctions based on religion, class and sex.' A number of respondents alluded to bribery being used as a means of avoiding conscription. This is reiterated by R #073, who stated, 'Favouritism and bribe[ry] are widely used to exclude some people.' In response to the question of whether the ENS was enforced with impartiality and equality R #084 stated, 'during the first stages probably, but later the wealthy people never stayed in the military for ever.' The gist of these different voices may be summarised as follows: all receive call up papers and all go to Sawa, but those who have wealthy and powerful relatives disappear gradually under different pretexts by obtaining *menqasaqesi* (travel permits) that can be extended indefinitely at a very high cost. When Aida was asked to explain the cost, she said, 'The holder has to renew the *menqasaqesi* before it expires through bribery.'

FROM BADGE OF HONOUR TO UNBEARABLE BURDEN

In light of many respondents' assertions that in the beginning the principle of forced equality in bearing the burden was almost absolute, the erosion of the principle of equality seems to be inextricably linked, on the one hand, to the degeneration of the ENS into open-ended forced labour, following the 1998–2000 border war (HRW 2009; Kibreab 2009b, 2013) and, on the other, to the generalised state of decay permeating the political and economic landscape. The consequence has been disenchantment and hopelessness among many who were previously enthusiastic about the ENS and the government. There are a number of reasons for this. Firstly, when the initiative of military training was launched in the first half of the 1990s the country was still in state of euphoria. There was unanimity amongst most Eritreans, except those who objected on the grounds of alleged religious conviction and political opposition to the government, that the ENS was an indispensable instrument of social cohesion, nation-building and post-conflict (re)construction in their multi-faith and multi-ethnic society. Participation in the ENS was therefore perceived as a badge of honour and national pride both among those who were within the age of conscription (eighteen to forty) and their relatives. Draft evasion and desertion were then spurned as an unpatriotic taboo. This study shows that during the first three or four rounds, the youths couldn't wait to join the ENS. Many even went as far as faking their ages, pretending to be eighteen or older in order to join the 'adventure' in Sawa. As R #084 stated, although it is necessary to adapt to hardship in the military, 'service for ever and the high level of intensity [pervading the ENS] inevitably takes away your [one's] national pride.'

Secondly, before the border war (1998–2000), the government adhered to the eighteen months duration stipulated in the Proclamation on the ENS, such that all were to be demobilised after eighteen months. All of this changed in the aftermath of the border war and with the introduction of the WYDC in May 2002, which rendered the ENS indefinite. It is important to note, however, that, although the border war is used as a pretext to render the ENS indefinite and open-ended, there has not been war between the two countries since May 2000. Even if there were an imminent threat of war, keeping the conscripts in arms without remuneration and against their will indefinitely has eroded rather than built Eritrea's fighting and defence capability (see Chapters 3 and 4). The threat of war is used as a pretext to mobilise an unpaid labour force and to avoid the potential security risk of mass youth unemployment.

The effect of the open-ended ENS on conscripts' incentive to participate, as reflected in draft evasion and mass desertion, has been dramatic. Before the border war the prospect of continuing one's education and pursuing different avenues of careers after serving the required eighteen months in the ENS was relatively high. This was because participation in the ENS was *sine qua non* for the exercise of citizenship rights, such as the right to education, to work, to engage in any form of income-generating activities such as self-employment, access to a business licence, land ownership, access to exit visas. Draft dodging or desertion was then rare, and whenever it did occur was stigmatised.

The powerful sense of optimism that permeated the social and political landscape began to fade after the ENS became open-ended, and this was exacerbated by the government's enmity of the private sector (see Kibreab 2009a) where most of the conscripts, subsequent to their demobilisation, hoped to derive their livelihoods from being employed or self-employed. Over time the Eritrean government's animosity towards the private sector assumed enormous proportions (see Kibreab 2009a) and this removed one of the main incentives for participating in the ENS. Many also took part in national service as a means of accessing higher education at the now defunct University of Asmara. The university was closed in 2006, removing one of the major considerations that incentivised some of the youth to join the ENS as an entrance ticket to higher education and careers.

Some respondents stated that the duty of serving in the ENS is not performed on the basis of equality due to highhanded attitudes and the actions or inactions of military commanders. R #143, for example, stated, 'Generally, all Eritreans participate in the ENS, but there are some weaknesses due to the irresponsible actions of some commanders.' According to Kidane, the problem of corruption and abuse of power evolved over time when the ENS became a never-ending burden. 'When the *agelglot* were required to serve for ever, they became like slaves and the relatives with the means left no stone unturned to rescue them. Bribing military commanders became widespread.' Habtom, Zere and Ahmed also said independent of each other that after the ENS became open-ended, the incentive to buy favours by bribing commanders became irresistible.

8

The Overarching Impact of the Eritrean National Service on the Social Fabric of Eritrean Society

Given its magnitude and indefinite duration, the ENS has affected, directly or indirectly, every aspect of Eritrean society's economic, social, cultural and political life. Nevertheless, in any socially and economically differentiated society, where power is concentrated on an unelected personal ruler and a few of his cronies, none of whom is accountable to citizens, and where actual and perceived levels of corruption are rife (Chapter 7), the impact of an open-ended national service on various sectors of society is likely to be highly differentiated.

Drawing on the experiences and perceptions of the respondents and the key informants, who served on average six years before fleeing the country, and supplemented by data derived from studies conducted by United Nations agencies, the International Monetary Fund (2003), the World Bank (2002b), the African Development Bank and independent analysts, this chapter assesses the overarching impacts of the national service on all aspects of Eritrean society. As expected, the conscripts, notwithstanding their shared experiences throughout the time they served in the national service in a variety of capacities, do not speak with a single voice. The ENS has profound impacts on the social fabric of the country. Here these impacts are documented and examined in detail. The incidence of sexual violence perpetrated by military commanders and military trainers against female conscripts is also discussed briefly. The question of sexual violence perpetrated by male conscripts against female servers is beyond the scope of the book. (On sexual violence see Kibreab 2017). The chapter also discusses the level of militarisation and securitisation of the educational system in the country. The plight of conscripts who suffer at the hands of ruthless traffickers and smugglers while en route to Israel via eastern Sudan and the Sinai desert, as well as to the EU+ countries through Ethiopia, Sudan, the Sahara desert, Libya and the Mediterranean Sea are discussed very briefly in the chapter.

THE IMPACT OF THE ENS ON THE COUNTRY

Since one of the main aims of the ENS is to (re)construct the war-torn economy of the country, the respondents were asked to assess the impact of the ENS on Eritrea's economy. The majority, 62 per cent, said that conscription has damaged the economy, with 33 per cent arguing that the effect of the ENS on the economy is positive. What the latter respondents consider positive contributions are the conscripts' participation in the construction of roads, houses, water reservoirs and micro-dams. Many of the conscripts also said that they participated in agricultural production and reforestation activities. It is noteworthy that nearly all the houses built by conscripts belong to the government, the ruling party and high-ranking military officers. The conscripts are also not paid, except the small amount of pocket money they receive from the ministry of defence. The majority of the respondents do not consider that the activities they undertake within the framework of the national service make any difference to the livelihoods of the large majority of the population and the coffers of the government. Nor do they think they contribute to overall economic performance. Zere, a key informant, for example, said, 'We build many micro-dams during the dry season and they get filled with sediment or the poorly constructed walls are washed away during the rainy season.' When I asked him, 'Why doesn't the government learn from its mistakes either by improving the quality of the construction or abandon them?' He said, 'Why should they? It does not cost them much because they don't pay the conscripts who do all the manual labour.' This view is edifying, because the government loses nothing and therefore it has no incentive to allocate labour to an activity where return is highest.

Five per cent of the respondents said that the ENS has neither a positive nor negative effect on the economy of the country. There is ample evidence to corroborate the views of the majority of the respondents concerning the negative impact of the ENS on the economy and society. For example, in 2002–2003 1,725,000 of the country's population faced serious threat of hunger (UN Office for the Coordination of Humanitarian Affairs 2003.) One of the major causes of the shortage of food crops was lack of labour. Sally Healy's study (2007) shows that the majority of the country's most productive labour force is either in the armed forces or in the militarised labour force within the framework of the ENS, and this situation continues unabated. Most of the country's able-bodied men and women are conscripted into the ENS, leaving their farms and livestock either unattended or to be looked after by older family members. The effect of this on agricultural production has been negative. According to the results of the joint FAO/WFP study, '[c]onscription to national service has [...] depleted the agricultural workforce in many areas' (FAO/WFP 2002) of the country. The report further states, '[t]he current rate of conscription to national service has had a significant negative impact on the availability of agricultural labour in many parts of the country. Eritrea has a very high incidence of female-headed households, which are often dependent on hired labour to cultivate their land on a sharecropping basis.' (FAO/WFP 2002). The shortage of labour is not only apparent in agricultural production. For example, an FAO-supported project that aimed at rehabilitating sub-regional veterinary clinics faced severe shortage of community animal health workers because of conscription of young men into national service (FAO/WFP 2002). A study by the International Fund for Agricultural Development (IFAD 2011: 2) also shows that the high level of mobilisation has had severe humanitarian and economic consequences.

The United Nations Office for the Coordination of Humanitarian Affairs states that 'service in the national military is mandatory for all able-bodied youth' and that this affects the economy of the country detrimentally (2013). In a recently published book, Andebrhan Welde Giorgis argues, '...indefinite active national service, far from catalysing national development, has exerted a powerful negative impact on the state of the Eritrean economy and the welfare of the Eritrean people. It has robbed private agriculture and animal husbandry, the mainstay of the national and household economies, as well as industry and services of vital work force...unlimited active national service has resulted in diminished domestic production...' (2014: 260).

Hundreds of thousands of skilled and highly educated professionals are forced to participate in the ENS, forgoing the opportunity cost of their labour time. The country's scarce resources are devoted to the military at the cost of the social and economic infrastructure of the country. In the long-term, not only does this devastate the economy of the country, but it also diverts massive resources away from its social and economic sectors. This may lead to resentment among citizens and lead to them viewing the government as illegitimate. This may in return precipitate repression, and more financial and labour resources may be devoted to the instruments of repression, further eroding the potential for economic development, social progress and political stability.

The mobilisation of most of the able-bodied men and women in the ENS during the 1998–2000 border war and the alleged state of no-war-no-peace that has prevailed has stifled the implementation and outcomes of many development projects. One such development was the ambitious human resources development project funded by the World Bank, which was considered the post-conflict Eritrean government's flagship project. This is clearly demonstrated through the findings of the World Bank (2004), in which it is stated, *inter alia,* that the border conflict between Eritrea and Ethiopia seriously affected implementation of the Human Resource Development (HRD) project and the resources available to it. The study states that during the border war, an estimated 60–70 per cent of the civil service was drafted into the army, along with between 80–90 per cent of HRD personnel (World Bank 2004: 14). More importantly, the World Bank correctly states, '[a]fter the ceasefire many of the conflict conditions prevailed...and the continuing high levels of mobilized skilled manpower in the army has had a very negative impact on HR capacity in the Government of Eritrea institutions' (World Bank 2004: 14). It is worth noting that the high level of militarisation and mobilisation under the alleged pretext of imminent threat to the country's national security has continued unabated and, as a result, shortage of labour has become so severe that the cost of production in manufacturing in Eritrea is the highest not only in the region but also world-wide (see World Bank 2002a). The negative consequence in a country where the technology in use is rudimentary and most economic activities are labour intensive is clear.

An extensive study of the performance of the manufacturing sector in Eritrea, conducted by the World Bank, shows that in spite of the severe scarcity of capital that permeates the economy of the country, firms are more capital intensive than in many sub-Saharan African countries. The study concludes, 'capital productivity is significantly lower than that of other countries in sub-Saharan Africa and beyond; it's almost to point of zero return' (2002: v). The World Bank attributes this problem to the labour shortage due to military mobilisation. It is stated that 'the lack of demobilization has deprived the private sector of a large segment of its skilled workforce and negatively affects the quality of overall management and performance' (2002a: v). The World Bank identifies scarcity of labour caused by mobilisation into the Eritrean national service and lack of foreign exchange as the most important bottlenecks affecting the manufacturing sector (2002a: v). It further states: 'The results of the survey analysis clearly indicate that the current overarching constraint is labour. The labour shortage affects firms' ability to grow and become competitive, either in the regional or international market place. Due to severe shortage of labour, firms are relatively less productive in Eritrea. The ratio of capital to labour is much higher than the optimal ratio and wages have been rising. Unit labour costs, a rough indicator of competitiveness show that *Eritrean labour is expensive relative to labour in other parts of the world*' (2002a: ix, emphasis added).

Based on the stark findings of the survey, the World Bank stated, '[i]mmediate demobilisation is necessary if the private sector in Eritrea is to function normally. Demobilisation will also make it easier to achieve macroeconomic stability' (2002a: ix). Although this recommendation was made over a decade ago, the degree of mobilisation has been intensifying since then and the damaging effect of the ENS on the economy and society continues unmitigated. The IMF's conclusion is similar to that of the World Bank, as they have stated that the economic crisis in the country has been aggravated by the continued mobilisation of large numbers of farmers into the armed forces (IMF 2003: 6). This is even admitted by the Eritrean government which, in a common assessment with the UN, states that because of the state of no-war-no-peace significant resources for defence that could have been used for the country's 'development effort, including investment in critical social infrastructure' are tied up (The State of Eritrea 2007–2011). According to Africa Economic Outlook (2012) one of the major factors influencing Eritrea's medium-term economic prospects is the large security infrastructure (2012: 9), which essentially means large-scale mobilisation.

Consistent with the available, extensive, evidence on the negative effects of the ENS on the Eritrean economy, the Bertelsmann Stiftung's Transformation Index (BTI) states, '[t]here has been no demobilization of army and national service recruits (at least 600,000 people) and unlimited national service that affects large parts of the working-age population remained in place' (2012: 2). The report further states, '[t]he Eritrean command economy was in a very poor state and remained under the control of the PFDJ leadership and military leaders. The conscription of more than 600,000 persons into the army and national service, where they had to perform forced labour without noteworthy payment for unlimited periods of time, worsened the distortion of the economy and led to severe shortages of basic consumer goods in the market at prices that are out of reach for the majority of the population' (2012: 15).[1]

The International Crisis Group (ICG), in its in-depth study, states that Eritrea is a highly militarised state in which, following the border war with Ethiopia, the national service has become in effect indefinite, such that young Eritreans have been swiftly absorbed into a military machine with little prospect of eventual demobilisation or even appropriate levels of leave (2010: 9). In their book, *The African Garrison State*, Tronvoll and Mekonen (2014) characterise the Eritrean state as one of the most militarised states in the world, resulting not only from the indefinite national service, but also as a result of the establishment of the people's militia comprising elderly citizens up to the age of 80 (2014: 165). Nicole Hirt also argues that the situation in Eritrea is permeated by 'excessive militarisation [...] justified by the no war, no peace situation' (2013: 7). In view of the empirical evidence presented in the above, the observation of the large majority of the respondents interviewed in the study, that the ENS has 'damaged the economy of the country,' is accurate.

In the following the extent to which female conscripts are subjected to sexual violence at the hands of military commanders and conscript trainers is discussed briefly.

SEXUAL VIOLENCE

Given the perceived gender equality that permeated the liberation struggle (see Pilar 1980; Cowan 1983) and in view of the fact that one of the central aims of the ENS has been to transmit the core values of the revolution to present and future generations, the findings of this study show that female conscripts are subjected to degrading and inhuman treatment. This includes rape at the hands of military officers, including conscript trainers. The ENS, which was launched for the first time in 1994, was preceded by a Summer Work Programme in which secondary school students throughout the country participated. The youths, both female and male, stayed in makeshift camps during the summer holidays. Many families were concerned that their daughters who were accustomed to strict parental guidance were suddenly stripped not only of parental control and guidance, but also of the taboos that permeate normal life, as well as the protective armour of family and home life.

The sexual morality of the youth is shaped by society along traditional lines in which the influence of religion, family and local communities are vital. The Summer Work Programme, and later the national service, removed all these influences and consequently unleashed pressures for sexual conduct previously unknown in the country. Most of the female

---

[1]   The figure of 600,000 is exaggerated (see Chapter 1).

participants in the Summer Work Programmes were underage and could not consent to sexual relationships voluntarily. The problem in the Summer Work Programme was not necessarily sexual abuse perpetrated by military commanders; the public was mainly concerned with the potential 'breakdown of sexual morality' among the youth.

This backdrop is important to understanding the response of the parents of the female youths who received call up papers to join the ENS when it was launched in 1994. This parental concern was not unfounded. For example, the UNHCR in its Eligibility Guidelines (2009) pointed out that there are women who avoid national service out of fear of sexual abuse.

> ...a pattern of sexual violence against female conscripts exists within the military. Some female conscripts are reported subjected to sexual harassment and violence, including rape. There have been reports of female conscripts coerced into having sex with commanders, including through threats of heavy military duties, harsh postings, and denial of home leave. Refusal to submit to sexual exploitation and abuse is allegedly punished by detention, torture and ill treatment, including exposure to extreme heat and limitation of food rations.

To escape the danger of sexual violence, many girls used pregnancy as a means of avoiding national service. One consequence of this is that many 'fatherless' children are born, as the attraction of getting pregnant was not to have children, but rather to avoid national service. Many parents are burdened with the responsibility of caring for their grandchildren, but, more importantly, those women who become pregnant without being married suffer stigma and ostracism at the hands of their families and communities and may consequently 'resort to committing suicide to escape the cycle of abuse' (UNHCR 2009). Many young girls also fall easy prey to traffickers in an attempt to flee the country in order to avoid being ostracised.

As seen earlier, in 2003 the Eritrean authorities, in an attempt to curb the number of draft evaders who flee the country, extended the duration of secondary school by one year and those who completed 11th grade were transferred to the Sawa Military Training Centre. Some of these students were underage and therefore unable to engage in consensual sexual relationships. The findings of the study show that sexual violence at the Sawa Military Training Centre and since is widespread (Kibreab 2017). As seen above, the central aim of the ENS is to preserve and transmit the values produced during the liberation struggle, which included gender equality. When the respondents in the study were asked whether female conscripts are subjected to sexual violence in the ENS, the large majority acknowledged the prevalence of sexual violence perpetrated by military commanders and conscript trainers against female conscripts. Only a few denied that such violations exist. R #009, one of many, said that sexual abuse 'is happening especially among those who continue their national service at Sawa. In the military camp of Sawa, there is no rule and any sergeant can do whatever he wants to do. [...] Most of them are forcing women and subjecting them to sexual abuse. ...' R #029 said that the commanders provide a variety of incentives, abusing their power to induce female conscripts to submit to unwanted sexual intercourse. This respondent further stated that there are no rules that regulate the behaviour of the military commanders in the ENS, and as a result they are at liberty to do whatever they please. He said that they say, 'We are the commanders and if you listen to us, you don't have to toil, you will have access to good food, be granted home leave, avoid serving in the frontline.' In order to avoid any form of difficulty, she [a female conscript] is forced to toe the line...' Another respondent said, 'conscripts are forced to do whatever their commander orders them to do. The power of the commander is absolute and as a result, nothing can stop him from doing whatever he wants, including sexually abusing female conscripts' (R #49). The widespread sexual violence that suffuses the ENS is contrary to expectation and to the aims and objectives of the ENS (see Chapter 1).

The prevalence of sexual abuse in the ENS is confirmed by other studies. For example, the Committee on the Elimination of All Forms of Discrimination against Women (2015),[2] under the sub-heading 'Women's rights in the context of the national service and the refugee crisis', states:

> The committee is deeply concerned about the negative impact of the indefinite national service on women's rights and at the insufficient measures taken by the State party to remedy this situation. It is particularly concerned about:
>
> 8   (a) Women and girls being forcibly recruited into the national service for an indefinite period of time and without formal pay, under conditions which amount to forced labour;
> (b) Reports that women in national service are frequently victims of sexual violence, including rape, committed by officers and male recruits and that those refusing sexual advances are often severely punished;
> (c) The large and increasing number of Eritrean women and girls, including unaccompanied children, who flee the country and become refugees in third countries to avoid national service. (2/14)

The US Department of State observes, 'There were frequent reports on rape in military training camps, during national service' (2014: 17). Cecilia Bailliet's study of female asylum-seekers in Norway (2007) found that female conscripts:

> ...attested to the rape of other women besides themselves, signalling the possibility of a systematic practice. They claimed abuses including detention (short and long-term), beatings, forced abortions (and attempted abortions), forced heavy labour [...] death threats, degrading treatment, continuous sexual violence and rape, as well as possible forced pregnancy and sexual enslavement. They also alleged that some women suffered sexual abuse by military leaders beyond the one they served directly.

She added:

> Refusal to submit to sexual abuse was punished by detention, torture, humiliation and ill treatment: including underground detention, binding of hands and feet and placement in stress positions, suspension from trees, limitation of food rations, exposure to extreme heat and insects, shaving of head, etc. [...] Applicants alleged that other women selected suicide as a mode of escape from the sexual violence.

Although Bailliet's findings are consistent with other available evidence, including this study, it is important to recognise the potential risk of bias. Her data are derived from female asylum-seekers who have an

---

[2]   Committee on the Elimination against Women considers the reports on Eritrea, 2015, available at http://www.ohchr.org/EN/NewsEvents/Pages/DsiplayNews.aspx?News.aspx?NewsID=1561&LangID=E (last accessed November 2015).

incentive to exaggerate the prevalence of sexual violence in the ENS in order to bolster their claim for asylum.

The Commission of Inquiry on Human Rights in Eritrea (2015: para. 1315) states:

> The Commission has received a large number of testimonies and submissions relating to the rape and sexual abuse of young women conscripts in military training centres. Despite the large number of testimonies reporting sexual violence within military training, the Commission considers that it may have only partially uncovered the full extent of the sexual violence suffered by women and girls in military training due to the cultural barriers and challenges associated with speaking about sexual violence. In light of these factors, the Commission is of the view that rape and other forms of sexual violence are perpetrated with frequency against women in the military training centres. The prevalence of such abuse in Sawa and Wi'a in particular is extremely high, but it is also found in other military training centres.

The widespread sexual abuse female conscripts suffer in the ENS is the result of an abuse of power. Some of the consequences of this have been proliferation of unwanted pregnancies, single motherhood, unsafe abortions and suicides motivated by the desire to avoid being stigmatised and 'dishonouring' families, burdening families with the responsibility to raise grandchildren whose fathers are in the open-ended national service, early and arranged marriages and increased risk of being trafficked at the Ethiopian and Sudanese borders, in the Sinai, the Sahara and Libya (see Kibreab 2017).

In the following a brief discussion on the degree of militarisation and securitisation of the system of education in the country is presented.

MILITARISATION AND SECURITISATION OF EDUCATION

> I want to insist that the intellectual is an individual with a specific public role in society that cannot be reduced simply to being a faceless professional ...the intellectual is an individual endowed with a faculty for representing, embodying, articulating a message, a view, an attitude, philosophy or opinion to, raise embarrassing questions, to confront orthodoxy and dogma [...] to be someone who cannot easily be co-opted by governments [...] whose *raison d'être* is to represent all those people and issues that are routinely forgotten or swept under the rug. (Edward Said 1993)

Isaias Afwerki, who rules the country with an iron fist, is anathema to intellectuals endowed with professional integrity and independence of thought. Because such intellectuals embody civil courage they are more inclined to defy rather than to bow to tyrannical authority. His animosity and suspicion of intellectuals is based on his personal experience during the formative years of the EPLF. When his dictatorial proclivities became clear at the beginning of the 1970s, he was for the first time challenged and nearly deposed from his position by a group of intellectuals from Haile Selassie University who joined the movement that later became the EPLF in the early 1970s (see Kibreab 2008).

Isaias and a handful of his clique defamatorily labelled the change-seeking reform movement as *Menqaê* (bat).[3] Over a short period of time the reform movement, *Menqaê*, won the hearts and minds of the oppressed rank and file fighters who demanded an end to: 'deprivation of fighters' freedom of opinion and expression, excessive securitisation, pre-emption and stifling of alternative views by divulging agendas to selected individuals prior to meetings, assaulting and detention of fighters...lack of accountability, transparency and maladministration...mistreatment of women' (cited in Kibreab 2008: 234). According to Markakis the main contentious issues raised by the reform movement were, '... undemocratic nature of the leadership and its methods. This was reflected in the fact that there had been no election of leaders, as well as resentment against their penchant for centralisation and secrecy. *Isaias in particular was accused of supervising everyone's work, of censoring all publications, thereby undermining the position of the cadres* (1990: 136, emphasis added). David Pool also states, '[m]uch of the criticism of the leadership was concentrated on Isaias Afwerki...' (2001: 76). Markakis further observes, '...the newly consolidated leadership was nearly outflanked by a group of newcomers [the *Menqaê*]' (1990: 135).

Following extensive documentation and analysis of the emergence, consolidation and extent of the imminent threat it posed to Isaias's unfettered control and the liquidation of its ringleaders, I wrote in my book, *Critical Reflections* (2008: 278), that the only time Isaias Afwerki was ever openly and defiantly challenged and forced into a defensive position before 2001 was by *Menqaê* in 1973. Indeed, when *Menqaê* was at its peak his fate 'hung in the balance' (Markakis 1990: 135). More importantly, *Menqaê*'s imminent threat has left a lasting impact on Isaias' mind-set and attitude toward higher education and intellectuals, as well as towards dissent. A former member of the People's Liberation Forces who was present throughout the 'turmoil' told me that Isaias has never recovered fully from the sudden and unexpected shock he suffered at the hands of the unforgiving Marxist cadres, the *Menqaê*, in 1973.[4] As the Dalai Lama surmised, '[o]nce bitten by a snake you feel suspicious even when you see a piece of rope'. After he narrowly escaped being ousted from power, he became excessively risk averse.

Since then, Isaias has been suspicious of university students and intellectuals. Essentially, he views university/higher education as a breeding ground for rebellion. His contempt for people with degrees is unequivocal. He describes them in a demeaning manner, as *seb bajella* or *bejella* holders.[5] Although he was the chancellor of the University of Asmara he never presided over the graduation ceremonies. The seeds of hatred toward intellectuals planted in his mind during the *Menqaê* days have informed his stances and actions on intellectuals and higher education ever since. Most of the measures he took against intellectuals

---

[3]   *Menqaê* is a mammal that looks like a bird and a mouse. Its idiomatic meaning is 'two-faced'.
[4]   Ali, London, 10 December 2015.
[5]   Bajella is a certificate given to primary school students at the end of the academic year.

and institutions of higher learning make sense when perceived from this historical perspective.

His hostility was further reinforced by the defiance exhibited by the Asmara students' union between 1999 and 2001. The defiance of the students seems to have discernibly rekindled the traumatic memory of what he experienced at the hands of *Menqaê* nearly three decades earlier. In 1999 the government, without warning or consultation, announced that all university students were required to participate in one month of summer work at the end of their first year of university education (Kibreab 2008: 100). They were ordered to pack and leave for Ali Gidir to work in the cotton plantation allocated to demobilised EPLF ex-combatants. The students defied the government's order on the grounds that it was during the summer holidays that they engaged in income-generating activities to fund their studies and to support their families (Kesete, cited in Kibreab 2008: 100). The students' defiance was highly significant. It was the first time that a civil society organisation had defied the government or an order from Isaias Afwerki in the post-independence period. More importantly, the students suffered no immediate consequences for their defiance. The profound consequences were to come soon after, however, culminating in the dismantling of the only university in the country.

The Summer Work Programme (SWP), which started in 1999, was interrupted by the intensity of the border war in 2000, but was reintroduced in 2001 subsequent to the signing of the Algiers Peace Agreement between the Eritrean and Ethiopian governments in December 2000. This coincided with the period of unprecedented but short-lived openness and growing discontent. The government feared that the prevailing discontent in the context of an ephemeral freedom of press and expression might radicalise students at the university. Taking advantage of the situation the student union criticised the government for its malevolent interference in academic affairs (Kibreab 2008: 100). The students' union's President, Kesete, scathingly criticised the government in a graduation ceremony speech. He articulated the students' grievances and announced that the students would not participate in the SWP unless their demands were met. The demands included that allocations of tasks in the SWP should be commensurate with the particular disciplines of students. In the student leader's view, only then would the students be able contribute positively to the economic development and social progress of the people. They also demanded fair remuneration.

In the midst of negotiations that took place between the Student Council and the president of the university, Dr Woldeab Yisak, the union's president, Kesete, was arrested on 31 July in 2001. The students refused to sign up for the SWP unless he was released and their other demands were met (Kibreab 2008: 102). As a BBC correspondent (2001) stated, '[i]n a defiant gesture, the students said they would only comply with the holiday work programme when their leader is either released or brought to court.' In a statement issued on 9 August 2001, the Student Council stated that it had a right and duty to defend its members' interests and it would not be intimidated into silence and abandon its duty to serve its members' interests (Student Council 2001). The Student Council further declared, '[w]e will not change our position until our questions have been answered sufficiently' (2001). The students' union filed writ of *Habeas corpus* twice asking the high court to order the authorities to bring Kesete to the court so that he would either be charged or released. The high court, under the leadership of the most able chief justice Eritrea ever had, Teame Beyene, ordered the police to bring the student leader to the court to be charged or released. The high court ordered the police to release Kesete as he had no case to answer. Teame was fired soon after because he criticised the executive's interference in the affairs of the court. He also condemned the decision of the president to establish the special court, which superseded the laws of the country. The special court was authorised to adjudicate without reference to the country's substantive and procedural laws.

The police requested more time and were allowed to interrogate Kesete further. When he appeared before the high court on 10 August 2001 about 400 students demonstrated in front of the court to demand his immediate release. The security forces rounded up the students and took them to a detention centre at Wi'a, about 30 kilometres south of Massawa, where the weather is scorching and unbearable. The police also rounded up about 1,700 university students and took them to Wi'a. They were accused of 'unruly behaviour and unlawful acts' (BBC 2001). To avoid being rounded up many students fled the country and it was feared that many lost their lives on the Mediterranean Sea when trying to cross to Italy (Kibreab 2008). The scorching temperature in combination with the appalling conditions in detention led to the death of two students, Yirga Yosief (14 August 2001) and Yemane Tekie (19 August 2001). The students were released from the detention camp at the end of September 2001, but five of the student leaders were kept in detention in a work camp in the lowland desert area (Kibreab 2008: 103).

The government, particularly the president and the PFDJ's head of political office, Yemane Gebreab, were taken aback by the audacity of the students who, in spite of the deafening silence permeating the Eritrean political landscape, defiantly rejected the government's order to participate in the SWP, unless their demands were met, including the immediate release of their leader or his being brought before the court. This, besides being unprecedented in the country's post-independence history, was, in the autocratic personal ruler's view, objectionable and excessive. The government feared that if such an ominous challenge was not rooted out it might, besides setting a dangerous precedent, constitute an imminent threat to national security, as well as to the 'sacrosanct' programme of nation building and post-conflict reconstruction. This excessive stance of securitisation, manifested in the dramatisation of the alleged 'threat', was intended to justify any future action taken to avert it. For the ruler, Isaias Afwerki, the university was a dangerous breeding ground for rebellion and hence it had to be dismantled so that the core of the rebellion would be destroyed. This was because it was thought that once the breeding ground was destroyed the agitators and their comrades would be thrown into disarray. To prepare the ground for this closure it was decided to phase out recruitment of new students to the university. The students who completed fourth year in the academic year 2001–2002 were sent to Sawa in July 2002 to receive six months military training and later to teach final year secondary school students at Sawa.

In 2003 the government introduced yet another major change, with the duration of secondary school education extended by one year. From the 2003–2004 academic year onwards students who complete 11th grade have been transferred to the Sawa military training camp to complete 12th grade under military discipline. Some of the students who completed 11th grade and transferred to the Sawa military camp were under eighteen. The Organisation for Child Soldiers states that although the proclamation on national service stipulates that only those who are eighteen and over are required to join the ENS, '...in practice for many it begins earlier'. Girls and boys under the age of eighteen years are among thousands of people who enter military training every year and who then spend most of the rest of their active working lives in military or other forms of national service. Although the Eritrean government denies allegations of unlawful conscription of under-eighteens, there is evidence that it occurs. This is, to a large extent, because many of the students who complete 11th grade are under eighteen years old.

After the government decided to close down the university, the student leaders were subjected to intense surveillance and endless harassment and intimidation (Interview, Iyob, London, 12 December 2015). Most of the student leaders were assigned to the military (army, navy and air force) within the framework of the national service so that they could be closely monitored. Thousands fled the country and others scattered to different post-secondary school tertiary colleges located in various villages where the educational infrastructure was either rudimentary or non-existent. This did not matter to the government because the rationale for the decision was to stem dissent and rebellion at the source rather than to promote scholarship. Nor did the risk of loss of institutional and intellectual memory and infrastructure worry the president or his cronies.

One damaging consequence of the government's decision to militarise education is that many parents feared, on the one hand, that their daughters might engage in sexual relationships with male conscripts in defiance of the cultural norms and, on the other, that they might suffer sexual violence at the hands of military commanders. As a result, many parents responded by withdrawing their daughters from school in order to avoid conscription. Many parents thought this was the only way they could protect their daughters from being abused by commanders, conscript trainers and male conscripts. Others forced their underage daughters into arranged marriages, often with men who were over forty and hence not affected by national service. Others encouraged their underage daughters to flee across the border to Ethiopia and Sudan, en route to the EU countries. The Committee on the Elimination of Discrimination against Women, for example, states that there are '[r]eports that many girls drop out of school, become pregnant and/or are forced to enter child marriage to avoid enrolment at the Sawa Military Training Centre and national service.'[6]

The architect of the whole scheme of the dismantlement and securitisation of higher education in the country, the head of state, saw the university environment as being ideologically contaminated. I asked Iyob, a graduate from university, why the government closed it down, and he said that the president thought 'the university was poisoned and whoever came to study, including many of the former combatants contracted the virus of rebellion.' In fact, it was thought that it would not be enough to close down the university to iron out dissent, root and branch. The process of decontamination had to begin earlier, in the final year of secondary education. Herein lay the rationale for the militarisation of education both at secondary and post-secondary levels at Sawa, Mai Nefhi and the other colleges. Since then the Eritrean polity, including education, has been characterised by a high level of militarisation (Reid 2009; Tronvoll and Mekonnen 2014). As Reid states:

> One of the problems for observers and teaching staff alike is that *the college [Mai Nefhi] appears to be run more along the lines of a military camp than an institution for further education.* Students cannot move freely in and out, and are closely guarded; parents cannot visit the students, nor can outsiders enter. An army officer is the *de facto* principal of the college, which lacks books and other essential equipment. In addition to a small but significant arsenal of automatic weapons on the site – presumably in anticipation of trouble – *there is a jail for students who fail to attend classes. On a visit in 2006, I was told that this jail was also home to a number of students who had recently been caught 'cheating in exams'.* (2009: 216, emphasis added)

The fact that truancy and cheating in exams are considered military offences that can result in corporal punishment and imprisonment is a clear indication of the degree of militarisation of the system of education in the country. This observation has been confirmed by the respondents and key informants who studied at Mai Nefhi after attending the *Warsai* School at Sawa. The students belonged to the same military organisational structure as they did at Sawa.

Tanja Müller (2008: 122) also states, 'Mai Nefhi is ran jointly by an academic vice-director and an army colonel [...] [it] resembles more a military camp than a place of higher learning.' She further observes, '[t]he different faculties are to be governed by branches of the respective ministries, and are thus exposed to direct political control and interference' (2008: 122). This indicates that Mai Nefhi and the other colleges are not typical higher institutions of learning with any façade of academic freedom. Amanda Pool also states, 'Mai Nefhi was being kick-started by the government as an alternative to the long-standing University of Asmara [...] it was a militarised school...' (2013: 67). Not only are the students at Mai Nefhi required to undertake military drills, but they also dig trenches and, more significantly, they are forced to work for the personal gain of military officers. The latter tasks are not even remotely linked to the goals of the ENS and nation building.

[6]   Para. 8 (d) Conclusion observations on the fourth and fifth periodic reports of Eritrea, Committee on the Elimination of Discrimination against Women, 6 March 2015, UN, CEDAW/C/ERI/CO/5.

Reid, for example, states, '[o]ne army officer was using this student labour to build his house in nearby Mai Nefhi village...' (2008: 216). As Reid observes, '[f]or many quiet critics of the government, Mai Nefhi College and education policy more broadly are symptomatic of the government's insensitivity and anti-intellectualism; its suspicious nature and tendency toward militaristic solutions to complex problems' (2008: 217). In spite of these critical and useful observations, Reid states, '[t]hese colleges are designed to equip students with the skills necessary to address peculiarly "Eritrean" problems, nothing more nothing less' (2008: 217). The data I gathered from conversations with several former activist students at the University of Asmara shows that the single most important purpose of the government's decision to close down the university was to decimate the critical mass which Isaias perceived as a threat to his autocratic rule and to PFDJ's cultural hegemony (Medhanie, interview, London 12, 14 and 16 December 2015). The government's alleged claim regarding the development of skills to meet the so-called 'peculiar Eritrean problems,' is a pretext concocted to stifle the development of critical thinking and freedom of thought among students (Interview, Isaac, London, 14 December 2015). There was no doubt in the minds of the informants who were among the key leaders of the 2001 confrontation that the single most important aim of the president and his cronies was to destroy the kernel of the resistance and to throw the student body into disarray. The students' interpretation of the events in which they actively took part makes sense. The so-called 'peculiar Eritrean problem' is a myth. The government's policy on education is no different from most educational policies elsewhere in developing societies. In the 1994 Macro-Policy, the objective of Eritrea's education is said to be the production of a population equipped with the necessary skills, knowledge and culture for a self-reliant and modern economy, developing self-consciousness and self-motivation in the population to fight poverty, disease and all the attendant causes of backwardness and ignorance, and making a basic education available to all. These educational goals are neither peculiar nor specific to Eritrea.

Those who flee from the open-ended national service in search of freedom and a better life have been falling easy prey to ruthless traffickers, avaricious smugglers and corrupt military officers in Eritrea and the transit countries, Ethiopia, Sudan, Libya and Egypt. This is briefly discussed in the following.

THE PLIGHT OF DESERTERS AND DRAFT EVADERS

As already discussed, the open-ended ENS and its negative effects on the economic, political and social fabric of Eritrean society has engendered inauspicious conditions that have resulted in the displacement of hundreds of thousands of citizens affected by the ENS. In the eyes of corrupt military officers in Eritrea and in the neighbouring countries, including Egypt, Sudan and Libya, as well as traffickers and smugglers, Eritrean conscripts and draft evaders who want to leave or have left Eritrea in search of safe haven and succour are perceived as precious commodities. As a result they are kidnapped, held as hostages and subjected to extortion and sexual violence. This is because these ruthless groups perceive the victims' diaspora connections as an invaluable resource to callously tap into. A study conducted by Meron Estefanos, human rights activist, and Mirjam van Reisen and Dr Conny Rijken of Tilburg University in the Netherlands shows that 'up to 30,000 Eritreans have been abducted since 2007 and taken to Egypt's Sinai to suffer torture and ransom demands' (cited in BBC 2013). The study further states, '[a]t least $600m (£366m) has been extorted from families in ransom payments [...] Victims are kidnapped in Ethiopia, Sudan and Eritrea and taken to Sinai' (cited in BBC 2013). HRW's Jerry Simpson, the author of *I Want to Lie Down and Die*, wrote, '[s]o far police and soldiers in Sudan and Egypt helping traffickers kidnap and torture refugees have nothing to fear. Some police in eastern Sudan are so emboldened by their impunity, they hand refugees over to traffickers in police stations' (HRW 2014a). Most of the US$ 600 million is made good by relatives in the diaspora.

A survivor of human trafficking in the Sinai told HRW (2014b): 'To make us pay, they abused us. They raped women in front of us and left them naked. They hung us upside down. They beat and burn us all over our bodies with cigarettes. My friend died in front of us and I wanted to lie down and die' (cited in UNHCR 2014).

According to the respondents and key informants interviewed for the study not only do diaspora Eritreans pay the huge ransoms demanded by hostage takers, but they also pay the exorbitant bribes demanded by corrupt military officers in Eritrea and in the neighbouring countries, as well as the fees to traffickers and smugglers.

Many families have lost their loved ones at the hands of ruthless traffickers in the Sinai desert while en route to Israel. For example, according to a joint study undertaken by the Physicians for Human Rights and the Hotline for Migrant Workers, two Israeli voluntary organisations that have been running clinics treating victims of human trafficking, 'an estimated 5,000 to 7,000 Eritrean refugees who arrived in the country [Israel] in the past three years had been tortured. Another 4,000 Eritreans have disappeared and many are presumed dead, according to testimony for the European Union' (Millman 2013). Dan Connell states that two distinct tragedies of the last two decades will leave an indelible mark across Eritreans' memories forever, namely, the flight of hundreds of thousands from repression and despair in Eritrea in search of safe haven and succour in 'democratic societies: the brutal kidnapping, torture and ransom of refugees in the Egyptian Sinai and the drowning of hundreds more in the Mediterranean Sea when their criminally unseaworthy and overcrowded boats went down, a running disaster epitomized by the October 2013 Lampedusa shipwreck' (2013). The catalogue of crimes and atrocities perpetrated against Eritrean asylum-seekers and refugees in Libya, Egypt, Eastern Sudan and Sinai are meticulously compiled in Rusom Kidane's Eritrean Human Rights Electronic archives (Rusom Kidane n.d.).

Many have also died in the Sahara desert en route to Libya. One of the many Eritrean youths who survived the ordeal told Martin Plaut from Libya, '[w]e started the journey [from Sudan to Libya] and it was very difficult and very bad. Nobody can cross the Sahara, it's too difficult. We had water but finished it. The car was spoiled (broken down). We stayed three nights and three days – we couldn't do anything. The driver had a phone. He tried to call, but the satellite communication was no good. We lost three friends there. But before that, we had seen several dead bodies in the Sahara' (Plaut 2007). This represents the tip of the iceberg. Many of the Eritrean asylum-seekers and refugees interviewed by the author reported that they had lost a number of their friends, relatives or countrymen and women when crossing the Sahara desert.

Members of the Rashaida tribe take hundreds of Eritreans hostage in Eastern Sudan. After ransom is paid to the Rashaida the hostages are further sold to Bedouin hostage takers in the Sinai (see Humphris 2013). Human Rights Watch, in a detailed study on human trafficking and torture in Eastern Sudan and Egypt, show harrowing treatment of Eritrean women and men, including minors taken hostage by the Rashaida and Bedouin near the Eritrean border in Eastern Sudan and the Sinai, respectively, in collusion with the police in Sudan and Egypt (Human Rights Watch 2014). Those who are taken hostage in Eastern Sudan are further transferred to the Bedouin in the Sinai whether they pay ransom or not. Human Rights Watch researchers spoke with 21 Eritreans who said that they were kidnapped by people they described as Rashaida in Eastern Sudan near the Eritrean border and in the refugee camp near the town of Kassala (Human Rights Watch 2014). They told Human Rights Watch (2014) that the 'traffickers detained them for days or weeks near Kassala, abused them to extort money from them, and then handed them over to kidnappers in Egypt. Seven said they were kidnapped in 2012, twelve in 2011, and one in 2009' (Human Rights Watch 2014). Eighteen of those interviewed told Human Rights Watch that the traffickers demanded that they pay between a few thousand dollars and US$10,000 in ransom: 'Whether they paid or not, all of those interviewed said that the traffickers then transferred them to other men in Egypt who also demanded payment' (Human Rights Watch 2014). The victims told Human Rights Watch that 'the Sudanese traffickers repeatedly beat and assaulted them in other ways, of whom three said the traffickers severely abused them and three said the traffickers threatened to kill them if they did not pay. One said that traffickers in Khartoum raped her and other female victims' (Human Rights Watch 2014). The study also shows that 'eight cases in which Sudanese police and Sudanese military handed Eritreans directly to traffickers who then abused them' (Human Rights Watch 2014). Harriet Sherwood summarises the plight of Eritrean youth in Sudan and Egypt (2014) as follows: 'Hundreds of Eritrean refugees have been enslaved in torture camps in Sudan and Egypt in the past ten years, enduring weeks or months of violence and rape and extorted by traffickers often in collusion with states security forces. Some of the refugees have died, and have been scarred for life – both physically and psychologically – as a result of mutilation, burning, beatings and sexual assault...'

It is not only en route to their planned destinations that Eritreans suffer, with their ordeal continuing once they reach countries such as Israel. This is briefly discussed in what follows.

MISTREATMENT OF ERITREAN ASYLUM-SEEKERS IN ISRAEL AND REMITTANCE

In total, 36,000 Eritreans have arrived in Israel, where application for asylum is not a straightforward affair. As a result only 1,950 have been able to apply for refugee status, out of which, '270 requests have been reviewed, *with just two of them being accepted*' (Connell 2013; Lior 2014) (emphasis added). Ironically, their mistreatment and the consequent loss of hope for any future in the country have engendered in them a greater propensity to send money to Eritrea. According to informants interviewed for this study, those in Israel remit more money and goods to their families and relatives in Eritrea than the rest of the Eritrean diaspora. This is because Eritreans in Israel see no future for themselves and their children as they are considered to be 'illegal infiltrators' waiting to be deported as soon as possible. In a scathing article published in the *Jerusalem Post*, Elliot Vaisrub Glassengerg (2014) wrote, 'Israel's treatment of asylum seekers has become a downright Hilul Hashem, desecration of the name of God, or in other words a dark blot on Israel's reputation and a shame for the Jewish people, especially when committed ostensibly in the name of Judaism and Jewish values'. He continues, '[a]s Jews we are taught we must love the stranger because we were once strangers in the Land of Egypt. We must not mistreat a runaway slave for we were once runaway slaves' (Glassengerg 2014).

HRW's report, 'Make their Lives Miserable: Israel's Coercion of Eritrean and Sudanese Asylum-Seekers to Leave Israel' (2014b), meticulously documents the gross violations of human rights perpetrated against Eritrean and Sudanese asylum-seekers by the Israeli government, contrary to international and Israeli law. The report shows, 'how Israel has used the resulting insecure legal status as a pretext to detain or threaten to detain them indefinitely, and has thereby coerced thousands into leaving Israel.' It further states, 'Israel's policies are well summed up in the words of former Israeli Interior Minister Eli Yisahi who said that as long as Israel cannot deport them to their countries, it should "lock them up to make their lives miserable"' (HRW 2014c). He also told the Channel 2 programme 'Meet the Press', 'If hundreds of thousands of migrant workers [read asylum-seekers] come here, they will bring with them a profusion of diseases: hepatitis, measles, tuberculosis, AIDS and drug (addiction)' (cited in Haaretz Services 2009).

In a similar vein, the Israeli prime minister, Binyamin Netanyahu, warned that 'illegal infiltrators [read asylum-seekers] flooding the country' represent a clear danger to the 'security and identity of the Jewish state' (cited in Sherwood 2012). Netanyahu further remarked, '[i]f we don't stop their entry, the problem that currently stands at 60,000 could grow to 600,000, and that threatens our existence as a Jewish and democratic state' (cited in Sherwood 2012). Netanyahu made this dramatic claim notwithstanding the fact that the barrier wall along the 150-mile border with the Egyptian Sinai which was completed in late 2013 has nearly completely stemmed the flow of asylum-seekers from Eritrea, Sudan and Ethiopia. According to Toga Tarnopolsky (2013), '[t]he fence's effect already appears to have been vast: according to estimates released in July by the Prime Minister's office, a mere 34 people entered Israel illegally in the first half of 2013 – compared to nearly 10,000 people in the first six months of 2012, a decrease of more than 99 per cent.'

The Israeli government's extremely inimical policy towards Eritrean asylum-seekers and refugees is also amply documented by David Sheen (2014). It is because of this hostile policy that Eritrean asylum-seekers in Israel, instead of investing in their 'future' in the country send most of their earnings to Eritrea, in anticipation that they may be deported there at any time in the near future. Their fear has now become real. The Israeli state has decided to deport Eritrean and Sudanese asylum-seekers to unspecified African countries, probably Uganda or Rwanda. The Zonszein (2015) *Guardian* wrote on 31 March 2015:

> Israel will begin deporting asylum seekers from Eritrea and Sudan to unnamed third countries in Africa even if against their will, the immigration authority announced on Tuesday. The assumption is that the third countries are Rwanda and Uganda, although Israel has not revealed details. According to the interior minister, Gilad Erdan, the move will 'encourage infiltrators to leave the borders of the state of Israel in an honourable and safe way, and serve as an effective tool for fulfilling our obligations towards Israeli citizens and restoring the fabric of life to the residents of south Tel Aviv.

Most Eritrean families who have members and relatives in Israel receive substantial amounts of remittances. Unlike in the case of other diaspora Eritreans where they have secure status, those in Israel are preparing the ground in case they are deported in the future. At least they will have something to return to: houses, savings and investment in social capital.

ASYLUM AND THE ERITREAN DIASPORA

The families of the conscripts who deserted from the ENS and subsequently made it to the global North and Israel successfully in spite of the suffering and abuse they might have experienced at the hands of corrupt and abusive government officials and military officers in Eritrea and in the transit countries, such as Ethiopia, Sudan, Egypt and Libya, as well as ruthless traffickers and covetous smugglers, have benefited tremendously from remittances. In Eritrea remittances play a key role in the livelihood of many families throughout the country. Temesgen Kifle, for example, states, '[i]n Eritrea, worker remittances from abroad play a significant role in the country's economy. Domestic output (GDP) is substantially augmented by remittances and many families in Eritrea depend on remittances for their livelihood' (2007). Given the variety of informal channels through which remittances are transferred from the regions where there are high concentrations of Eritrean diaspora, including hundreds of thousands who deserted from the ENS and currently reside in regions such as the Gulf States, Western Europe, North America, New Zealand and Australia, figures on the total amounts remitted are difficult to come by. The available figures for recent years, based on nothing more than educated guesses, suggest that about US$350–400 million are transferred to the country a year (Styan, cited in Healy 2007: 6). Other estimates suggest the total is US$411 million (IFAD, cited in Oucho 2008), although the actual amount is likely to be much more than this. There are two main reasons for this. Firstly, the number of Eritreans who have been fleeing from the ENS and seeking asylum in the global North, particularly in the EU+ states, has been soaring since 2008 (see Table 4.1 in Chapter 4). The amount remitted to Eritrea is likely to increase with the rising number of Eritrean refugees working and studying abroad. It is not only workers, but also students, who send money to their crisis-stricken families and relatives. Secondly, because of the government's restrictive economic policy and the indefinite national service, most families' options to fend for themselves have been eroded and, as a result, many rely on remittances received from their exiled relatives for sustenance and survival. The claim that the amount of remittances has declined in recent years due to the economic downturn in the global economy (see World Bank 2012) and UN sanctions (see Africa Economic Outlook 2012; AfDB, OECD, UNDP 2015) cannot be taken seriously. It is not because diaspora Eritreans have surplus income that they send money and goods to their families and relatives at home, it is because they feel they have a responsibility to do so, even at the expense of their own families' and children's wellbeing and education in the West. The effect of the sanctions has been on the mechanisms of transfer of remittances rather than on the amount remitted, as the UN sanctions have no effect on the informal channels of remittances transfer. Although there is no assessment of the impact of the UN sanctions on economic activities and on overall economic performance in the country, the amount of remittances sent by diaspora Eritreans to their families are likely to be inversely related to sanctions. The more the sanctions bite, the more likely diaspora Eritreans are to send more money in order to offset the negative impact on their families.

For our purpose, it suffices to say that in the context of severe constraints permeating the reality on the ground, reflected, *inter alia*, in a state of no-peace no-war (see World Bank 2012; Plaut 2014; Mosley 2014; Andebrhan Welde Giorgis 2014), indefinite national service (see Human Rights Watch 2009; Kibreab 2009b, 2013), militarisation (Hirt 2010; Tronvoll and Mekonnen 2014), severe restrictions imposed by the government on economic activities (Kibreab 2009a; ICG 2010; AfDB, OECD, UNDP and UNECA 2012; World Bank 2015b) and its isolationist policies and practices (Muhmuza 2013; Oxford Analytica 2013), as exacerbated by unfavourable weather conditions (FAO/WFP 2003; FAO 2015), remittances from family members and relatives in the diaspora constitute the backbone of the country's economy and of households' incomes.

The indefinite and universal ENS has engendered suffering which has left hundreds of thousands of conscripts with no acceptable alternative but to flee from conditions that have degenerated into forced labour (Human Rights Watch 2009; Kibreab 2009b). According to the European Asylum Support Office (EASO, 2014), there has been a significant increase of Eritrean applicants for international protection arriving in EU+ countries since July 2013. The highest influx in 2014 (till August) was observed in Sweden, Denmark, Switzerland, Norway, Netherlands and the United Kingdom. The month of July 2014 was marked by a very large influx of Eritrean nationals applying for asylum, exceeding the peak registered in the summer of 2013. The total number of Eritreans who applied for asylum in the 28 EU+ member states in 2013 was 14,485, but the figure increased to 46,750, a dramatic increase from 12,000 in 2012.

The inrease between 2013 and 2014 was 154.9 per cent (see Table 4.1 in Chapter 4). In 2013, Eritrean asylum-seekers were the eighth largest group who arrived in the 28 EU+ countries. In 2014, it became the fourth largest producer of asylum-seekers in the 28 EU+ member states after Syria, Afghanistan and Kosovo (European Commission 2015).

According to EASO's Asylum Quarterly Report (2014), '[f]or the second consecutive quarter, Eritreans were the third largest citizenship of applicants in the EU+, reaching more than 19 000 applicants for inter-national protection and accounting for 10% of the EU+ total in the third quarter of 2014.'[7] According to UNHCR (2014), '[s]o far [during the first ten months of] this year, nearly 37,000 Eritreans have sought refuge in Europe, compared to almost 13,000 during the same period last year' (UNHCR 2014). In 2014, a total of 36,930 Eritreans sought asylum in Europe (European Commission 2015). However, during the second quarter of 2015 Eritrean asylum-seekers represented the sixth largest, or 4 per cent, of the total number of asylum seekers in the EU (Eurostat 2016). Between January and August 2015 a total of 6,100 Eritreans sought asylum in the EU for the first time.[8] The figures show that the proportion of Eritrean asylum-seekers in the EU during the first eight months of 2015 had declined from the mid-2014 peak.

The open-ended ENS, its detrimental effects on the livelihoods of families and the havoc it has wreaked on the national economy and social fabric of the society have, therefore, been the most important drivers of forced migration in the post-independence period (see Kibreab 2013). The EASO (2014),[9] for example, stated, '[t]he grounds cited by Eritrean applicants as a basis for their asylum application seem to be similar in most EU+ countries. *A majority of Eritreans leave the country because of*

---

[7]   EASO Asylum Quarterly Report, Quarter 3.
[8]   A monthly breakdown of the numbers shows that between for the first eight months of 2015 were as follows: January (870), Feb. (520), March (405), April (530), May (830), June (1,245), July (965) and August (735). In *Ibid.*
[9]   EASO, Report of the EASO Practical Cooperation Meeting on Eritrea 15–16 October 2014, 17 November 2014, available at http://reliefweb.int/sites/reliefweb.int/files/resources/Quarterly-Asylum-Report-Q3.pdf (last accessed November 2015).

the open-ended national service' (emphasis added). This is because '[t]he open-ended Eritrean national service (ENS) is by many EU+ countries considered as sufficient grounds to grant Geneva Convention status because of imputed political opinion, in line with the UNHCR Eligibility guideline' (UNHCR 2011). A substantial proportion of those who fled and safely arrived in the global North have been granted asylum.

Notwithstanding the fact that nothing had changed on the ground concerning the Eritrean government's bleak record on human rights and on the ENS, towards the end of 2014 the Danish Immigration Service produced a discredited and politically motivated report on Eritrea whose sole *raison d'être* was to stem the flow of Eritrean asylum-seekers into the country, as numbers had reached unprecedented heights in the summer of 2014. However, not only was the discredited Danish Immigration Service's report on Eritrea (2014), ferociously criticised by Kibreab (2014), *The Local* (2014), UNHCR (2014), Human Rights Watch (2014), Amnesty International's spokesman in Denmark (World Bulletin 2014) and many others, but also two of the three Danish researchers, Dr Jens Weise Olessen and Dr Jan Olsen, who were part of the three-man fact-finding mission in Eritrea, publicly distanced themselves from it, 'claiming their superiors had distorted the truth' (*The Economist* 2015). In a documentary aired on 5 March 2015 on Danish TV called 'DR2 Investigates: Eritrea – the failed mission' one of the researchers in the fact-finding mission, Jens Weise Olessen, said that the head of mission, 'Glynstrup put pressure on them to arrive at a predetermined conclusion. He was fixated on a particular conclusion in this report. I have absolutely no doubt about that. It was obvious from the moment that Jakob [head of mission] landed [in Eritrea] that his focus was on whether we could reach a conclusion in support of rejecting asylum' (Danish Immigration Service 2015). Jens Weise Olesen and Jan Olsen were also interviewed by Amnesty International and the full report, *Vi skulle jo også kunne sove om natten*, has been published by Amnesty Danish section (Amnesty International 2015), in which Olesen said '[i]t was a dream scenario for our bosses to be able to present brand new information on the situation in Eritrea.' The report was considered so flawed that, '[l]ast December the Danish Immigration Service decided to disregard the findings of its own report' (*The Economist* 2015).

Despite these floods of scathing criticisms, the UK's Home Office decided to adopt new guidelines, by literally recycling the discredited Danish Immigration Service report on Eritrea. As expected, the UK Home Office's guidance was also heavily criticised by many analysts and human rights organisations, such as the author (Kibreab 2015), UNHCR, and the Independent Chief Inspector of Borders and Immigration's Independent Advisory Group on Country Information who said the report was of 'dubious quality' and unreliable (IAGCI 2015). The guidelines were also heavily criticised by Human Rights Watch and Right-to-Remain.

Astonished by the UK Home Office's misguided guidance, *The Economist* states, '[i]f such controversy makes the Home Office's decision to adopt the Danish findings seem odd, then the decision to stick with them is even more baffling.' It was further stated, in June 2015, that 'the UN Human

Rights Council found that 'systematic, widespread and gross human-rights violations' were being committed in Eritrea. Yet the Home Office's latest reports on Eritrea, released in September, still rely heavily on the Danish evidence, which is cited more than anything else. The Home Office, which is under political pressure to reduce immigration, claims the updates take into account more recent sources, but offers no further explanation.

According to Home Office statistics, '[i]n the year ending June 2015, the largest number of applications for asylum came from nationals of Eritrea (3,568), followed by Pakistan (2,302) and Syria (2,204).' Recognition rates for Eritreans was 73 per cent in the first quarter of 2015, but this plummeted to 34 per cent during the second quarter of 2015 (UK Home Office 2015b; Lyons 2015). With the sharp rise in rejections of asylum applications filed by Eritrean asylum-seekers, the number of appeals lodged in the past six months has also increased dramatically. The judges who consider the appeals also seem to disagree with the Home Office's decisions, as 'Eritreans' success rate on appealing against rejections soared to 86% in the third quarter of this year, up from 31% in the same period last year. The number of appeals lodged in the past six months is greater than in the previous six years' (Lyons 2015).[10]

One of the consequences, as discussed previously, of the large-scale conscription of hundreds of thousands into the ENS has been the deprivation of Eritrean families of indispensable sources of income, resulting in the collapse of their livelihoods. However, with the worsening conditions in the ENS, the number of conscripts who have been fleeing and seeking asylum in the EU+ countries and elsewhere has been soaring and so have remittances. Remittance has become the single most important source of livelihood for many families. To underscore the importance of remittances to Eritrean families' survival, a key informant, Andom, said, 'In the past, people in the rural areas, who wanted to know about the wellbeing and economic status of a family used to ask, "how big is your farm and how many heads of cattle, goats, sheep, donkeys and chickens do you have?" These questions have become obsolete.' He continued, 'The routine question these days, including in the urban areas is, "How many daughters and sons do you have abroad?"' He further stated, 'This is because the families that are better off in Eritrea these days are those who have family members in exile and preferably females as they tend to be more selfless than male relatives.' Asmeret, a female key informant, stated, 'throughout Eritrea, remittance has become the backbone of most families' livelihoods. Economic differentiation is no longer dependent on ownership of land, property, livestock and businesses, but rather on the number of children one has in the diaspora.'

The families of those who are stuck in the open-ended ENS and those who are tortured and disappeared in the process are the main losers. However, for the lucky families whose loved ones make it safely to the EU+ countries, North America, Australia and New Zealand, even after

---

[10] In October 2016, the UK Upper Tribunal (Immigration and Asylum Chamber) in a landmark Country Guidance case rejected the much-criticised UK Home Office's policy on Eritrean asylum-seekers. See postscript on p. 191.

suffering harrowing experiences, the intolerable conditions in the ENS are a blessing in disguise. Not only have the families of the former conscripts and draft evaders who have joined the diaspora been able to overcome the livelihood crisis they previously faced, but also some of them have become conspicuous consumers whilst their neighbours whose loved ones are either stuck in the indefinite and oppressive ENS or died in the Sinai and the Sahara deserts or the Mediterranean Sea are suffering from agonising bereavement and grinding deprivation. As Ahmed stated, 'if you see a nice house, a nice car, women with too much jewellery, well-dressed and well-nourished individuals, you can bet that they have family members in Western Europe, North America, Australia and the Gulf States.' Saba agreed with Asmeret and stated, 'In present day Eritrea, the basis of social and economic differentiation is no longer ownership of the means of production or commercial enterprise. It is remittance.'

Although the total amount of remittances received by Eritrean families from their sons, daughters and relatives who exited from the intolerable conditions permeating the indefinite ENS is difficult to estimate, the numerous mushrooming neighbourhoods in different parts of Eritrean cities and towns, such as Senafe, Adi Keyih, Dekemhare, Debarwa, Keren, Barentu, Mendefera, and Bet Mekaė are testament to the large amounts of remittances received by families of ex-conscripts. Ironically, the government has been demolishing many of the houses built through remittances on the alleged grounds that they were built without planning permission (Eritrea: PFDJ Troops Shot 2015).

Other groups that have not been mentioned earlier among the beneficiaries are high-ranking military officers, smugglers and mediators. Although there is no evidence to show that the Eritrean government necessarily sanctions the illegal and corrupt activities of some high ranking army officers who are heavily involved with those organising the smuggling of draft evaders and conscripts, there is ample evidence to show that an unknown but considerable proportion of those who are fleeing the country have been doing so through highly organised networks operating under the direct or indirect auspices of high ranking military officers and their agents. The author has interviewed several informants who said that they were picked up by trucks belonging to the Eritrean Defence Forces from previously agreed locations inside Asmara. The key informants, interviewed independently of each other, said that either their relatives made the arrangements with the 'men behind the scene' who are usually high-ranking army officers or their agents, or they were approached by young men who operate as messengers for smugglers. The messengers are usually streetwise young boys who approach young men and women in the neighbourhoods and elsewhere and ask, 'Do you want to flee from the ENS? Help is available and we can arrange a meeting with a person who can provide safe passage to Sudan or Ethiopia.'

Given the high level of fear engendered by government agents no one admits to such a desire during the first two or three encounters. Some degree of trust must be established before such an intention could be indicated. Even when such an intention is voiced it is accompanied by a flurry of misinformation and innuendo concerning one's name, background, address and so on. Once a certain degree of rapport is established between the messenger and the would-be absconder, the former suddenly disappears from the scene and his place is taken by an agent of the 'boss' who has been operating behind the scenes. All the negotiations regarding the fees, methods of payment, transportation, timing and reception arrangements in Kassala town, Eastern Sudan, are negotiated with the agent of the 'boss'. At this stage, even on the date of departure, no money is exchanged. At the agreed date and time the individual is asked to mount a truck belonging to the Eritrean Defence Force. All such departures take place in the evening at about 8 or 9 p.m. The informants said that the lights are switched off at the back of the trucks and one could not recognise those who are travelling in the same truck. Those who left the country before the checkpoints were dismantled in 2011, the truck drivers or the agents, used certain signs or passwords to communicate with those guarding the checkpoints. The trucks were let through without being searched. In addition through prior arrangement no searches took place at the Sudanese border.

In Kassala they were taken to accommodation belonging to the smugglers or their agents. From there, relatives, mainly in the diaspora, were contacted and advised to transfer the fee to a bank account in Dubai, sometimes in Asmara or anywhere agents or collaborators of the smugglers reside. Once the fees were paid the individual concerned was released immediately. Others who needed further services would stay put until the smugglers made the necessary arrangements for further emigration. This might have involved travelling, for example, to Uganda, Kenya, South Africa, Libya or the Gulf States. Some smugglers' networks are transnational and they are involved throughout the chain, beginning from Eritrea, through the transit countries, namely Ethiopia, Sudan and Libya, and on to the final destination, the EU+ countries.

Not only has the construction of the wall at the Egyptian-Israeli border at the Sinai desert in 2013 brought to an end the secondary movement of Eritrean asylum-seekers and refugees from the Sudan to Israel through the Sinai desert, but also since then the Eritrea-Ethiopia-Sudan-Sahara desert-Libya-Mediterranean Sea route has flourished, where smuggling rather than trafficking has become the single most important mode of transnational migration. Eritrean smugglers, who collaborate with corrupt military officers in the transit countries, as well as subcontracting different parts of the operations to Sudanese and Libyan operators, exclusively run this route. Not only has the smuggling operation been perfected over time, but it is horizontally organised such that clearly defined duties are allocated to different actors, at the top of which chain are Eritreans and a few Ethiopians. The smuggling operations are highly lucrative multi-million dollar transnational activities in which corrupt police, army and immigration officials in both the transit countries and countries of origin are heavily involved.

The losers are the families whose sons and daughters are still trapped in the indefinite ENS, and those whose loved ones have perished in the Sinai desert at the hands of ruthless kidnappers and traffickers, those who fall victim to traffickers, who die of thirst and hunger in the Sahara desert, as well as those who die in the Mediterranean Sea. Families whose offspring and relatives are languishing in the bleak transit centres and refugee camps in northern Ethiopia and Eastern Sudan are bereft. Those families whose relatives and offspring are suffering in the various detention centres and prisons in the neighbouring and transit countries, as well as in Libya, Egypt, Yemen and other countries, are also among the losers, as well as the relatives of those who are sleeping rough in the central stations of Rome, Milan and Paris. To this must be added the thousands of Eritreans who, after surviving agonies at the hands of traffickers, smugglers, corrupt police and security officials in Eritrea and in the transit countries, the Sahara desert and Mediterranean Sea, languish in the French port of Calais en route to the United Kingdom.

Although the port town of Calais is located in one of the most developed countries in the world, France, and is within a stone's throw of the UK, the conditions under which the asylum-seekers from Afghanistan, Eritrea, Ethiopia, Sudan and Syria are living are so squalid that it is an affront to human dignity. Senior members of the UK government have been using dehumanising and highly unfitting descriptions of the asylum-seekers and migrants in Calais. The former British prime minister, David Cameron, for example, told ITV news on 30 July 2015 'that there was a "swarm of people coming across the Mediterranean" to seek a better life in Britain' (cited in Elgot and Taylor 2015). The foreign secretary, Phillip Hammond, also said 'millions of marauding African migrants pose a threat to the EU's standard of living and social structure' (in Perraudin 2015). Not only are such claims not evidence-based, but they are unfitting of a prime minister and foreign minister of a democratic country with a proud history of providing safe haven and succour to those who flee in search of safety and protection.

The history of post-independence Eritrean refugees and asylum-seekers is a history of survivors. We know nothing about those who perished throughout the displacement cycle, namely those who were killed at the borders as a result of the 'shoot to kill' policy of the Eritrean government. We also know nothing about those who died due to snakebites, attacks by wild animals or road accidents. We also don't know how many have perished at the hands of vicious traffickers and smugglers in Eastern Sudan, in the Sinai, the Sahara, Libya and the Mediterranean Sea. There are thousands of Eritrean families who are shedding 'red tears' due to the lack of information regarding the whereabouts of their loved ones. We also don't know the extent of sexual violence suffered by female asylum-seekers throughout the displacement cycle. The above brief discussion clearly indicates that, with few exceptions, the impact of the ENS on Eritrean conscripts, their families and the country has been calamitous.

9

Impact of the Open-Ended ENS
on Families and Conscripts

When I went home on a short leave, I found my parents in a wretched state. Most of their livestock died because there was no one to look after them. Weeds overtook all their farms except the small plot near the village, including the irrigated farm. I found my family reduced to abject poverty. This was the most painful thing I ever witnessed in my life. I crossed the Rubicon (*mewedata betsihe*) the moment I saw my mother and father on the verge of starvation. I love my country and I recognise that I have a duty to defend it against an external enemy. However, the government's claim notwithstanding, in 2005 there was no evidence whatsoever to indicate that Eritrea's sovereign existence was under threat. In the absence of a real threat to Eritrea's national security, my primary duty became to alleviate the plight of my family by any means.

Tekle (Interview, London, 17 February 2014)

This chapter analyses the impact of the Eritrean National Service (ENS) on the livelihoods of families, and conscripts' careers, survival and wellbeing. Further, the dissenting opinions of a few respondents who see the ENS as the ultimate good and worth sacrificing one's own and one's family's present and future interests are considered briefly. Eritrean society is predominantly agrarian. The large majority of households and individuals derive their livelihoods from subsistence agriculture and other related or unrelated off-farm income-generating activities. Agriculture and allied activities, such as crop production, livestock herding, forestry, and traditional fishing constitute the basis of livelihood for about 80 per cent of the population (World Bank 2015a). Given the rudimentary nature of the technology in use, agricultural production in the country is labour intensive. Due to a shortage of capital, a lack of credit facilities and small farm sizes, the overwhelming majority of subsistence farmers depend on family, rather than hired, labour. Given the arid and semi-arid nature of the environment within which nearly 80 per cent of the population eke out their meagre existence, rain-fed farming is a highly risky enterprise and, as a result, food security remains one of the major pre-occupations in the country (Kibreab 2009a, 2009c; World Bank 2015a). The Eritrean government's food security assessment at the household level, conducted as part of poverty assessment in the country, found that 68.8 per cent of the rural population lived below the poverty line, with the corresponding figure for urban areas at 31.2 per cent. According to the report, 66 per cent of Eritreans were 'poor and unable to obtain sufficient food (in terms of calories) and other essential goods and services to lead a healthy life' (Government of the State of Eritrea 2004: 7). A brief report by IFAD states, 'Poverty and food insecurity are wide spread and are on the increase. Even in years with adequate rainfall, about half of the food that the country requires has to be imported' (IFAD n.d.).

One of the consequences of livelihoods deriving from subsistence agriculture in arid and semi-arid regions is that the income farmers earn from farming, including from associated activities such as livestock herding, rarely covers the annual subsistence needs of families. In response, farmers adapt to the adverse situation by allocating their family labour to diverse economic activities, in order to spread the risk of failure and diversify their sources of income. This is achieved by expanding the possible range of economic activities within and outside of the agricultural sector. Diversification enables those families endowed with sufficient labour supply to earn incomes from diverse sources, such as seasonal rain-fed crop production, livestock herding, non-farm wage employment, transfers in the form of remittances, incomes earned from self-employment and migration. In rural Eritrea, incomes derived from the sale of animals and animal products supplement the incomes and diets of some families.

Household income diversification is, however, equally important in urban areas. Households in both rural and urban areas diversify their income sources for at least two reasons: namely, for the purposes of accumulation among the better off families, and among the worse off families for risk minimisation and coping with shocks caused by diminishing factor returns, including unfavourable weather conditions. Given the multiplicity and diversity of economic activities Eritrean families are engaged in, both in rural and urban areas, it can safely be stated that diversification of income, assets and economic activities constitute the foundation on which sustainability of the majority of households' livelihoods depend.

The best way to assess the impact of the open-ended, compulsory and universal ENS on the livelihoods of families and individual conscripts is therefore to examine how it affects the ability of the families and individual conscripts in both rural and urban areas to diversify their income sources, activities and assets. In order to understand the extent to which the ENS competes for families' scarce labour time, within both the rural and urban areas, the respondents who deserted from the ENS after serving for an average of six years were asked to state whether they had siblings who served in the Eritrean national service. In view of the compulsory and universal nature of the ENS, not surprisingly 84 per cent said that one or more than one of their siblings had served. Each respondent was asked to state how many of his or her siblings had served, with the results showing that 25 per cent, 28 per cent, 18 per cent, 7 per cent, 4 per cent, 2 per cent and 1 per cent had one, two, three, four, five, six and seven siblings, respectively, in the ENS at some time between 1994 and 2012.

In view of the fact that a considerable number of conscripts have been 'voting with their feet' in order to escape from what is considered by many analysts to be open-ended forced labour (HRW 2009; Kibreab 2009b, 2013; UNHCR 2015), as well as its negative effects on families' and conscripts' livelihoods, it is necessary to find out how many of the respondents' siblings were in active national service in 2012 when the interviews for the study were carried out. The results show that 37 per cent, 25 per cent, 10 per cent and 2 per cent have one, two, three and four siblings in the ENS, respectively. The data clearly show that a large majority of the respondents have one or more than one family members still participating in the open-ended ENS. The impact of this on the livelihoods of families and individuals has been devastating.

As evidenced earlier, at the heart of sustainable livelihood systems in the country lies the ability of families, both in the rural and urban areas, to allocate their family labour to diverse income-generating activities and to pull together the incomes of each family member in order to meet basic needs. In order to have some idea about the level of diverse economic activities the families of the respondents engaged in prior to the introduction of the ENS in May 1994, and how this changed as the result of the ENS, two key informants, one from an urban and another from a rural area, were interviewed in depth and were asked to describe the economic activities each of their family members engaged in and the extent to which they contributed to the family budget to meet the consumption needs of their families. They were also asked to state how this had changed as a result of conscription.

Abdu was from Asmara and comes from a large family. He has eight siblings: two sisters and six brothers. He was the third oldest in the family. When asked to state how each of his siblings contributed to the livelihood of his family before the introduction of the ENS he said:

> My oldest brother, Ibrahim, was a freedom fighter and did not make it to independence. He was martyred in 1990. My next oldest brother, Yasin, had a vegetable stall in the market. He bought vegetables from small horticulturalists and displayed and sold the commodities on his stall at reasonable profit margin. One of my young siblings, Suleiman, worked with Yasin after and before school hours. Yasin and the rest of the family pulled together their savings and paid for my sister, Zeneb, to emigrate to Saudi Arabia to work as domestic worker. My brother, Abdelwohab, worked as a tailor in a clothing shop and made women's dresses. Abdulaziz worked as a shop assistant at my uncle's business. Mahfuza, my young sister, was a student and helped my mother with the domestic chores outside her school hours. I had a small shop where I sold commodities to families in our neighbourhood. Each of us handed over our incomes to our mother and she gave us small amounts of pocket money. My sister, Zeneb, sent most of her income to my mother from Saudi Arabia. (Interview, London 25 February 2014)

When Abdu was asked to describe the situation of their family, he said, 'Although we were not affluent, we ate well, dressed well and our house was relatively comfortable. Life was relatively good.' At the heart of the success of the livelihood of the family lay the participation of the different members of the family in diverse income-generating activities which both enabled the family to spread the risk of failure and allowed for the strategy of pulling together the incomes of each family member to meet the collective subsistence and other needs of the family managed by the central figure, the mother, as head of the household. In fact, Abdu said that the combined incomes of the family members were not only enough to meet the basic consumption needs of the family, but he said that their mother was able to save enough to build an extension which provided sufficient accommodation for all of them. Abdu said, 'my mother had also an ambition to buy a second house for the future need of the family'.

He said that a few years after independence, in 1994, the government announced that all citizens aged between eighteen and forty should report to the authorities to undertake six months military training at Sawa as part of the eighteen months ENS, which had already received wide coverage in the government media outlets. As a result, Abdu and three of his siblings were called up in the first round. The family suddenly lost four of its main breadwinners. When asked how this affected his family's livelihood, he said, 'Our family's earnings were reduced by over 90 per cent instantly.' Nevertheless, he stated that 'The only positive thing at that time was that everybody knew that the duration of the service was limited to eighteen months only. My mother made some arrangements to fill the gap that was created by our departure.' Abdu said that a sister and brother were called up during the second round, so that six members of the family were then mobilised, which had a dramatic impact on the family's income. After serving for eighteen months all were demobilised and resumed their previous occupations. When all of the adult members of Abdu's family subsequently went into national service, the family suffered a considerable loss of opportunity cost, not only in terms of income but also, more importantly, in terms of loyal customers. Two of Abdu's siblings were also called up during the third and fourth rounds. He said, 'although the effect on our family's income was considerable, it was far from being disastrous. At that time, most Eritreans, including my mother were in favour of the national service. It was a small price that had to be paid to re-build the war-torn economy and to foster national unity.' He added, 'My mother saw this as a tribute of honour to our martyred brother, Ibrahim, and his fallen comrades.'

According to Abdu, everything changed after the border war broke out against Ethiopia in May 1998. He said:

> Six of us were mobilised to fight in the border war and this broke the backbone of our sustainable livelihood. After we were re-called, each of us was assigned to the war fronts in different parts of the country. Throughout the two years, some of us lost contact with each other. Although it was clear that so many lives were lost, the government was unwilling to inform the families regarding the whereabouts of their loved once. My mother could not cope with the situation and developed heart problems. She passed away in 2005.

He said that when the government finally announced the names of the 19,000 martyred Eritreans, 'my brother, Yasin, was in the list. This broke our hearts. Our family's stable economy and wellbeing were shattered.'

As is the case with all conscripts, those who survived were not demobilised either. Abdu said, 'With most of us in the indefinite national service, our family's livelihood collapsed and we felt completely hopeless to deal with the situation.' He added:

> In desperation, three of us decided to flee the country independently. My brother, Abdelwohab, was caught at the border and was taken back to Eritrea and subjected to horrendous kind of torture and subsequently detained in a shipping container for a long time. Abdulaziz and I made it to the Sudan, but

unfortunately, my brother Abdulaziz, was taken hostage in the Sinai desert when trying to cross to Israel. The hostage-takers demanded US $20,000 of ransom for his release and threatened to raise it to US $30,000 if not paid within the given period. Our uncle contacted our relatives in Jeddah who kindly contributed part of the ransom, but we were forced to sell our house to secure his release. After he was released, Abdelaziz managed to cross into Israel and has been sending money to our family in Eritrea. Zeneb and he sent me money, which I used to pay for smugglers first to go to Libya across the Sahara and through the Mediterranean Sea to Italy. From Italy, I managed to come to Britain via Calais, France.

I asked him whether the economic status of his family in Eritrea has improved. He said, 'My sister in Saudi Arabia, my brother in Israel and I send a substantial proportion of our incomes to our family in Asmara and thanks God, our family is no longer in a desperate situation although my siblings are still living in a rented accommodation.' He further pointed out that two of his siblings are still in the ENS, fourteen years after they were first called up.

Tekle is from rural Eritrea where mixed farming is the main basis of livelihood. I asked him to describe the basis of his family's livelihood and said:

> I am the oldest among six siblings, five boys and one girl. My father was a farmer who cultivated small plots of land where we produced rain-fed food crops and hay for animal feed. We planted varieties of crops, which provided our family adequate nutrition. We had also a small-irrigated plot where we planted different types of vegetables for sale. We consumed a small portion of the vegetables. Most of the produce was sold in the nearby market. My father used the proceeds to pay taxes, to buy commodities, such as red pepper, salt, cloths, kerosene and farm tools. (Interview, London, 17 February 2014)

When asked to describe how each family member contributed to the family budget, he said:

> It depended on the season. A few weeks before the planting season, my father, my brothers, Berhane, Wolday and I cleared the land. We terraced it to conserve soil and water. We also carried manure on our backs from our village to the farms and prepared the land for planting. When the rains fell, my father planted the crops using oxen ploughs. My mother and sister picked up the weeds by following after the plough. This activity besides being less labour intensive, did not take longer than two weeks. Whilst my father, mother and my sister planted the crops, three of us migrated to the nearby towns and engaged in different income-generating activities. During the dry seasons, Berhane worked as an assistant in a construction site, Wolday as a waiter in a teashop and Teages worked as an assistant in a vegetable stall. Three of us lived together in a single room to cut the costs of living. My brother, Hagos, looked after our livestock. After making good the expenses, we sent most of our remaining earnings to my father. My fifth brother, Tesfay, emigrated to the Gulf States and sent most of his income to my parents. My father pulled together our incomes and bought water pump and planted vegetables. Not only did this enable us to expand our irrigated plot, but also we were no longer dependent on the erratic and unreliable rainfall. This stabilised the sources of our income and made life more predictable.

In Tekle's view, had it not been for the ability of each family member to do his or her bit to contribute to the family's livelihood by pooling together their incomes derived from diverse economic activities, everybody in the family would have been worse off and the wellbeing of the family would have sunk to an abysmal level.

In an extensive one-to-one interview I asked Tekle to state how the ENS, and later the Eritrea-Ethiopia border war, affected the wellbeing and livelihood of his family. He said:

> [t]he war and the open-ended ENS destroyed the wellbeing and the livelihood of our family. Our family's livelihood was detrimentally affected when five of us were called up to participate in the ENS in the first three rounds. However, the negative effects on our family were reversed when four of us were demobilised after serving for eighteen months. When the war broke out, we were called back to defend the country. None of us objected when we were recalled in anticipation that we would be discharged once the war was over. To our dismay, when the war was over, the government instead of demobilising the hundreds of thousands intensified its mobilisation efforts throughout the country. As a result, not only did the livelihood of our family collapse, but also the wellbeing of our parents and of every member of our family deteriorated.

Tekle further pointed out that his parents' health and wellbeing deteriorated, not only because of loss of income, but also due to the government's failure to announce the names of those who were martyred in the border war. He said, 'the uncertainty about whether my brothers were dead or alive consumed my parents. Their wellbeing and health deteriorated. Finally, when the government announced the names of the martyrs, two of my brothers were in the list. This tragic news almost killed my mother. She has never recovered from the devastating shock she suffered when the she heard the news.'

Tekle pointed out that he went home on a short leave in November 2005 and found his parents in a wretched state. Most of their livestock had died because there was no one to look after them. Weeds overtook all of their farms except the small plot near the village, including the irrigated farm. He said that he found his family reduced to abject poverty. 'This was the most painful thing I ever witnessed in my life,' he said. When I asked him what he did to ameliorate the situation, he said, 'I crossed the Rubicon (mewedaêta betsihe) the moment I saw my mother and father on the verge of starvation. I love my country and I recognise that I have a duty to defend it against an external enemy.' However, the government's claim notwithstanding, in 2005 there was no evidence that indicated that Eritrea's sovereign existence was under threat. 'In the absence of a real threat to Eritrea's national security, my primary duty became to alleviate the plight of my family by any means'. When asked to explain the means by which he could do that, he said,

> The government has brought our country to its knees (*amberkikoma*) and hence no solution could be found from within for the time being. I had to seek a solution elsewhere. There was no way I could return to my unit. Instead, I decided to flee the country disregarding the potential risks. Before I left, I managed to pass a message to my brother who was in the ENS. I fled to Sudan and arrived at Kassala after one week safely.

I asked him whether he used the services of smugglers to cross into Sudan. He said, 'smugglers are ruthless exploiters. One needs a lot of money to benefit from their services. I could not afford such a thing. Luckily, most of my assignments were in the Eritrea-Sudan border area. I was familiar with the location and had no difficulty in crossing without paying a penny to the bloodsuckers and soldiers.'

He said that he contacted his brother, Tesfay, who was already in the Gulf States, and other relatives who were in North America and Western Europe seeking help. After he received the remittances he needed, he hired the services of a smuggler and began the dangerous journey to Italy through the Sahara desert, Libya and Mediterranean Sea. He was detained twice in Libya and the decrepit boat they used to cross the Mediterranean Sea capsized. He was one of the few rescued by the Italian navy within the Mare Nostrum programme. From Italy he went to Calais with the help of smugglers and, after spending about one month in the 'jungle', he crossed into the UK where he sought asylum and was soon granted refugee status. As his primary goal was to escape from the open-ended ENS and to alleviate the plight of his starving and ailing parents, he wasted no time in finding a job. He worked day and night below the minimum wage and sent most of his earnings to his parents.

Tekle said that he received a message from his brother, Wolday, in May 2012 saying he had deserted from the ENS and he was in the Shagarab refugee camp in eastern Sudan where the risk of kidnapping was imminent (see UNHCR 2013; CAPERI 2014; UN News Centre 2015). He was waiting to receive help from him and his brother, Tesfay, to proceed to Khartoum en route to Italy via the Sahara desert, Libya and across the Mediterranean Sea. He said:

> I had no savings at all and I had to borrow money from my friends to send him the amount he needed to help him come to Europe. He made all the necessary arrangements using the money Tesfay and I sent him. After spending some time in detention in Libya, he set off to cross the Mediterranean Sea in a rickety boat. After he left for Italy, I lost contact with him and my life turned into a living hell. A couple of weeks passed without any news from him or about him. I heard later, i.e. in July 2012, a boat that left for Italy had capsized off the Tunisian coast and all the passengers except one Eritrean perished. After all attempts to find him failed, I assumed that he was one of the dead.

I checked and indeed such a tragic accident had taken place on 9 July 2012. On 12 July the UNHCR reported, '[i]t is with great sadness that UNHCR received the news that 54 people perished attempting the sea journey from Libya to Italy. According to the sole survivor, an Eritrean man, 55 people boarded the boat in Libya in late June. He reported that all the other passengers died of dehydration during a fifteen-day ordeal' (2012). Tekle said, 'the first mindboggling question that sent shock waves down across my spine was: what do I say to my parents?' He added, 'I also feel guilty for having contributed to his death. If it were not for the money I sent to him, he would not have been able to attempt to cross the Mediterranean Sea.' This form of agonising guilt was shared by a number of interviewees and respondents who sent money to their relatives to join them in Western Europe and Israel, who subsequently vanished in the Sahara, Sinai or on the Mediterranean Sea.

Before he recovered from his deep sense of loss and bereavement he received a message from his brother, Teages, who said that he was in the Shagarab refugee camp in eastern Sudan and asked for his help to continue the perilous journey to Western Europe through the Sahara desert, Libya and the Mediterranean Sea. Tekle said that although he was delighted about his brother's safe arrival in Sudan he was not sure whether he could again be a party to a risky action which had already cost him and his family the life of a loved one. He said, 'I don't know how to deal with the dilemma. Leaving him in Sudan means condemning him to suffering and exposing him to the risk of kidnapping and trafficking and helping him to try the dangerous route via the Sahara and the Mediterranean Sea may also mean potential death.' He said, 'I was paralysed and lost my ability to think objectively in a balanced and rational way [...] How could I when I had contributed to the tragic death of my own brother?' I asked him what he intended to do and he said, 'I wish I knew. For the time being my brother and I have helped him to come to Khartoum and we are sending him money regularly to meet his basic needs, but the challenge regarding his future seems to be still insuperable at the moment. We are postponing the critical decision hoping against hope that the tyrants in Asmara would be removed from power and those citizens who are languishing in the camps in Sudan and Ethiopia, Egypt as well as in the squalid detention camps in Libya would be able to return in safety and dignity.' He also stated, 'I know I am dreaming, but dreamers are agents of change. If I don't dream, I cease to live.' The ENS has had tragic and devastating effects on the livelihoods of conscripts' families and has disrupted conscripts' education and careers. As we shall see later, those who are driven out of the country by the open-ended national service frequently suffer severe punishments, lack of freedom, an end to economic and career development opportunities and family pressures, as well as facing life-threatening risks at the hands of ruthless traffickers and smugglers, and corrupt military officers in Eritrea, Ethiopia, Sudan, Egypt and Libya.

The data presented earlier elicited from two in-depth interviews with deserters are almost identical to the data gathered from the respondents. The latter respondents were asked to state whether the ENS has positively or negatively impacted on conscripts' families. Ninety-six per cent said that the impact of conscription on families' livelihoods, wellbeing and overall survival has been catastrophic. This is not surprising because, as previously noted, most families make ends meet by pulling together the meagre incomes earned by every family member from diverse income-generating activities. By depriving families of their most invaluable resource – family labour – the ENS has shattered the nerve centre of most families' livelihoods and consequently brought unbearable pressure to bear on conscripts. The national service has become like a cancerous growth that eats into the livelihood systems of families, both in the rural and urban areas. For example, the World Food Programme (WFP 2004) states: '[t]he recruitment [...] in the productive age into the national service deprives households from a breadwinner and imposes an additional burden on the families left behind. Often, these families are then dependent on the income of female household members, whose livelihood opportunities are extremely limited by tradition and culture and who have to assume this responsibility in addition to their multiple roles as mothers, caretakers, housewives, farmers, etc. Not surprisingly, the Eritrean Rural Livelihood Security Assessment classifies half of the households depending on a female's income as poor.' It was stated further, 'At the time of the mission one of the most important constraints to sustainable livelihoods in rural areas was shortage of labour; in large part due to the ... the number of able bodied men (and to a lesser extent women) in national service. Even areas of Eritrea that had benefited from adequate rains were not fully sown to crops in 2003' (FAO 2003: 45).

A study conducted by the FAO/WFP reached the same conclusion, stating that the conscription of the able-bodied productive labour force into the ENS has broken the backbone of families' coping strategies: 'Casual labour is the most normal alternative form of income generation or coping strategy for the majority of Eritreans. *The current severe shortage of labour caused by the absence of many young men in National Service is not only affecting the performance of normal productive activities, such as ploughing and weeding, but is also curtailing coping strategies, further exacerbating food insecurity at household level*' (FAO/WFP 2002: section 6.4, emphasis added).

One of the consequences is that malnutrition has become rampant. Although the FAO's study was conducted at a time when the Eritrean government had not completely phased out food aid, the effect of the shortage of labour on the nutritional status of most families who lost their productive members to the open-ended ENS is remarkable. The FAO stated: '[m]alnutrition has become a major concern in Eritrea. Forty per cent of all Eritrean young children and an estimated 41 per cent of all women are chronically malnourished. Reports indicate that 38 per cent of children below three years of age are stunted, 16 per cent are wasted and 44 per cent are underweight. Micronutrient deficiencies are common' (FAO/WFP 2002). The United Nations Office for the Coordination of Humanitarian Affairs (OCHA 2012) also states, 'UNICEF and WHO support over 260 community-based and facility based therapeutic feeding centres in the country, indicative of persistent food insecurity at household levels.' In spite of the problem of widespread malnutrition throughout the country, the government continued with its restrictions on NGOs and UN bodies. The US Department of State (2011), for example, said that the Eritrean government refused to allow humanitarian food distribution by NGOs and the WFP, but allowed UNICEF to continue its supplementary feeding programmes under the supervision of the Ministry of Health (US Deartment of State 2011). The government, by requiring NGOs and UN organisations to obtain permission to travel outside the capital, effectively denied access to relief organisations to the rural areas. Although the WFP has an office it does not have any programmes operating in the country. The report states, '*Several UN organizations and NGOs cited high levels of malnutrition as a concern which could not be adequately addressed with the current limited feeding programs*' (Ministry of Health 2011, emphasis added). The FAO and WFP (2005) concluded in a joint study:

> *The shortage of labour was observed everywhere. The main cause of this shortage is the conscription of men into defence forces and national service for long periods of time...* Due to continued critical shortage of labour, the wage rates this year have been observed to be very high ranging from 30 to 50 ENN/day for digging wells or for house construction activity. Since farmers cannot afford to pay such high

wages for different farming activities; critical field operations such as weeding have generally been neglected. Eritrea has a very high incidence of female-headed households, which are often dependent on hired labour to cultivate their land on a sharecropping basis. This is further enforced by the traditional disapproval of a woman operating a plough, especially in the highlands. (FAO/WFP 2005, emphasis added)

According to the Human Development report 2011, Eritrea has a Human Development Index (HDI) of 0.349, ranking 177th out of 187 countries. In comparison to sub-Saharan Africa's HDI, which increased from 0.365 in 1980 to 0.463 today, Eritrea's HDI is far below average. The country's HDI value and rank for 2013 was 0.381, which placed it 182nd out of 187 countries. Between 2010 and 2013 the country's HDI value increased by 2.1 per cent, and '[b]etween 1980 and 2013, Eritrea's life expectancy at birth increased by 19.6 years, mean years of schooling stayed the same and expected years of schooling increased by 0.7 years. Eritrea's GNI per capita decreased by about 21.2 per cent between 1995 and 2013' (UNDP 2014). Except for life expectancy at birth, these data demonstrate the bleak state Eritrea is in.

The proportion of the country's population living below the national poverty line is estimated at an average of 66 per cent. According to the national poverty assessment the incidence of food poverty, as reflected in total number of people who are unable to meet their basic food requirements, is very high: 70–80 per cent of the population (Compressive Africa Agriculture Development Programme (CAADP) 2013: 4). Eritrea thus has high stunt rates relative to countries in the same region and income group (World Bank 2011). UNICEF's report, based on rapid screening using mid-upper arm circumference and conducted in April and May 2010, also showed that global acute malnutrition rates among children under five range from 5 per cent to 11.7 per cent in the six regions of the country. Diarrhoeal disease related to poor sanitation is also among the three major causes of underage mortality (UNICEF 2011). According to the FAO (2009) two-thirds (66 per cent) of Eritrea's total households are food insecure and the country's global ranking of stunting prevalence is 19th highest out of 136 countries (UNICEF 2009, cited in World Bank 2011).

The qualitative data generated from the open-ended questions answered by respondents shows that the ENS has a devastating impact on the families of conscripts. According to R #003 the 'Duration has been extended from eighteen months to eighteen years and the negative effect of this on families has been dramatic and as a result, life has become extremely burdensome to families who lost their sons and daughters to the national service.' Implicit in this respondent's observation is that had the duration of the ENS been limited to eighteen months as was originally stipulated in Proc. 82/1995, its effect on families of conscripts would have been less dramatic. R #006 stated, 'Families are left without support and consequently lose economic and moral support of their offspring and as a result suffer different adversities.' In Eritrean society family members are, as seen earlier, sources of income as well as moral and social support. In view of the fact that the majority of Eritrean families live dangerously close to the subsistence margin, the marginal utility derived from each family member's contribution to a family's income is high. The families who lost their offspring to the ENS suffered substantial loss of income. This respondent further stated, 'your life is wasted for nothing. Your parents suffer due to lack of support from their offspring.' Given the socially defined responsibility of each family member to support and sustain their families, this respondent views the inability to provide support to one's family as a waste of life. R #008 stated, 'Families are left heart-broken. Married men leave their wives and children alone for unlimited period. It is terrible.' When conscripts join the ENS most parents are uncertain whether their loved ones will safely return, especially after May 1998 when the border war against Ethiopia broke out resulting in the death of 19,000 Eritreans[1] and the maiming of an unknown number, but probably tens of thousands. It is with this in mind that the respondent said that parents are left heartbroken when their loved ones join the ENS. With regard to the impact of the ENS on the respondents' families she stated, 'The effect on my family has been calamitous. They invested in me to go to university so that I could earn an income and help them. They were afflicted with chronic illnesses such as blood pressure. They are disaffected like all Eritrean families who lost their loved ones to the ENS.'

Given the importance of each family member's contribution to the livelihoods of families, especially among the poor, the opportunity cost of sending children to school instead of working to earn an income is very high. Families send their children to school in anticipation of rewards later for the parents and the students concerned, thereby forgoing the benefits they could have had from their income. It is not surprising therefore that the respondents' parents were afflicted with illnesses such as blood pressure issues when they were left without carers. To underscore the critical role children play in the maintenance of their parents during their old age, R #112 said, 'Families have been left without someone to look after them in their later years. Children are held hostage and businesses die.' It is not only older parents who are suffering due to lack of carers, but also businesses that are collapsing because of lack of labour, in this respondent's view. As we saw before, the findings of the IMF and the World Bank show that the ENS has, by creating an acute shortage of labour, dramatically reduced the country's competitiveness in the regional and international markets, because of the high costs of production caused by this shortage (World Bank 2002a; IMF 2003). The respondent's account is consistent with the findings of the World Bank and the IMF. It is not only businesses that rely on hired labour that are affected negatively, but equally those that depend on their own family's labour supply. This is because business owners who were within the age of conscription were ordered to close down their firms and join the ENS. R #119, for example, stated, 'Many of the families that owned businesses were negatively affected because the breadwinners [the owners] were conscripted and their children were left on their own helplessly' without anyone to support them. The respondent

[1] 'Eritrea 19,000 Eritrean soldiers killed during the war', Afrol News, 22 June, available at http://afrol.com/News2001/eri005_war_vicitms.htm (last accessed 28 November 2001).

further stated that the ENS has '*destroyed the fabric of the family and its livelihood*' (emphasis added).

Some families lost all their sons and daughters to the ENS and were left without breadwinners and carers. This was the case with R #009's family. She stated, 'On my own experience: I am the only daughter with three brothers in my family and going to Sawa left my family with no one to look after them and this was the cause of my mother's death.' When the family lost four of their children to the ENS the pressure became unbearable, resulting in the death of the respondent's mother. This reminds me of the misfortune that befell the family that used to live next door to our house in Asmara before they moved into their own home in Mai Temenay in the early 1980s. When I returned to Eritrea in the immediate post-independence days in 1991, I visited the family and found out that they had lost all their children in the war of independence. Only their granddaughter, who was born in the base areas of the EPLF, survived. When none of their children came home, the father suspected that they had been martyred and he suffered from prompt paralysis. He was deeply religious and when I tried to console him he said, 'We should be grateful to God. At least, our granddaughter has survived.' I visited the family again in January 2000 and found that the father had passed away. When I asked the mother where her granddaughter was, she said, 'She is in *hagerawi agelglot* (national service).' When I asked her, 'how could the government do that to a family who paid so much for the liberation of the country?' the mother said, 'Is there any family in Eritrea who has not lost children in the liberation struggle? *Kem seba* (like everybody else).' This case indicates, on the one hand, the insensitivity of the system and, on the other, the virtuousness and powerful sense of patriotism of the mother, and probably of other mothers in her situation.

When R #010 was asked to assess the impact of the ENS on families of conscripts he said, 'I need to be very clear here. If the ENS has been applied as it was in the law, it would have been good for both [the country and families] but I can understand the regime has taken my golden age for nothing...' It was not only this respondent who thought that the main cause of the damaging effect of the ENS on families and conscripts was not its compulsory and universal nature but its open-endedness. In this respondent's view, had the ENS been limited to eighteen months, as stipulated in the proclamation on national service, the benefits to be had by both conscripts and families would have outweighed the costs. R #123 agreed, stating, 'Had the Eritrean national service been similar to other national services over a limited period, it would have been good for all concerned. However, the Eritrean national service is forcible and when three to four members of a family are conscripted for an indefinite period, the family becomes impoverished.' In a similar manner, R #152 states, 'Because the ENS [is] dysfunctional, its impact on families has been devastating. Had it been implemented in accordance with the spirit and letter of the proclamation on the ENS, its impact on families would have been positive.' R #159 also observed, 'It [the ENS] is compulsory and sometimes three to five siblings serve simultaneously.'

It was only after its indefinite extension that the costs outstripped the benefits and destroyed the foundation – family labour – on which the livelihoods of most families were rooted. Along the same line, Saba, female graduate from the defunct University of Asmara, in an in-depth personal interview said:

> The Eritrean government is within its sovereign right to impose on its citizens the duty of performing national service legally, but this has to be framed and enforced in a manner that respects the fundamental human rights of servers and should be beneficial to them and their families, as well as the country. Servers may benefit from learning and bonding with their compatriots hailing from different religious, geographic and cultural backgrounds. They may also acquire skills that enable them to earn an income after demobilisation. Families may benefit from the transformative effect of national service, including inculcation of discipline and responsibility. The country may benefit from the unifying effect of national service, labour contribution and building of infrastructure and defence capability. (Interview, Geneva, 23 November 2013)

Although she thought that eighteen months as stipulated in the Proc. No. 82/1995 may be considered long, had the government respected its own law and demobilised each conscript after this time, and collaborated with international donors and financial institutions, such as the World Bank, United Nations and international and national NGOs within a political framework based on good governance, the benefits accruing to conscripts' families, the conscripts themselves and the country would have outweighed the losses.

It is interesting to note that even the only respondent who considers the impact of the ENS to be generally positive thinks that its indefinite nature is negative. The respondent (R #128) said, 'In the ENS, one learns a lot of things. That is why in our country all people accept the idea of national service because of its positive effect. *But the indefinite national service's influence is definitely negative*' (emphasis added). Among the respondents I interviewed none of them supports the extension of the obligation beyond the eighteen months stipulated in Proc. 82/1995. Chronologically, this can be traced to the post-1998–2000 border war and the introduction of the WYDC in May 2002 (see Kibreab 2009b).

In a similar vein, R #013 said, 'Families forgo the benefits they could [have] derived from their children.' R #016 said, 'Parents expect a lot of help from their offspring, but when all go to national service, they are left alone and suffer as a result. I am the oldest in the family. In my absence, my parents faced lots of problems when they fell ill.' In the views of these respondents' the ENS is depriving families of a crucial resource with high opportunity cost. It is common in Eritrea for parents to forgo their short-term interests to invest in their children's upbringing, training and education, partly to help them to be economically and socially independent later in life, but also in anticipation of future help in their old age. This kind of help provided by offspring during their parents' old age in societies where there are no provisions of public or private insurances is indispensable. This is exacerbated by the fact that in post-independence Eritrea there is no workplace or state pension, so that individuals are solely dependent on their own savings or family support when they retire.

In view of this, the ENS is not only eroding the livelihood systems of the society but also threatening the survival of elders after retirement. If their children spend most of their productive lives in the ENS they will be unable to support themselves and their own families later in life, let alone their retired parents. From this perspective the ENS is stifling the present livelihood systems in the country, but also has considerable future implications on the subsistence security and welfare of most families.

When asked to state how the ENS affected her family, R #022 said, 'we all went to national service as a result, the economy of our family collapsed. The negative impact is obvious if a family member goes to national service and does not return.' As seen earlier, at the start of the chapter, at the heart of families' subsistence security lies family labour, and it is not surprising therefore that this respondent's family's sources of sustenance collapsed when all those who were able to work and contribute to the economy of the family were taken away to serve in the open-ended ENS without remuneration. Similarly, R #027 stated, 'It is impossible to look after one's family and therefore the negative impact of the ENS on families is considerable.' According to the National Living Standard Measurement survey (LSMS), 'the overall poverty estimate for Eritrea is 66 per cent, with 37 per cent living in extreme poverty (below the food poverty line)' (Government of Eritrea 2005: 4). This suggests that two-third of the population live from hand to mouth and the loss of any able-bodied family member, let alone up to five or more, is likely to undermine and over time obliterate the basis of subsistence security for most families.

In 2013 life expectancy at birth was 62.9 (UNDP 2014). Although the stipulated age range in the proclamation on national service is eighteen to forty years, after the border war and the introduction of the WYDC in May 2002, it has become open-ended and therefore there are tens of thousands over fifty years old still serving in the army and in the civil sector within the framework of the ENS. Unless the government changes its policy in this regard, many of the conscripts are likely to reach the end of their lives without ever having been able to fend for themselves and their families. This is exacerbated by the government's decision in 2012 to expand the militarisation of Eritrean society by distributing arms to older civilian citizens up to the age of seventy, due to either its worry 'about a future threat from outside' or in order 'to make up for desertions from the military' (*Indian Ocean Newsletter* 2012, cited in Tronvoll and Mekonen 2014: 181). The consequence of this high level of militarisation on the livelihood systems of the country and families is cataclysmic. When asked to assess the impact of the ENS on families R #028 said, 'For a person with a family to work without pay for a long time in the context of the high rate of inflation, the picture is vivid.' In Eritrea, especially in the rural areas, boys and girls establish families at an early age. Even without the extension of the duration of the ENS many of those who are required to participate in the service are likely to have families of their own. This became far worse after the ENS became open-ended. Even those who joined the ENS when they were single now have families of their own without the means to support them. The common practice is to leave children with their grandparents, further exacerbating the burden on families who have already lost their breadwinners.

It is not only the nature of the service that is the problem, but also the fact that the conscripts are paid a pittance and, as a result, most families that lose their children to the ENS become impoverished. This is what R #040 was referring to when he said, 'The *agelglot* (conscripts) are not paid enough and families suffer poverty as a result.' After serving for eighteen months, conscripts receive 450 Eritrean Nakfa (ERN) which, according to the official exchange rate, is equivalent to US$ 30 and at the black market rate US$ 9 a month. The UN Special Rapporteur on the Situation of Human Rights in Eritrea described the consequence of the ENS on the livelihoods of families and on the social fabric of the society aptly, observing insightfully that it has been 'affecting the very fabric of Eritrean society, and its core unit, the family' (Keetharuth 2013: 17–18). Along the same lines, R #042 states that the indefinite ENS impoverishes the conscripts as well as their families. This is because, she observes, 'One's family forgoes manpower and income that would have been derived from family members that are lost to national service.' The cause of impoverishment, according to this respondent, is the high opportunity cost forgone by conscripts and their families. For example, as R #151 observed, 'when all children belonging to a family are conscripted, parents are stripped of their labour supply and fall into the poverty trap.' R #153 used an apt metaphor to describe the predicament of Eritrean families who lose their children to the ENS. She said, 'Eritrean parents are losing their children like a chicken whose chicks are snatched by a vulture bird. They are faced with endless problems.' The use of the metaphor 'vulture' is instructive. A chicken whose chicks are snatched by vultures can do little else but helplessly watch the vulture as it flies away with the chick. Reflecting on her family's situation, R #176 lamented, 'My family have fallen into abject poverty and are forced to lead a squalid life.'

The respondents were asked to comment on the generalisation that 'the national service is a waste of time and resources'. Out of 187 who commented on the generalisation, 36 per cent strongly agreed, 29 per cent agreed, and 26 and 7 per cent disagreed and disagreed strongly, respectively. The majority, 65 per cent, think that the ENS is a waste of time and resources, whilst only 33 per cent think it is not. This is because of the high opportunity cost and high level of inefficiency permeating the programme. The respondents were asked to comment on the generalisation that the 'ENS is inefficient because it is difficult to motivate the conscripts and it is without an end, as well as without opportunities for promotion or pay increase'. Out of the 189 who answered the question, 52 per cent and 33 per cent respectively strongly agreed and agreed with the generalisation. Only a small minority of 12 per cent disagreed, and 3 per cent disagreed strongly. The damaging effects of the ENS on the conscripts and their families can also be surmised from the following data. The respondents were asked to comment on the generalisation that 'the ENS wrecks the lives of *agelglot* (conscripts) and their families'. Not surprisingly, 87 per cent agreed and strongly agreed with the generalisation. Only 12 per cent disagreed with the generalisation.

In the same vein, R #046 states, 'The national service exposes one to hunger and poverty', further stating: 'Beyond the stipulated time of eighteen months, national service becomes a waste of time.' There was general agreement among the conscripts that had the national service been limited to the legally stipulated eighteen months it would not have constituted such a waste of time and resources. The impact of the ENS on farming families that depend on family labour is remarkable. R #048, for example, said, 'Our farms are left without protection and destroyed by elephants. Many families have suffered as a result.' She added, 'When my brothers and my husband left our family to join the national service, my mother-in-law and I were left alone and we could not look after the livestock.'

According to the ideology that governs the gender-based division of labour in Eritrea looking after livestock, especially cattle and camels, is a masculine activity. Hence, although she did not elaborate further, unattended livestock often become easy prey for wild animals. R #049 stated, 'All economic activities and businesses based on family labour have collapsed because all the labour force has gone to NS. The reason the Eritrean youth is in a sad state of indefinite limbo is because of the ENS. They can neither marry nor establish families. Their lives are in danger because of the indefinite ENS.' In this respondent's view, not only has the indefinite ENS strangled all types of economic activities based on family labour, but also the conscripts are in a liminal state and consequently suffer from uncertainty and insecurity. Although this respondent states that the conscripts can neither marry nor establish families, the data collected for this study show that when the conscripts lost hope of demobilisation they married each other without having the means to support families. Not only has this exacerbated the economic hardship of parents who are forced to look after their grandchildren and their mothers, but also thousands of children are raised without being cared for by their fathers.

Families who had only one son or daughter were the worst affected when called up for national service. For example, R #053, who was the only child in his family, said, 'I used to support my parents. When I went to national service, they had no one to look after them.' In a country where there is no provision of state or voluntary-sector sponsored social welfare, the loss of the single breadwinner can be devastating for families. Some families lost all their family members to the ENS and their livelihoods collapsed as a result. For example, R #055 said, 'My parents lost three of their sons to the national service and were left with no one to help them.' The effect of the ENS was the same on R #069's family. She said, 'My parents were left with no one to support them economically, and had no one to care for them when they fell ill.' In Eritrea, where there are no nursing homes or care centres, the elderly are solely dependent on their families. The same is true of those who are disabled or suffer with long-term illnesses. Because the government makes no exceptions on the grounds of family needs the number of elderly people and those with physical and mental disabilities, as well as long-term illnesses, who are left without carers is high. With regard to this, Zerom, a key informant, said, 'The Eritrean government's cruelty and immorality is boundless. There is nothing worse than depriving ailing old parents and disabled people of their carers and breadwinners without making alternative provisions. Eritrea today is full of uncared old, disabled and poorly citizens.' R #151 reinforced this view by observing, 'Because I went to NS, my parents were left with nobody to look after them.' R #167 reinforced the devastating effect of the ENS on families, stating, 'The effect is adverse because many of the *agelglot* are forced to abandon their families and their work. Their spouses, parents and their children are left without anyone who can work and care for them.' A similar view was expressed by R #152 who stated, 'I am the youngest in my family. Two of my older brothers were in national service simultaneously with me. Our elderly parents were left with no one to help them to fetch drinking water. Both our parents and us spent the time lamenting and crying.' Depending on the location of respondents' villages, in some parts of Eritrea, owing to the arid and semi-arid nature of the environment, water sources, especially during the dry season, can be far from villages and its collection can be arduous and highly labour intensive. Not only do the families who lose all their offspring to the ENS suffer from food shortage, but also from water and firewood poverty.

R #073 captures the predicament of the families who lose their breadwinners to the ENS, stating, 'limitless conscription puts many families on the verge of starvation as their breadwinners are held captive in the military'. The word 'captive', used by the respondent to describe the plight of the conscripts who are forced to serve against their will at the risk of inhuman treatment in the indefinite ENS, which has over time degenerated into a modern form of slavery or forced labour, is edifying (see HRW 2009; Kibreab 2009b, 2013; HRC 2014: 69–76, 2015). The consequences of this, according to the respondent, are, 'isolation, poverty, weakening of responsibility. People have been denied the ability to help their families.' The Eritrean government has been depriving families of their breadwinners and carers without providing a substitute and, as a result, its policy of indefinite national service has degenerated into an instrument of economic and social impoverishment and deprivation. As R #101 put it, 'The NS is a means by which the *agelglot* are deprived of their rights and reduced into slavery.' In the same manner, R #152 stated, 'They should call it [the ENS] slavery rather than national service. To run away from the national service, many are falling prey to dangerous wild animals. *Eritrea has lost its youth and as a result its future has become bleak*' (emphasis added). A recent article in *The Wall Street Journal* used a similar metaphor, stating, 'Eritrea's future is running away from it' (Stevis and Parkinson 2016).

A number of key informants emphasised the damaging effect of the ENS on families who derive their livelihood from mixed farming, that is cultivation and livestock herding. In Eritrea hyenas and other wild animals prey upon livestock without the protection of shepherds. Abreha from the Barka region, for example, said, 'Before the government introduced the national service, our family allocated each family member's labour time to different activities and the incomes derived from these diverse activities were the basis of our livelihood.' When asked to spell out the types of activities they engaged in he said, 'My parents and sisters stayed in our village and looked after the farms and the small animals, such as goats, milking cows and donkeys. My brothers migrated to Gash-Setit with our cattle seasonally where there was abundant pasture and water.' He added, 'One of my brothers was a trader. He smuggled goods to Sudan and from Sudan to Eritrea.' This, he said, 'was a lucrative activity, especially during the war'. Another of his brothers owned a small shop in their village. I asked him what happened after the introduction of the ENS. He said, 'All of us joined. Two of my brothers died during the border war. Not only did our family's livelihood collapse, but also most of our cattle perished because they could no longer migrate in search of pasture and water. There was no one to look after them.'

The predicament of families who lose their members to the ENS is not only due to loss of income and care, but also the additional responsibility of raising their grandchildren and supporting their daughters-in-law. This is because not only is the children's father in the indefinite ENS, but also because he earns no income excepting a pittance of pocket money. This is aptly described by R #080, who states, 'When the breadwinner joins national service, the parents bear the burden of raising their grandchildren.' The inability to look after one's family, including children, is incompatible with one of the defining elements of Eritrean culture. As Hirt and Mohammad (2013: 147) perceptively stated:

> In Eritrea, as a poor society, aspirations may be more moderate, but of course, founding a family and providing for it is the most basic goal...The lineage or extended family is the basic form of social belonging and has so far guaranteed survival in the absence of a governmental social security network. Many Eritreans depend on support from their relatives...We assume that basic cultural goals which are common to all Eritreans irrespective of their specific ethnic or religious belong, and which at the same time are incompatible with the nationalist demands of the PFDJ are the following:
>
> To establish a nuclear family and regularly spend time together with one's spouse and children as well as with one's extended family.
>
> To sustain one's self and safeguard the subsistence of one's family through work. (emphasis added)

They further state, 'By introducing the [national service], the government is preventing a whole generation from reaching these internalised cultural goals through legitimate means' (Hirt and Mohammad 2013: 147). To these internalised goals one must add the duty to care for aging and ailing family members. The open-ended ENS has wiped out all of these essential cultural roles.

In the same vein, R #150 states, 'Because the national service is endless, not only do families forgo the benefits that they would have got from their children in terms of labour, income and care, but [also] the families are forced to support their conscripted children's and their families [wives].' A similar view is expressed by R #153, who said, 'My brother and I were in national service and as a result, our father and my brother's children were left without anyone to help them. We felt sad as a result.' In a similar vein, R #166 stated, 'The negative side of the ENS is on families. It has created a big gap in their lives. Many families have become impoverished, as well as devastated (orphaned).' The use of the word 'orphaned' is deeply instructive in the context of the Eritrean culture. Often the term orphan is used to describe a parentless child, but in the Eritrean context it also applies to aging parents and grandparents without sons, daughters and grandchildren to look after them. This is because there are no government social security and/or state or occupational pension benefits.

Not only is the burden on families who lose their breadwinners excruciating both economically and emotionally, as well as being socially debilitating, it also has considerable implications on the wellbeing and nutritional statuses of children and their mothers. It is not due to random occurrence that Eritrea's global ranking of stunting prevalence is 19th highest out of 136 countries in the world (UNICEF 2009, in World Bank n.d.). This is further reinforced by the fact that the total number of Eritreans who are unable to meet their basic food consumption needs is 70–80 per cent (CAADP 2013: 4). Although this is the result of inextricably linked complex multiple factors, including policy failures and the shortage and erratic distribution of rainfall, the tying down of the large majority of the country's most productive labour force into the ENS instead of them being able to fend for themselves and their families is a major part of the explanation.

R #082 underscores the damaging effect of the indefinite ENS on families stating, 'the absence of their children inflicts economic difficulties and demoralisation'. The respondent explains, 'The reason I say the impact of the national service has been bad for the country, families and the conscripts is because it has no end and citizens cannot fend for themselves and their families.' In this respondent's view the difficulties befalling families are not due to the ENS per se, but rather due to its indefinite nature: because the ENS is universal it affects most families detrimentally. R #084 stated, for example, 'Almost every household has been affected because the breadwinners for the families have to stay in the military for a long period without any payment. This affects families and the nation at large.' Referring to his own family's experience the respondent said, 'the breadwinner of our family (my brother) has been in the military with no payment for the last seven years. If I were not here [in the diaspora], our family would have been severely affected economically.' As we shall see later, the lucky families whose child or children flee from the ENS and make it to Northern Europe, evading the anguishes or deaths that befall many at the hands of hostage-takers/traffickers, or avaricious smugglers in eastern Sudan, the Sahara, Libya, Sinai, the Mediterranean Sea or Calais, are able to benefit from remittances. In the damaging context of the ENS, had it not been for remittances, many Eritrean families, as this respondent said, would probably have faced starvation.

R #146 states, 'When the productive members of the family are conscripted, the family faces real danger' and when assessing the impact of the ENS on her family she said, 'The national service had created lots of problems for our family because five of us were conscripted.' When a family loses five members of its productive labour force the negative consequences are severe. According to some respondents, the detrimental effects of the ENS are not limited to economic deprivation and the impoverishment of families, but they also reported that their parents' quality of life was eroded because of separation and concern about their loved ones' potential risk of death and injury. As a result, many parents fell into depression and angst. The conscripts were also affected because they were separated from their parents just when parental care and guidance were most needed, which was particularly difficult for younger conscripts. R #023, for example, succinctly summarised the social impact on parents and conscripts as follows: 'parents are worried about their loved ones' risk of death, separation and injury. Conscripts are detrimentally affected due to separation and deprivation of parental love.' Parents of female conscripts who flee to avoid or escape from the open-ended ENS additionally suffer from the severe anxieties and fear that stem from the potential risk of rape at the hands of soldiers, smugglers, traffickers and government officials in their own country and transit countries. A female key informant, Hiriti, for example, said, 'I was kidnapped by the Rashaida in eastern Sudan at the time when Eritrean hostages were subjected to inhuman treatment. When I was released after my relatives paid the ransom they demanded, my parents told me that they could never sleep and as a result developed varieties of debilitating illnesses.' Although she was reluctant to say, it is not difficult to imagine the gruesome treatment she might have suffered at the hands of her captors.

When asked to state the main impacts of the ENS on families and conscripts, R #040 said, 'Separation and poverty.' Eritreans come from tightly knit households and children are socialised from early childhood to internalise the values and norms transmitted to them from their parents. Key in this socialisation process is the inculcation of values that foster responsibility that encourage each family member's contribution to their family's economic and social wellbeing. For this to succeed, however, the autonomy and integrity of the family needs to remain intact. The ENS, by separating families from each other, has thwarted their ability to play the roles that are culturally transmitted and socially sanctioned. By separating and disintegrating families, the ENS assaults the foundation of the edifice on which the coping and survival strategies of Eritrean families are based. An important consequence of this has been, as many respondents stated, abject poverty, and erosion of long-standing survival strategies that had survived the test of time.

Similarly, R #049 said, 'Not only has my family been suffering from depression and desperation but they are [also] forced to live on hand-outs.' Given the Eritrean government's hostility to food and foreign aid, hand-outs, even for the most deprived and destitute families, are hard to come by. For example, BBC News, on 3 January 2010, stated, '[t]he drought gripping the Horn of Africa means nearly 20 million people are going to need emergency food aid, according to the United Nations. However, Eritrea is refusing food aid and restricting humanitarian access inside its borders' (BBC 2010). In *The Economist* (2006) in a piece titled 'Eritrea:

the Myth of Self-Reliance' it was written that '[t]he secretive ex-guerrilla government has always been good at concealing its real intentions. But Eritrea's policy on aid has become unusually bizarre. *One of the poorest countries in the world, with some of its population now facing food shortages, Eritrea is deliberately rejecting help.*' It was further reported, '[t]his week, the United Nations special humanitarian envoy for the Horn of Africa, Kjell Magne Bondevik, made his first visit to Eritrea, where the UN faces a tricky dilemma. Eritreans are tired and hungry, but the government sticks to a mantra of self-reliance. *In early 2005, the UN estimated that two-thirds of Eritrea's 3.6m people needed food aid, making Eritrea one of the most food-aid-dependent countries in the world*' (emphasis added). Luc van Kemenade (2011) also wrote, 'Eritrea, a nation of 5 million people that borders Sudan, Ethiopia and Djibouti, has also seen failed rains and widespread food shortages. *But its autocratic government, which faces international sanctions, refuses to acknowledge a drought has swept its territory. Satellite images show that the Red Sea nation has been hit by drought conditions similar to those in Somalia, Ethiopia and Djibouti*' (emphasis added).

Alem Fesshatzion (2015), for example, brazenly boasted, 'Why is Eritrea thriving while Ethiopia is starving?' Since both countries are located in the same ecological zone (see van de Giessen 2011) the risk of hunger facing Ethiopia is likely to affect Eritrea equally, even though the government of Eritrea does not acknowledge this. The difference is not that Eritrea is immune to drought and its negative effects and Ethiopia is not, but rather that whilst Ethiopia admits the threat of impending starvation and tries to feed its people in collaboration with its international partners, Eritrea tries to go it alone because the ruler, Isaias, perceives potential partners, such as NGOs and Western governments, as foes. For example, he told the local media, 'NGOs ...are obstructing the establishment of effective and competent governments and governmental institutions in Africa, especially in states that won their independence recently like us... *We reject the work in the field of relief aid and employing it as a cover up as well as using religious names, which have got their weight and exploiting this in the field of spying, espionage, sabotage and terrorist acts*' (cited in Redeker Hepner and O'Kane 2009: xvi–xvii, emphasis added).

There has been a lot of talk about the worst drought Ethiopia is facing (UNICEF 2016), but the Eritrean government has not yet expressed concern. If Ethiopia is threatened, it goes without saying that Eritrea is equally affected. As Martin Plaut and Mirjam van Reisen observe, '...drought is no respector of borders. While Ethiopia has faced up to the scale of the crisis not a single word has been issued by neighboring Eritrea. Yet the evidence is beginning to mount up that the country is facing similar crisis' (2015). The looming crisis is likely to be exacerbated by the negative effects of the ENS.

The observation of the following female with a post-graduate degree, Selam, portrays the predicament of Eritrean families in a bleak light. With regard to the devastating impact of the ENS on families and the economy of the country in the context of a government that rules with contempt, she observed:

> The Eritrean people are plagued with a number of misfortunes. Firstly, they inhabit arid and semi-arid region where crop failures due to lack or erratic distribution of rainfall is common. The consequence of this is that agricultural production even during favourable weather conditions is not enough to cover the annual consumption needs of the population. Secondly, Eritreans are ruled by the most callous, repressive and ignorant government, which pursues myopic foreign policy that damages not only the short and long-term economic and security interests of the country and its population, but also which leaves the country and its people isolated and impoverished. (Interview, Pretoria, 7 November 2013)

She continued, 'What Eritrea needs is a high-minded, smart and friendly government that is aware of the country's economic limitations and strengths, as well as understands the rule of the game and acts accordingly in the best interest of the country and its people.' Selam's claim that, even in the best seasons, Eritrea is unable to produce sufficient amount of food to feed itself is backed by a variety of sources, including the World Bank, who have stated, '[b]y virtue of its location in the Sahel, Eritrea suffers periodic droughts and chronic food shortages hampering development efforts. *Even in times of good rainfall, domestic food production is estimated to meet 60–70% of the population's needs*' (2015, emphasis added). Mussie Tesfagiorgis (2010: 106) also states, '[e]ven during good rainy seasons, most of the rural communities cannot manage to produce enough food to meet their subsistence consumption requirements.' Abraham Haile's study confirms this: 'Historical records from 1975 to 1999 reveal that the crop production in Eritrea only covered 20 to 60 per cent of the basic food needs of the population' (2007).

It is in spite of this ecological menace that the Eritrean government has deprived Eritrean families of their most critical resource, family labour. The culture of denial and policy of rejection of food and foreign aid have exacerbated the plight of the Eritrean people. The loss of breadwinners to the ENS has such a severe and unbearable impact that in at least one case a parent lost his life because of stress and lack of carers. R #171 said, 'My father passed away because of sorrow and none of his children attended his funeral.' The acceptable cultural norm in Eritrea is that funeral rituals are organised and attended by all family members, especially direct descendants of the deceased. This is considered dignifying both for the deceased and their families. Unless the deceased person's offspring are prevented by mental or physical illness, they are expected to organise and attend the funeral. It is not uncommon for Eritreans to travel from all over the world to attend family funerals. Notwithstanding this long-standing tradition and cultural practice, the Eritrean authorities rarely grant leave of absence to conscripts to attend their parents' and siblings' funeral services and rituals. The shortage of labour resulting from the ENS is so severe that many communities are unable to find able-bodied residents to dig graves to bury the dead. Such a level of labour shortage was previously unheard of in the country.

The denial of leave for the purpose of funeral attendance, besides showing the government's disrespect for the religious and cultural practices of the population, also discounts the fact that depriving conscripts of a historically transmitted and socially expected role and responsibility –

attendance of one's parent's funeral – is likely to be emotionally stressful, if not damaging. There is also evidence to show that for some parents, the psychological effect of the loss of their children to the indefinite ENS is so destabilising that it affects them fundamentally. R #175, for example, said, 'My parents found life without us unbearable and impossible and as a result were forced to flee to Sudan.' The respondent did not elaborate how fleeing the country would ease their depression or stress. It was either in anticipation of their conscripted children's flight to Sudan or the loss of means of livelihood that prompted their decision to flee. R #176's assessment succinctly encapsulates the impact of the ENS on families and their conscripted children: 'After having struggled to raise their children, parents lose them at the time they need them most. This becomes a source of pain both to the conscripts and their families.'

In the following, the views of the minority of respondents who were strongly in favour of the ENS are presented.

DISSENTING MINORITY VOICES

As emphasised throughout this book, the conscripts, in spite of their common experiences, do not speak with a single voice. Although the overwhelming majority of the respondents think that the ENS as it is currently implemented constitutes a waste of time and resources, there are a few who still think that the price paid by the conscripts and their parents is worthwhile. This is not only because of the differential impact of the burden, but a handful of the respondents also seem to be strong supporters of the government and its policies. For example, although R #121 did not deny the negative effects of the ENS on the families of the conscripts, he thought it to be a price worth paying for the sake of the country. He said, 'The ENS affects families negatively, but the family is an integral part of the nation and therefore notwithstanding the problems it faces, the country is being built.' In this respondent's view, building the country at the expense of conscripts' and their families' livelihoods and interests is worthwhile. The much-loved cliché from supporters of the Eritrean government and the party – 'Eritrea is being built by the sweat and blood of its patriotic sons and daughters' – is highly contested. The pro-government group in the diaspora justifies this by arguing that, in the short-term, the nationals within the age of conscription and their families may suffer but, in the long-term, all Eritreans will be better off. This fallacy reminds one of John Maynard Keynes' celebrated observation: 'But this long-run is a misleading guide to current affairs, in the long-run we are all dead' (1922: 186). An interesting question one can ask in regard to this is: 'Who bears the cost?' Diaspora Eritreans can afford to be positively predisposed to the endless ENS because neither they nor their immediate families bear the cost. When I asked Saba, 'Why do you think some Eritreans in the diaspora support the indefinite ENS and condemn those who flee the country to avoid it?' she said, 'They have nothing to lose. Their children are safe and are pursuing their studies and careers. Their parents at home do not suffer because of the remittances they receive from them.' This may suggest that, except in the case of those who oppose the ENS on matters of principle, the attitude people have towards it is based on personal interest.

The common metaphor used by the supporters of the government is: '*adi tihnetz ala*' (the nation is being built). R #136 said, 'The ENS makes one a good and a committed citizen and this is beneficial to families.' In this respondent's view, by performing the ENS conscripts undergo change and transformation and become good citizens as a result, which benefits them and their families, as well as the country. Similarly, R #146 said, 'Yes, it [the ENS] was a very powerful, educational [weapon] which inculcates love for the country.' The same respondent also thinks that the ENS transforms and shapes the conscripts. He stated, 'The effect on families is good and bad because the children of some families are unruly and idlers and the national service shapes their character.' In exactly the same vein, R #150 said, 'The national service is good for families because their children will return with different behavioural traits, culture, experience and work habits.' It is important to underscore the fact that this group represents a tiny fraction of the total respondents interviewed for the study and, interestingly, all are male. The basis of this minority's support seems to be that the ENS is good for the country, for families and for the conscripts themselves. These views are inconsistent with the opinions of the exponents of the philosophical foundations of national service.

10

Conclusion

There is no easy walk to freedom anywhere, and many of us will have to pass through the valley of the shadow of death again and again before we reach the mountaintop of our desires.

Nelson Mandela (1953)

THE BUILDING OF ERITREA'S DEFENCE AND FIGHTING CAPABILITY

Theoretically, the decision of the post-independence Eritrean government to adopt and implement a universal and compulsory national service was legitimate and groundbreaking. There were a number of reasons for this. Firstly, for a small country with limited resources and small population recovering from a devastating thirty years' war (1961–1991), it was prudent to limit the size of the standing army and boost its defence and fighting capability through compulsory conscription, provided the duration of the latter is limited and strictly regulated by law. Secondly, the remarkable victory of the Eritrean People's Liberation Front (EPLF) over sub-Saharan Africa's largest army was chiefly due to the devotion of the volunteer combatants who served their country, not only without any remuneration, but also at the expense of their interests, including their lives. Although the realities of the two periods, namely the liberation struggle and the post-independence era, are fundamentally different, the government's attempt to build a defence capability based on the historical success of the liberation struggle is an innovative idea. Justifiably, one of the central aims of the Eritrean National Service (ENS) is to establish a strong defence force by drawing on the experiences gained during the liberation struggle. All things being equal, the approach might have provided an opportunity for safeguarding the sovereignty and territorial integrity of the country cost-effectively.

Nevertheless, in spite of this initially worthy endeavour (which later went woefully wrong, partly due to the fact that, rhetoric notwithstanding, the ruler of the country, Isias Afwerki, is not committed to the development of an autonomous, professional and institutionalised military), the findings of the study based on the perceptions of the conscripts interviewed show that the national service has failed to build

Eritrea's defence and fighting capability. Contrary to its stated objectives, the national service has become one of the factors accelerating the process of its erosion by depleting the country's most invaluable resource: labour power. In any developing country this is the fulcrum of a robust defence capability. Although the cause of decay of the Eritrean Defence Forces, the successor of the 'once widely admired as one of the most effective fighting organisations in the world' (ICG 2010). Unlike the Eritrean People's Liberation Army (EPLA), the ENS has failed to augment Eritrea's fighting and defence capability.

The ENS's failure to build post-independence Eritrea's defence capability is not surprising because no country suffering from an excessive loss of its population has ever been able to build a robust defence capability. Additionally, the Eritrean military is micromanaged by the head of state and this has demonstrably resulted in a dearth of autonomy in recruitment and promotion, as well as in formulating strategic and operational policies. The president's incessant interference, among other things, has resulted in a high turnover of senior commanders. Unlike in the post-independence period, in which tens, if not hundreds of thousands, within and approaching the age of conscription have fled the country to seek protection and a livelihood elsewhere, the reason the EPLF was able to win the war of independence, against all odds, was because during the liberation struggle, Eritreans inside the country, in Ethiopia and Sudan, as well as in the diaspora, abandoned their lucrative professions, jobs, businesses, careers, families and studies to join the liberation struggle and lay their lives down for their people and country. The converse is the case at present, as reflected in the decision of hundreds of thousands to 'vote with their feet' to seek protection, careers, employment and educational opportunities. During the liberation struggle, these personal ambitions and interests were either sacrificed or frozen until the war of independence ended, which intensely preoccupied most Eritreans.

After the ENS became open-ended and degenerated into forced labour in the context of economic decay, the rate of attrition reached an unsustainable level. Flight in search of protection and livelihood has become the norm among the victims. It is not surprising therefore that the Eritrean defence forces, the successors of the heroic EPLA which had an excellent track record during the liberation struggle, are in disarray, reflected, *inter alia*, in the inability of the Eritrean state to exercise sovereignty over its borders. This is evident in the exodus of hundreds of thousands of draft evaders and deserters. As Albert Hirschman (1978: 94) observes, '...the existence of the state is incompatible with the virtually costless availability of exit and with sort of citizens to it as a routine response to dissatisfaction.'

The Eritrean Defence Force (EDF) has also been unable to stop the successful exit of the Tigray People's Democratic Movement (TPDM/ Demhit) from Eritrea. The commander of the Ethiopian dissident group and his 683 soldiers were able to walk across the Eritrea-Sudan border unhindered by the presence of the EDF.

The EDF have also been unable to protect the country's territories against Ethiopia's aggression, as in March 2012 when the Ethiopian military launched an assault inside Eritrea unscathed. Ethiopia also continues to occupy large swathes of sovereign Eritrean territory in defiance of the Eritrea-Ethiopia Border Commission's decision. Nevertheless, this is not to be blamed on the Eritrean government, but rather on the Ethiopian government's impunity, which is premised on the assumption that the Eritrean military is unable to defend the country. It is not suggested here that Eritrea should try to use force to regain its lost territories, as this is likely to reignite the conflagration. Negotiation and compromise, rather than military confrontation, are the only ways forward.

Although the development and consolidation of an effective defence capability is a function of inextricably linked multiple factors, among which professionalism, technical capability and autonomy from executive interferences are critical, some of the main reasons for the ENS's failure to boost the defence capability of the country include the indefinite, open-ended and compulsory nature of the service which is imposed on all citizens aged between eighteen and fifty-four for men and eighteen and forty-seven for women (except the mentally infirm and the severely disabled) without remuneration and exception. There is also evidence to show that some of the commanders, the majority of whom are former combatants, have turned the ENS into a mechanism of personal enrichment rather than an instrument of building the country's defence and fighting capability.

In addition, the former conscripts who deserted from the national service after serving on average about six years state that one of the factors that reduced the ability of the ENS to build a robust defence capability is the incessant conflict between the military commanders (*yikealo*) (former combatants) and the *warsai* (the conscripts). In the Eritrean government's and the ruling party's view, the *yikealo*, who embody the core values of the liberation struggle, would transmit to the *warsai* the qualities and character traits that impelled them to accept the moral obligation to fight and lay down their lives for the nation. It was thought that these values and resources, if successfully transmitted to the *warsai*, would motivate the latter to be the key driving force in building an invincible defence capability.

The findings of the study show that, firstly, the *warsai* neither perceive the military commanders, the *yikealo*, as being the repository and epitome of the core values of the revolution, nor as positive role models worthy of emulation. Secondly, a transmitter of value should generally command the respect of the would-be recipient. The findings of the study show that the majority of the *warsai* perceive the large majority of the commanders in the ENS, the *yikealo*, as vile and callous individuals who mete out severe punishments without any regard for the physical safety and wellbeing of the *warsai*. As a result, they are inclined to reject rather than embrace the values and behaviour associated with them. Thirdly, the assumption that the core values the commanders internalised during the liberation struggle would persist in the post-independence period in spite of competing demands on their loyalties and resources, as well as in the context of shifting aspirations in the post-independence period, is flawed. During the war of liberation the ex-combatants had no competing or conflicting interests and, as a result, were ready and willing to sacrifice their interests, including their lives, in the service of their country. In the post-independence period these primary values have become conflicted and diluted because of the changed circumstances and aspirations. Fourthly, the findings of the study show that the relationships between the commanders and *warsai* have become poisonous, in the former conscripts' views, due to the commanders' callousness and corruption. It is not surprising therefore that the ENS has failed to contribute substantially to Eritrea's defence and fighting capability.

PRESERVATION AND TRANSMISSION OF THE CORE VALUES OF THE LIBERATION STRUGGLE

The second major goal of the ENS is to preserve and transmit the core values developed during the liberation struggle to the present generation, the *warsai*. The architects of the ENS perceive these core values as constituting the edifice of the foundation on which a united Eritrean nation would be built, thrive and be sustained. The main core values the Eritrean authorities wanted to transmit to the *warsai* included a powerful sense of sacrificial nationalism, patriotism, common secular national Eritrean identity, dedication, thick social networks, solidarity, unity, a powerful sense of common purpose and mutual trust across the social cleavages of religion, region, ethnicity, class, sex and political opinion. The architects of the ENS strongly believe that the internalisation of these core values would produce the glue that would hold Eritrean society together regardless of ethnic, religious and regional differences.

These were the core values that determined the successful outcome of the liberation struggle. Had this not been the case, Eritrea, which not only lacked superpower patronage but also solidarity and unity derived from a myth of common ancestry, would have been unable to defeat Ethiopia, which had massive superpower backing and access to greater financial and labour resources. During the liberation struggle most Eritreans stood together, relegating their identity and particular interest-based differences to the background. It is these values and character traits that the Eritrean authorities wished to transmit to the *warsai* via the *yikealo* in the course of their performance of national service.

It is also important to note that the other core values the architects of the ENS wanted to transmit to the *warsai* were obedience and a non-questioning acceptance of authority, as was the case during the liberation struggle. Therefore the important question that needs to be addressed is the extent to which the core values engendered during the war can be reproduced in the absence of an existential threat presented by an external enemy. The Eritrean government and the party feared that the glue that held Eritrean society together during the war might be eroded once the enemy had been thwarted. This was the reason the Eritrean national service was conceived as a mechanism of maintaining and transmitting the core values produced during the liberation struggle.

In the absence of other means of measuring the effectiveness of the ENS as a mechanism of preserving and transmitting the values of the thirty years' war, the perceptions of the *warsai* interviewees and key informants are a good measure of the extent to which the national service has been able to achieve this primary goal. In addition, the respondents were asked to state the virtues and vices they learned in the course of performing national service. They were provided with a set of eight potential 'virtues' and seven 'vices' and were asked to identify the ones they learned in the national service. Of the total respondents, a majority, 65 per cent, said that they had learned to be hard working. The internalisation of hard work as a value undoubtedly constitutes a virtue. However, under the rigorous punishment regime that permeates the ENS, refusal to work hard can lead to torture and detention. Therefore, in the context of such a punishment regime, it is difficult to distinguish between acquiescence precipitated by fear of punishment and that by commitment to the value of hard work. According to some of the respondents the conscripts work hard either to please their commanders and/or to avoid severe punishment, but this tends to become a habit over time. To reinforce this, some respondents reported that the former conscripts are now known for their discipline and hard work thanks to the experience they gained in the ENS. Habtom, who was granted asylum in the UK after serving in the ENS for thirteen years, for example, said, 'hard work is one of the key defining features of my life. I feel anxious when I am not working thanks to the habit I developed in the national service.'

Slightly more than half of the respondents said that one of the core values they internalised in the course of performing national service was dedication to public causes, such as nation building, national unity and economic and social development. It may only mean that participation in the ENS did not make them more committed to public causes than they were before. The other core values the respondents reported they developed and internalised in the process of performing national service were solidarity, cooperation, patriotism and reliability. These findings show that the ENS has been, to a limited extent, an effective mechanism for transmitting the core values developed during the liberation struggle. Inasmuch as these core values contributed to the success of the liberation struggle, they are vital to nation building and post-conflict economic, political and social (re) construction. It is worth noting, however, that with the exception of hard work, fewer than half of the respondents said they internalised the other core values developed during the liberation struggle.

The corresponding values derived from interviews with EPLF combatants are 100 per cent. This is consistent with expectation because war fought against a common enemy is an engine that engenders a powerful sense of solidarity, feelings of camaraderie, internal cohesion and a powerful sense of common purpose, mutual trust and dedication to a common cause, as well as acquiescence. Such values produced under conditions of war tend to wane gradually in post-war periods. The fact that a considerable proportion of the conscripts said that they still hold and cherish such core values is an indication of the ENS's effectiveness in transmitting and maintaining the key core values created and reproduced during the liberation struggle.

It is worth noting, however, that in the course of performing national service the conscripts also learned some vices that have nothing to do with nation building, good citizenship and character building. In fact, they run counter to the stated aims of the ENS. In comparison to those who said they had learned and internalised invaluable virtues and values in the course of performing national service, a minority said that they developed some vices that may, if unabated, defeat the goals of the ENS. The findings of the study show that among the total number of respondents a minority have learned fraudulence, cheating, deceit, lying, opportunism, sycophancy, submissiveness and laziness.

Not only do these findings evidence values antithetical to the core values produced during the liberation struggle, but they are incompatible with the goals and objectives of the national service. The conditions under which the core values were created have changed fundamentally with the cessation of war. The former combatants, who are supposed to transmit the core values of the liberation struggle, have also changed in the post-war period. It is therefore unrealistic to expect that the core values produced during the war would remain intact in peacetime. It is equally naïve to expect that the former combatants' commitment to the national core values would remain intact in spite of their shifting priorities, aspirations and interests. Nevertheless, it is still instructive to understand where the vices the minority of the conscripts internalised stem from.

The data gathered from the interviewees and key informants show that the interests, priorities, attitudes and aspirations of the former combatants are no longer the same as they were during the liberation struggle. During the struggle the combatants were single-mindedly committed to the common good of Eritrea, and, in their view, the commanders in the ENS pursue their personal interests with the same passion and determination. As Aida (a key informant) put it, 'They are determined to accumulate wealth by any means to make for the lost time.' The majority of the respondents and key informants interviewed for the study said that most of the commanders (who are former combatants) they met in the ENS are corrupt, vile, excessively self-interested and cruel. These are supposed to be the 'bearers and transmitters' of the core values of the liberation struggle. In view of the widespread abject poverty pervading the country, resulting from a variety of institutional and structural factors, among which myopic economic policy, lack of democracy, conscription and unfavourable weather conditions are most important, the selfish traits exhibited in the behaviour of the *warsai* are not surprising. Magnus Treiber found the same traits among draft dodgers who lived in Asmara, hiding from the feared military police. With regard to one of his informants Treiber said, 'He daily understood how the security authorities' permanent threat and Eritrea's increasing poverty, which had finally arrived in the capital and affected literally everyone corrupted people's minds and actions creating doubt, mistrust, and envy between generations, age-mates, and even close friends' (2009: 94).

The commanders in the ENS ran shops and private farms, and engaged in a variety of income-generating activities, exploiting the conscripts' labour power and pocket money for personal gain. They also collect substantial amount of bribes in return for selling *menqasaqesi* (travel permits) that enable the holders (conscripts) to stay away from their units. The *menqasaqesi* can be renewed repeatedly against payment of monthly fees. Some of the commanders have turned the ENS into a mechanism of personal enrichment. It is not surprising therefore that some of the conscripts have learned vices through emulating the corrupt practices and behaviours of their commanders.

FOSTERING NATIONAL UNITY

The third major goal of the ENS was to foster national unity among the Eritrean people by eliminating sub-national feelings and allegiances. The findings of the study show that the outcome of this goal has been the greatest achievement of the ENS. When asked whether the national service fosters social cohesion, harmony and national unity, 90.5 per cent of respondents said that the ENS is a key mechanism of enhancing national unity and social cohesion. Only 9.5 per cent had a dissenting view. The corresponding views of the key informants were 100 per cent. The respondents strongly believe that bringing together nationals from diverse regions, religious and cultural backgrounds promotes mutual love, understanding, unity and cohesion. By participating in the ENS, the servers visited and worked in different parts of Eritrea and inhabited by different ethno-linguistic groups. This has enabled them to learn about other places and ethnic groups, their cultures and their way of life.

Eritrea is home to nine disparate ethno-linguistic groups. The compulsory and universal national service brings these groups together in one place, at the Sawa military training camp, where all conscripts live, eat, study, play, train and sleep together. Prior to their arrival at the Sawa military training camp, some of those who did not go to school were not even aware of the existence of citizens who were linguistically, culturally and racially different from them. Many of the youths, especially those from the rural areas, belonged to ethno-linguistic groups oblivious to the world outside them. In the national service not only are these conscripts acquainted with their countrywomen and men but also over time they undergo change and transformation. A female informant, Hiriti, with a post-graduate degree in anthropology, used the rites of passage metaphor to explain the changes and transformations the youth undergo in the ENS: 'the national service strips the individuals of their original sub-national identities, allegiances and roles by inducting them into a common Eritrean national identity'. Solomon (Interview, London, 4 September 2014) used the metaphor of exfoliation or shedding of a particular identity to describe the process of change the youths hailing from disparate ethno-linguistic backgrounds undergo in the national service. When asked to explain, he said:

> Have you ever heard or seen a snake shedding its old skin? That is precisely what the Eritrean youth experience at the national service. They shed their previous secluded identities in favour of common Eritrean national identity. The youth are initiated into the Eritrean nation. The process affirms a sense of community, solidarity and common purpose.

The views expressed by the key informants and respondents are identical. The ENS, by mixing together youths originating from different classes, faiths, sexes, ethnicities, regions, cultures and occupational and educational backgrounds in one place, namely, the Sawa military training camp and by subjecting them to intense processes of military training, political socialisation and indoctrination in a common language, has enabled them to gain common experience and to know and learn from and about each other and their communities. Although military training is conducted in Tigrinya, lessons in political socialisation are provided in five additional languages, namely, Tigre, Hedareb, Nara, Kunama and Saho. Members of the Blin join the classes where Tigrinya and Tigre are used, the Afar join the Saho. Such an environment is auspicious for the construction and consolidation of common national identity and social cohesion. It is in this sense that the eminent sociologist Amitai Etzioni referred to national service as a 'sociological mixer'.

The significance of this in a multi-ethnic and multi-faith traditional society, such as Eritrea, cannot be stressed enough. As noted previously, Charles Moskos' description of America and the role the institution of national service could play in fostering social cohesion applies equally to Eritrean society. He said, '[o]ur cohesion depends upon a civic ideal rather than on primordial loyalties' (1988: 9) The findings of this study show that the conscripts' knowledge and familiarity with the different communities, their ways of life, cultures and geography have been enhanced. As a result, trans-faith, trans-ethnic and trans-regional friendships and dense social networks have flourished. The findings show conclusively that the ENS functions as a vehicle of social cohesion and national unity.

The ENS, by bringing citizens from all corners of the country and every walk of life, has been able to create a genial environment where citizens of disparate ethnic, geographic, religious, occupational, educational and regional backgrounds interact repeatedly with each other, and, over time, they have learned to know and trust one another, to interconnect with each other and to share experiences, values and norms that encourage cooperation, openness and compromise. Therefore, national service has produced the glue that interconnects hundreds of thousands of conscripts across the cleavages of faith, ethnicity, class, and occupational, educational and regional backgrounds.

It is worth noting, however, that had the ENS been implemented in a context of a democratic system of governance in which conscripts could question, challenge and influence not only the parameters within which the ENS works, but also its goals and the methods of its implementation, it would have been a vital mechanism for promoting citizenship and democratic institutions. A process of national unity that results from such an open and free conversation regarding the aims, scope and outcome of such an all-encompassing programme would have been transformative rather than being an instrument of social engineering in which the conscripts are treated as recipients of change rather than as agents of change and transformation. Such an approach would also have been good for retention. As seen throughout the book, after the ENS became open-ended and consequently degenerated into forced labour, an unknown but significant number of conscripts deserted, risking their lives in search of protection and livelihood elsewhere. Between 2000 and 2014 133,385 conscripts, draft evaders and children have fled and sought asylum in the EU+ countries (Table 4.1 in Chapter 4).

The question that arises is: what happens to the social capital when such a large number flee in search of protection and livelihood elsewhere? Over the past three years, the composition of those who have fled the country has changed dramatically. A substantial proportion of those who flee the country are not necessarily conscripts or even people approaching the age of conscription. Many of those fleeing to the neighbouring countries, Ethiopia and Sudan, and those with relatives in the diaspora en route to the EU+ countries, are unaccompanied and separated children far below the age of conscription. According to statistics obtained from the Administration for Refugee and Returnee Affairs (ARRA) as of 15 December 2015, there are 2,600 underage Eritrean asylum-seekers and refugees in refugee camps in Ethiopia, consisting of 993 in Mai Aini, 713 in Htsats, 591 in Adi Harush and 303 in Enda Aba Gun.

Although the number of Eritrean minors among the post-independence refugees and asylum-seekers in Sudan is likely to be much larger than those in the Ethiopian refugee camps, their exact number is difficult to ascertain because they are continuously on the move. The large majority of those who arrive in the northern Ethiopian refugee camps do not stay there but rather move on to Sudan en route to Khartoum, and from there to Libya and Europe across the Mediterranean Sea. A sizable proportion of those who are kidnapped and taken hostages by the Rasahida and Bedouin Arabs are underage Eritreans. Even at a time when the scale of trafficking is assumed to have reduced dramatically after the flow of Eritreans to Israel via the Sinai desert was stemmed following the construction of the Sinai wall, built by Israel, the kidnapping of Eritrean refugees en route to Eastern Sudan from Eritrea, from the Shagarab refugee camps and from the Sahara desert en route to Libya and inside Libya has continued unabated, albeit on a smaller scale. For example, on 5 June 2015, the UN stated:

> An armed group opened fire on a convoy transporting Eritrean asylum-seekers in eastern Sudan and kidnapped 14 of them, *including six boys and one girl*, the United Nations refugee agency reported today and urged the Sudanese Government to spare no effort in apprehending those responsible and bringing them to account.
>
> The Office of the UN High Commissioner for Refugees (UNHCR) said the incident occurred on Thursday when an armed group in a pickup truck opened fire on a convoy organized by the Sudanese Commissioner for Refugees (COR), which was transporting 49 Eritrean asylum-seekers from Wad Sharifey reception centre near Kassala to Shagarab refugee camp. (UN Newscentre 2015, emphasis added)

Although all the respondents and key informants interviewed for this study were conscripts, since 2014 a large number of Eritrean asylum-seekers in Ethiopia, Sudan and in the EU+ have been minors who are not within or even approaching the age of conscription. It is therefore difficult to estimate how many of those who are 'voting with their feet' are conscripts, draft evaders and children not directly affected by national service. If, for analytical purposes, we assume that the large majority of those who have been leaving the country are draft evaders and unaccompanied and separated children who have not been in the national service, it can be said that the stock of social capital produced in the national service is not completely lost to the country. Undoubtedly, an unknown but significant proportion of the conscripts of the ENS have fled the country and it is apposite to ask: what happens to the social capital produced in the ENS? Those who are still in the country are likely to continue benefiting from it, as would the country, but whether those who deserted and left the country will be able to continue drawing on it in their efforts to build transnational social networks and organisations in pursuit of common goals is difficult to predict. This is because there are no empirical studies to date to show whether the deserters who are scattered throughout the world remain interconnected transnationally in pursuit of common ideals.

PROMOTION OF EQUALITY

Its architects conceived the ENS as a leveller that would affect all Eritreans within the age of conscription equally regardless of their sex, ethnicity, religion, class and region. During the liberation struggle the principle of equality among combatants regardless of rank was the defining feature of the EPLF. This does not nevertheless indicate that the power of decision-making was not concentrated in a few hands. The distribution of tasks and resources was strictly governed by the principle of equality, and the rigour with which this principle was enforced nurtured mutual trust, commitment to the cause of the liberation struggle and willingness to sacrifice one's life in defence and promotion of the common good of the Eritrean nation. As a former EPLF combatant stated, 'We owed our lives to the revolution. We measured the importance of our lives in terms of the contributions we were able to make to the success of the revolution and preservation of our comrades' lives and the Front's possessions.' One of the aims of the ENS is therefore to foster the principle of equality in terms of sacrifice resulting from bearing the burden of serving the nation and its citizens. The ENS was therefore conceived as a mechanism for transmitting one of the important core values of the liberation struggle, equality, to the conscripts.

The findings of the study show that before it became open-ended, every citizen within the age of conscription, save the physically disabled and mentally infirm, was equally affected without discrimination. In the beginning, the enforcement of the principle of equality was substantially enhanced by enthusiastic responses of the youth to the national service.

Then participation in the ENS was considered a badge of honour. Not only were the majority of the youths, except women and men from some of the rural areas, enthusiastic regarding bearing responsibility for defending and building the country, but also some of the youths fraudulently faked their ages to qualify for conscription, because the minimum age before 2003 was eighteen.[1] Before the border war broke out against Ethiopia in 1998, the powerful sense of enthusiasm permeating the stance of the youths towards the national service engendered intense fervour which incentivised the citizens within the age of conscription to join and serve their country.

Nevertheless, after the national service became open-ended not only did the powerful enthusiasm that permeated the stance of Eritrean youth decline, but also many of the conscripts and their relatives developed a whole industry based on malfeasance, cheating and corruption intended to avoid or minimise the burden of serving in the open-ended ENS. Once those with resources and connections managed either to avoid conscription or minimise its effect by paying bribes to their commanders to secure preferential treatment in terms of securing assignment in the capital city, Asmara, the wish to imitate their corrupt behaviour proliferated. The veracity of Alexis de Tocqueville's critical observation, namely, '...it is the unequal distribution of the weight, not the weight itself, that commonly occasions resistance' cannot be overemphasised. When all citizens within the age of conscription participated in the ENS voluntarily and enthusiastically the default position of the overwhelming majority of the youths was to join the national service either before or after they received call up papers, as clearly demonstrated through the findings of the study. However, once the national service became open-ended and those with resources and connections managed either to free ride or to diminish its severe consequences, over time, the level of resistance reflected in draft evasion and desertion by any means escalated dramatically. This was facilitated by widespread corruption and nepotism in the army, especially among commanders in the ENS.

One of the anomalous findings of the study is that, notwithstanding the widespread perception that power rests in the hands of the Tigrinya-speaking ethno-linguistic group, the lion's share of the burden of serving in the ENS has fallen on the youths hailing from the so-called bearers of power, the Tigrinya speakers. Most of the respondents and key informants stated that the ethno-linguistic groups in the country do not equally share the burden of serving in the ENS. The Tigrinya-speaking youth are over-conscripted and the large majority of the respondents reported that the ENS does not affect members of the Rashaida, the Hedareb, the Beni Amer and the Kunama. In comparison to the Tigrinya-speaking youths, those who belong to the other ethnic groups, such as the Afar, the Saho and the other minority groups from the remote rural areas are less affected. More often than not, the marginalised groups live in hard to reach places where the transaction cost of search and capture (*giffa*) is too high.

---

[1]   After the transfer of students in year 12 to the Sawa military camp, many of the students were below the age of eighteen.

The other interesting finding is that although Proclamation No. 82/1995 on the ENS stipulates that the duty to serve is heedless of religious differences, to a large extent, Muslim women from the rural areas, and to some extent even from urban areas, are far less affected without necessarily being formally exempted. As a matter of public policy, the authorities repeatedly rejected the plea of Muslim elders to exempt Muslim women from the obligation to serve, on the grounds of religion, but in reality the authorities have been less forceful in compelling Muslim women, especially from the rural and remote areas, to be conscripted against their will. The findings of the study show that, over time, the ENS has lost its potency for promoting equality, and at the heart of this failure lays political expediency to allay Muslim disaffection, corruption and absence of regulatory and enforcement structures that constrain abuse of power of commanders. For example, when the respondents interviewed for the study were asked to express agreement or disagreement with the following generalisation, namely, 'The national service has become corrupt and delivers political favours rather than equal service to all,' 48 per cent strongly agreed and 25 per cent agreed with the statement. Based on their own and their families experiences, 72 per cent of the total respondents perceive the ENS as being littered with corruption and nepotism, contrary not only to its declared goals but also to the core values produced during the revolution.

OVERARCHING IMPACT ON THE SOCIAL FABRIC OF THE POLITY

The universal and open-ended ENS has had a profound impact on every aspect of the social fabric of Eritrean society, including family livelihoods, conscripts' careers, education, wellbeing and the economy of the country. The findings of the study show that before the ENS robbed the families of a key resource – family labour – they used to meet their subsistence and other consumption and savings needs by allocating their family labour to diverse income-generating activities and by pulling together the incomes of all family members derived from diverse economic activities. Not only did such a long-standing survival strategy enable Eritrean families to diversify their sources of income, but also to spread the risk of failure. Before losing their members to the ENS, Eritrean families with an adequate supply of labour allocated the same to different sectors, namely, farming, herding, manufacturing, agricultural wage labour, trade and commerce in the service sector, including construction and self-employment in the informal sector. Diversification of family income resulting from diverse allocation of family labour was equally critical to subsistence security in the rural areas.

Many families were able to avoid the risk of subsistence crisis because a failure in one sector was compensated by incomes derived from other activities in other sectors. The universal and open-ended ENS has dealt a mortal blow to this historically transmitted survival strategy developed over time based on trial and error. A survival strategy that took centuries to develop, refine and consolidate has been debilitated by a single political act motivated by a rigid ideological dogma alien to Eritrean economic, social and cultural reality. The policy on the ENS was declared and implemented without forethought of the short, medium and long-term deleterious effects on the livelihood systems and ways of life of Eritrean society. Not only has the universal, compulsory and indefinite national service led to the collapse of most Eritrean families' livelihoods, but it has also turned the country into one of the most militarised societies in the world. As if the large-scale mobilisation into the national service and the shifting of the upper limit of the age of conscription to forty-seven for women and fifty-four for men were not enough, all men in the cities and rural areas, including in the pastoral areas, up to the age of seventy are forced to join the peoples' militia. Those in the peoples' militia are forced to attend compulsory weekly and bi-weekly drills, sacrificing the high opportunity cost of their precious labour power. They are also subjected to intensive indoctrination. The findings of the study show that the ENS, like a cancerous growth, has been eating into the Eritrean polity.

One of the many damaging consequences of the national service has been a severe shortage of labour in all sectors of the economy, including in the subsistence sector. The consequence of this has been that the cost of production in Eritrea is the highest in the world, and consequently goods produced in the country are the least competitive on the regional and world markets. The overall consequence of the national service in all sectors, including on conscripts' and their families, has been catastrophic. These findings are consistent with the findings of the World Bank, IMF, FAO, WFP and UNICEF presented earlier. The available evidence, based on studies conducted by these organisations, shows that 66 per cent of the population lives below the national poverty line and between 70 and 80 per cent are unable to meet their basic food requirements. Most economic activities in Eritrea are labour intensive and the severe shortage of labour caused by the open-ended ENS has been one of the main causes of impoverishment.

It is not only the families of conscripts who have lost their breadwinners that are detrimentally affected by the ENS, as the whole economy has suffered from a severe shortage of labour. Although the central purpose of the ENS is to contribute to the country's socio-economic development and social progress, 62 per cent of the respondents and 100 per cent of the key informants said that the ENS has substantially damaged the economy and impoverished the country. One of the interesting findings of this study is that the free hire of labour in the national service encourages inefficient allocation of labour, such as assigning the wrong people to the wrong jobs, as the costs are disguised. The national service represents a waste of conscripts' time and labour, as well as destroying their future educational and professional careers.

Another profoundly detrimental impact which is incompatible with the core values of the liberation struggle, which the government intends to transmit to the conscripts through the institution of the ENS, is sexual violence perpetrated by military commanders against female conscripts, including at the Sawa military training camp and the *Warsai* School.

The findings of the study show that sexual violence is rife, with the large majority of the former conscripts and key informants interviewed for the study stating that female conscripts suffer sexual violence at the hands of military commanders who behave with impunity. As a result, early and unwanted pregnancies, suicides, single motherhood and early and arranged marriages without affection have become widespread throughout the country. Many parents also withdraw their daughters from school to avoid their exposure to sexual violence.

Although one of the central aims of the ENS is to produce devoted nation builders willing to sacrifice their personal, and their families', interests for the common good of the country and its citizenry, a large number of those who are supposed to build and defend the nation have fled to escape from the indefinite national service and its devastating effects, which has paralysed the normal functioning of the society and its economy. During the past five years a large proportion of those fleeing to Ethiopia and Sudan have been minors who are far below the age of conscription. They have been 'voting with their feet' because they see no future in the country. As Matina Stevis and Joe Parkinson, writing in *The Wall Street Journal*, have stated, 'Eritrea's future is running away from it' (Stevis and Parkinson (2015). Over time, the ENS, instead of producing nation builders and defenders, has set in motion a process of depletion, robbing the country of its most prized resource: labour. Although educated guesses suggest that at the time of writing (2016) up to 5,000 Eritreans leave the country every month, this should not be mistaken for a fact. The total number of Eritrean asylum-seekers and refugees in Ethiopia and Sudan is also difficult to state with certainty because they are permanently on the move. The only relatively objective evidence is on the total number of Eritrean asylum-seekers and refugees that are in the 28 EU+ countries. The total between 2000 and 2014 was 133,385. Between June 2014 and June 2015, the total number of Eritreans in the EU+ countries was 34,515, and between Q1 and Q2 2015, the total increased by 191 per cent. However, between Q2 2014 and Q2 2015, the number decreased by 18 per cent. This decline is in contrast to the dramatic increase in the number of Syrians, Afghans, Albanians, Iraqis and Kosovars which, according to EUROSTAT data, increased by 104, 323, 354, 470 and 386 per cent, respectively.[2]

One of the major findings of this study is the dearth of institutional rules within which the ENS is implemented. This lies at the heart of the fundamental problems afflicting the national service. It is not governed by regulations and guidelines, which are left to the discretion of commanders and, as a result, the different forms of abuses, including sexual victimisation of female conscripts, exploitation of conscripts' labour power for personal gain, and infliction of inhumane punishments permeate the national service. The absence of regulatory arrangements and monitoring mechanisms gives the military commanders in the national service *carte blanche* in the form of unlimited and unaccountable power, which over time has bred impunity.

---

[2] http://ec.europa.eu/eurostat/statistics-explained/index.php/Asylum_quarterly_report (last accessed 10 March 2016).

Postscript

The UK Upper Tribunal (Immigration and Asylum Chamber) Country Guidance on Eritrea

Prior to the most recent Country Guidance on Eritrea, eighty-seven per cent of those who were refused under the Home Office Country Information and Guidance, Eritrea: National (incl. Military) Service, August 2016 and Country Information Guidance Eritrea—Illegal Exit, September 2016, had their refusals overturned on appeal. In October 2016, the Upper Tribunal (Immigration and Asylum Chamber) in a country guidance case—MST and Others (national service – risk categories) Eritrea CG [2016] UKUT 00443 (IAC) rejected the much-criticised UK Home Office policy on Eritrean asylum-seekers by concluding:

> *Accordingly, a person whose asylum claim has not been found credible, but who is able to satisfy a decision-maker (i) that he or she left illegally, and (ii) that he or she is of or approaching draft age, is likely to be perceived on return as a draft evader or deserter from national service and as a result face a real risk of persecution or serious harm.* (Para. 10) (Emphasis in original)

The UK Home Office Country of Origin Information, which influences the decisions of judges and case workers was based on the flawed assumption originating from the much-criticised and discredited Danish Immigration Service report on Eritrea which concluded that if an Eritrean deserter from the ENS or draft evader who exited from the country illegally signed a repentance letter and paid the 2 per cent diaspora tax, he or she is free to return to Eritrea without facing any risk of persecution. The UK Upper Tribunal categorically rejected this flawed conclusion stating in para. 334:

> Suffice to say for the purpose of this section, that we do not accept that the evidence goes anywhere close to establishing that the payment of the tax and the signing of the letter would enable draft evaders and deserters to reconcile with the Eritrean authorities. In relation to the letter of regret, we also have serious doubts that it can properly be described as a basis for reconciliation, since its terms amount to a confession of guilt by the person who signs it to what the Eritrean regime considers "appropriate punishment" in the context of a regime with a very poor human rights record.

The Upper Tribunal in para. 346 further noted, 'The question is, therefore, what further characteristics are needed to place a person at real risk of persecution or serious harm on return.' The exceptions the Upper Tribunal identified are exactly the same as those in MA (Draft evaders – illegal departures – risk) Eritrea CG [2007] UKAIT 00059 and MO (illegal exit – risk on return) Eritrea CG [2011] UKUT 00190 (IAC) where I was the only expert witness as was the case in MST and Others (national service – risk categories) Eritrea CG [2016] UKUT 00443.

In para. 347, the Upper Tribunal observed:

> We consider two further characteristics are needed: (i) that they will be perceived on return as evaders/deserters; and (ii) that they will be persons subject to forcible return. Even then, however, we continue to think that this category is subject to certain exceptions and that they are exactly the same as those identified in MO, namely (1) persons whom the regime's military and political leadership perceives as having given them valuable service (either in Eritrea or abroad); (2) persons who are trusted family members of, or are themselves part of, the regime's military or political leadership. A further possible exception, requiring a more case specific analysis is (3) persons (and their children born afterwards) who fled (what later became the territory of) Eritrea during the War of Independence. *We do not accept the position identified in the latest version of the Home Office CIG on Illegal Exit published on 4 August 2016 that the scope of these exceptions has widened.* (Emphasis added)

The Home Office prayed the Upper Tribunal to adopt an open-ended fact-specific approach, but this was rejected on the grounds that:

> ... [her] [Home Secretary's] argument is dependent on the premise that those who have left Eritrea illegally as evaders or deserters have the ability to regularise their position by payment of the diaspora tax and letter of regret. For reasons given above at [333] we reject this. Persons who are likely to be perceived as deserters/evaders will not be able to avoid exposure to such real risk merely by showing they have paid (or are willing to pay) the diaspora tax and/have signed (or are willing to sign) the letter of regret.

References

Abraham Haile (2007) *Tradition in Transition, Water Management Reforms and Indigenous Spate Irrigation Systems in Eritrea* (London: Routledge)

Administration for Refugees and Returnees Affairs (ARRA) 'Underage Asylum-Seekers from Eritrea', 15 December 2015

AfDB, OECD and UNDP (2015) 'Eritrea 2015' available at http://www.africaneconomicoutlook.org/fileadmin/uploads/aeo/2015/CN_data/CN_Long_EN/Eritrea_GB_2015.pdf (last accessed 20 January 2015)

AfDB, OECD, UNDP, UNECA (2012) 'Eritrea 2012', available at http://www.youthpolicy.org/national/Eritrea_2012_Youth_Employment_Briefing.pdf (last accessed 20 January 2015)

Africa Economic Outlook (2012) 'Eritrea 2012', available at http://www.youthpolicy.org/national/Eritrea_2012_Youth_Employment_Briefing.pdf (last accessed 20 January 2015)

AI (2003) 'Amnesty International Report 2003 – Eritrea', available at http://www.refworld.org/docid/3edb47d41a.html (last accessed 20 January 2015)

AI (2003) 'Eritrea continued detention of prisoners of conscience and new arrests of members of religious groups, 17 September', available https://www.amnesty.nl/nieuwsportaal/pers/continued-detention-prisoners-conscience-and-new-arrests-members-religious-groups (last accessed 20 January 2015)

—— (2004) 'Eritrea: "You Have No Right to Ask" Government Resists Scrutiny on Human Rights', 18 May, available at https://www.amnesty.org/en/documents/AFR64/003/2004/en/ (last accessed 20 January 2015)

—— (2010) 'Annual Report: Eritrea 2010', 28 May, available at www.amnestyusa.org/research/reports/annual-report-eritrea-2010 (last accessed 20 January 2015)

—— (2011) 'Annual Report: Eritrea 2011' 28 May, available at http://www.amnestyusa.org/research/reports/annual-report-eritrea-2011 (last accessed 20 January 2015)

—— (2015) 'Vi skulle jo også kunne sove om natten', 10 Sepember, available at http://amnesty.dk/nyhedsliste/2015/vi-skulle-jo-ogsaa-kunne-sove-om-natten (last accessed 20 January 2015)

Alem Fesshatzion (2015) 'Why is Eritrea thriving while Ethiopia is starving', available at www.dehai.org/guests/feb-apr06.htm (last accessed 20 January 2015)

Alemseged Tesfai (2002) *Two Weeks in the Trenches: Reminiscences of Childhood and War in Eritrea* (Trenton, N.J.: The Red Sea Press)

Andebrhan Welde Giorgis (2014) *Eritrea at Crossroads: A Narrative of Triumph, Betrayal and Hope* (Strategic Book Publishing & Rights Agency)

Anti-Slavery Organisation (2015) 'What is Modern Slavery', available at

http://www.antislavery.org/english/slavery_today/what_is_modern_
slavery.aspx (last accessed 20 January 2015)

Awate Team (2014) 'Eritrea 2014: Isaias Afwerki & His Musical Chair', available at http://awate.com/eritrea-2014-isaias-afwerki-his-musical-chair/ (last accessed 20 January 2015)

Bailliet, Cecilia M. (2007) 'Examining Sexual Violence in the Military Within the Context of Eritrean Asylum Claims Presented in Norway', *International Journal of Refugee Law* 19 (3): 471–510

Bandow, D. (1990) 'National Service: the Enduring Panacea', CATO Policy Institute, No. 130, 22 March

Barnett, C. (1979) *Britain and Her Army 1509–1970* (Harmondsworth: Penguin)

Barry, B. (1964) 'The Public Interest', *Proceedings of Aristotelian Society*, Supplementary Volumes 38: 1–18

BBC (2001) 'Eritrea defends political crackdown', 10 October, available at http://news.bbc.co.uk/1/hi/world/africa/1591835.stm (last accessed 20 January 2015)

BBC News (2010) 'Eritrea refuses food aid', 3 January, available at http://news.bbc.co.uk/1/hi/world/africa/8438207.stm (last accessed 20 January 2015)

—— (2012) 'Ethiopia "launches military attack inside Eritrea"', 15 March, available at http://www.bbc.co.uk/news/world-africa-17386161 (last accessed 20 January 2015)

—— (2013) 'Thousands of Eritreans "abducted to Sinai for ransom"', 4 December, available at http://www.bbc.co.uk/news/world-africa-25222336

—— (2015) 'Eritrea footballers "gain Botswana asylum" after World Cup qualifier', 28 October, available at http://www.bbc.co.uk/news/world-africa-34664026 (last accessed 20 January 2015)

Beattie, P. M. (2001) *The Tribute of Blood: Army, Honor, Race, and Nation in Brazil, 1864–1945* (Durham: Duke University Press Books)

Bellamy, E. (1888) *Looking Backward, 2000–1887* (Leipzig: Bernhard Tauchnitz)

Bernal, V. (2014) *Nation as Network: Diaspora, Cyberspace & Citizenship* (Chicago: The University Press of Chicago)

Bloch, A. (2007) 'Methodological Challenges for National and Multi-sited Comparative Survey Research', *Journal of Refugee Studies* 20 (2): 230–47

Bloomfield, S. (2009) 'Eritrean Soccer Team Defects in Kenya', 17 December, available at http://www.npr.org/termplates/story/story.php?storyId=121549470 (accessed 1 October 12)

Board, R. (2006) *Conscription in Britain 1939–1964: The Militarisation of a Generation* (London and New York: Routledge)

Bourne, R. (1982 [1916]) 'A Moral Equivalent of Universal Military Service' in Anderson, M. (ed.), *The Military Draft* (Stanford: Ca.: Hoover Institution Press), pp. 397–402

Briez, P.C.J. cited in Hippler, T. (2007) *Citizens, Soldiers and Armies: Military Service in France and Germany, 1789–1830* (London: Taylor and Francis)

Bryman, A. (2008) *Social Research Methods* (Oxford: Oxford University Press)

BTI (2012) 'Eritrea Country Report', available at http://www.bti-project.org/uploads/tx_itao_download/BTI_2012_Eritrea.pdfat (last accessed 20 January 2015)

—— (2014) 'Eritrea Country Report', Gütersloh: Bertelsmann Stiftung, available at http://www.bti-project.de/uploads/tx_itao_download/BTI_2014_Eritrea.pdf (last accessed 20 January 2015)

Burgess, D. (1989) 'Women and War: Eritrea', *Review of African Political Economy* 16 (45/46): 126–32

CAPERI (2014) 'Reports: Bedouins attack Eritreans in refugee camp in Sudan', 26 December, available at http://www.caperi.com/reports-bedouins-attack-eritreans-in-refugee-camp-in-sudan/ (last accessed 20 January 2015)

Carr, E. H. (1942) *Conditions of Peace* (London: Macmillan and Co. Ltd)

Chapman, B. (2002) 'A Bad Idea Whose Time is Past: The Case Against Universal Service' Brookings Institute

Clapham, C. (2001) 'War and State Formation in Ethiopia and Eritrea', Failed States Conference, Florence, 10–14 April 2001

Cliffe, L. (1999) 'Regional Dimensions of Conflict in the Horn of Africa', *Third World Quarterly* 20(1), 89–111

Cohen, E. A. (1985) *Citizens and Soldiers: The Dilemmas of Military Service* (Ithaca and London: Cornell University Press)

Cohen, H. (2013) 'Time to bring Eritrea in from the cold', 16 December, available at http://africanarguments.org/2013/12/16/time-to-bring-eritrea-in-from-the-cold-by-hank-cohen/ (last accessed 20 January 2015)

Coleman, J. (1990) *Foundations of Social Theory* (Cambridge: Harvard University Press)

Commission of Inquiry on Human Rights in Eritrea (2015) 'Report of the Commission of Inquiry on Human Rights in Eritrea', 4 June, A/HRC/l29/42

Committee on the Elimination of Discrimination against Women considers the reports of Eritrea (2015) available at http://www.ohchr.org/EN/NewsEvents/Pages/DisplayNews.aspx?NewsID=15617&LangID=E (last accessed 20 January 2015)

—— 'Concluding observations on the fourth and fifth periodic reports on Eritrea', CEDAW/C/ERI/O/5, 12 March 2015

Comprehensive Africa Agriculture Development Programme (CAADP) (2013) 'East and Central Africa Regional CAADP Nutrition Program Development Workshop Nutrition Country Paper – Eritrea', 2013, available at http://www.fao.org/fileadmin/user_upload/wa_workshop/ECAfrica-caadp/Eritrea_NCP_190213.pdf (last accessed 20 January 2015)

Connell, D. (1997) *Against All Odds: A Chronicle of the Eritrean Revolution* (Trenton, N.J.: The Red Sea Press)

—— (2007) 'War & Peace in Sudan: The Case of the Bejas', 27 February, available at http://hornofafrica.ssrc.org/Connell/index1.html (last accessed 20 January 2015)

—— (2010) *Historical Dictionary of Eritrea* (Lanham: Scarecrow)

—— (2013) 'The Rerouted Trafficking in Eritrean Refugees', *Middle East Research and Information Project*, 10 August

Cowan, Nicola (1983) 'Women in Eritrea: An Witness Account', *Review of African Political Economy* 10 (27/28): 143–52

Crick, B. (2000) *In Defence of Politics* 5th edn (London: Continuum)

Danish Immigration Service (2014) 'Eritrea – Drivers and Root Causes of Emigration, National Service and the Possibility of Return Country of Origin Information for Use in the Asylum Determination Process', August and October 2014 (November)

—— (2015) 'Head of division defends Eritrea report', 5. March, available at http://www.dr.dk/Nyheder/Andre_sprog/English/2015/03/05/122325.htm (last accessed 20 January 2015)

Dawit Teclemariam Bahta (2016) 'Girls' Enrollment in Secondary Schools in Eritrea: Status and Hindering Factors', *African Research Journal of Education and Social Sciences* 3 (1): 1–10

Dawson, D. (1982) 'Posse Comitatus', in Anderson, M. with Honegger, B. (eds), *The Military Draft: Selected Readings on Conscription* (Stanford, California: Hoover Institution Press Stanford University), pp. 3–12

de Tocqueville, A. (1945) *Democracy in America*, trans. Henry Reeve (New York: Vintage)

Debessai Ghide (2004) '*Teateq*' (Get Armed), Special Issue 7 July

—— (2016) '29th Round National Service Members Graduate: 7th Eri-Youth Festival Opens', *Eritrea Profile* 23 (39): 8

Dietz, H., Elkin, J. and Roumani, M. (eds) (1991) *Ethnicity, Integration, and the Military* (Boulder, CO: Westview)

DiLorenzo, T. J. (1990) 'National Service: A Solution in Search of a Problem', *The Freeman* 40 (3), available at http://fee.org/freeman/national-service-a-solution-in-search-of-a-problem/ (accessed 5 February 16)

Dybnis, A. (2011) 'Was the Eritrea–Ethiopia Claims Commission Merely a Zero-Sum Game?: Exposing the Limits of Arbitration in Resolving Violent Transnational Conflict', *Loyola of Los Angeles International & Comparative Law Review* 33 (2): 255–86

Dzurek, D. (1996) 'Eritrea-Yemen Dispute Over the Hanish Islands', *IBRU Boundary and Security Bulletin*, Spring, pp. 70–7

EASO (European Asylum Support Office) (2014) 'EASO Quarterly Asylum Report Quarter 3', available http://reliefweb.int/sites/reliefweb.int/files/resources/Quarterly-Asylum-Report-Q3.pdf (last accessed 20 January 2015)

EASO (2014) 'Annual Report on the Situation of Asylum in the European Union', July, available at http://www.bfa.gv.at/files/berichte/EASO_Annual_Report_2014.pdf (last accessed 20 January 2015)

—— (2015) 'EASO Country of Origin. Information Report. Eritrea Country Focus', 2015, available at http://www.refworld.org/docid/557a94724.html (last accessed 20 January 2015)

Economic Intelligence Unit (1995) Country Report Ethiopia, Eritrea, Somalia and Djibouti, 4th Quarter, Economic Intelligence Unit, London

Elberly, C. (1988) *National Service: A Promise to Keep* (Rochester: John Alden Books)

Elgot, J. and Taylor, Matthew (2015) 'Calais Calais crisis: Cameron condemned for "dehumanising" description of migrants', *The Guardian*, 30 July

Enegwea, G. and Umoden, G. E. (1993) 'NYSC: Twenty years of national service', Abuja, Nigeria: National Youth Service Corps, Directorate Headquarters

Enloe, C. (1980) *Ethnic Soldiers: State Security in Divided Societies* (Athens: University of Georgia Press)

—— (2004) *The Curious Feminist: Searching for Women in The New Age of Empire* (Berkeley and London, University of California Press)

Eritrea (2014) 'Index of Political Freedom', available at http://www.heritage.org/index/country/eritrea (last accessed 20 January 2015)

Eritrea-Ethiopia Claims Commission (2005) 'Report of International Arbitral Awards Recueil Des Sentences Arbtrales Eritrea-Ethiopia Claims Commission – Partial Award: Jus Ad Bellum – Ethiopia's Claims 1-8 19', December, Volume XXVI: 457–69

Eritrea: PFDJ (2015) 'Troops Shot and Killed Civilians in Adi Keyh as Townspeople Confront Home Demolition Crew', 5 March, available at http://www.asmarino.com/articles/articles-video/4315-eritrea-pfdj-troops-shot-and-killed-civilans-in-adi-keyih-as-townspeople-confront-home-demolition-crew (last accessed 20 January 2015)

Eritrean Government (1995) 'Proclamation on National Service, Proclamation No. 82/1995', *Eritrean Gazette,* No.11, 23 October

Eritrea Profile (1994) 'National Service – the facts ', *Eritrea Profile*, 4 June

Etzioni, A. (1983) *The Immodest Agenda: Rebuilding America Before the Twenty-First Century* (New York: McGraw-Hill Book Company)

—— (1990) ''Foreword' in Sherraden, M. and Eberly, D. (eds), *The Moral Equivalent of War? A Study of Non-Military Service in Nine Nations* (New York: Greenwood Press), pp. ix–xi

—— (2001) *Spirit Of Community: The Reinvention of American Society* (New York: Simon and Schuster)

—— (2015) 'Common Good', in *The Encyclopaedia of Political Thought*, 1st edn, Michael T. Gibbons (ed.) (John Wiley & Sons, Ltd), pp. 1–7

European Commission (2015) 'Asylum in the EU', *Eurostat* 9 June, available at http://ec.europa.eu/dgs/home-affairs/e-library/docs/infographics/asylum/infographic_asylum_en.pdf (last accessed 20 January 2015)

European Union (2015) 'Countries of Origin of Asylum Applicants to the EU 28', available at http://ec.europa.eu/dgs/home-affairs/e-library/docs/infographics/asylum/infographic_asylum_en.pdf (last accessed 20 January 2015)

Eurostat (2016) 'Asylum in the EU Member States. Record number of over 1.2 million first time asylum seekers registered in 2015 Syrians, Afghans and Iraqis: top citizenships', 44/2016- 4 March 2016, available at http://ec.europa.eu/eurostat/documents/2995521/7203832/3-04032016-AP-EN.pdf/ (last accessed 20 January 2015)

Evers, W. M. (1990) *National Service: Pro & Con* (Stanford: Hoover Institution Press)

FAO (2009) 'The State of Food Insecurity in the World: Economic Crises – Impacts and Lessons Learned'

—— (2015) 'Countries requiring external assistance for food', December, available at http://www.fao.org/giews/English/hotspots/index.htm (last accessed 20 January 2015)

FAO/WFP (2002) 'Special Report FAO/WFP Crop and Food Supply Assessment Mission to Eritrea', 3 October, available at http://www.fao.org/docrep/005/y7678e/y7678e00.htm (last accessed 20 January 2015)

Field, F. (2003) *Social Capital* (London: Routledge)

Fisher, I. (2000) 'After victory, Ethiopia looks toward other fronts: Signs all of Eritrea could be battlefield', *The New York Times*, 20 May

Flynn, G. Q. (2002) *Conscription and Democracy: The Draft in France, Great Britain, and the United States* (Westport, Connecticut/London: Greenwood Press)

Gebru Tareke (2009) *The Ethiopian Revolution: War in the Horn of Africa* (New Haven: Yale University Press)

Gettleman, J. (2008a) 'A Conflict's Buffer Zone: Rocks, and Inches', *New York Times*, 25 May

Gettleman, J. (2008b) 'Eritrea and Djibouti square off over wasteland at the Horn of Africa', *The New York Times*, 25 May

Gil, P. (1980) 'Women in the Eritrean Revolution: Eye Witness Reports and Testimonies on the Role of Women in the Eritrean Revolution', in *Women in the Eritrean Revolution* (ed.) by National Union Eritrean Women: National Union of Eritrean Women

Glassengerg, E. V. (2014) 'It's time to change Israel's refugee policies', 15 September, available at http://www.jpost.com/Opinion/Its-time-to-change-Israels-refugee-policies-375440 (last accessed 20 January 2015)

Global Security, Eritrea Army (2015) available at http://www.globalsecurity.org/military/world/eritrea/army.htm (last accessed 20 January 2015)

Gorham, E. B. (1992) *National Service, Citizenship and Political Education* (New York: State University of New York)

Government of Eritrea (1997) 'The Constitution of Eritrea', ratified by the Constituent Assembly, 23 May, available at http://www.africanchildinfo.net/clr/policy%20per%20country/eritrea/eritrea_foodsecurity_2004_en.pdf I(last accessed 20 June 2015)

—— (2004) 'Eritrea: Food Security Strategy' Asmara, April

—— (2005) 'Support to NEPAD-CAADP implementation' (NEPAD Ref. 05/10 E), January, available at ftp://ftp.fao.org/docrep/fao/008/ae741e/ae741e00.pdf (last accessed 20 January 2015)

Gray, A. (2006) 'Eritrea/Ethiopia Claims Commission Oversteps its Boundaries: A Partial Award', *European Journal of International Law* 17 (4): 699–721

Gunaratna, R. (2002) *Inside al Qaeda: Global Network of Terror* (London: Hurst)

Gutmann, A. (1987) *Democratic Education* (Princeton: Princeton University Press)

Haaretz Services (2009) 'Yishai: Migrant workers will bring diseases to Israel: Interior Minister says he has to choose between "popularity and hypocrisy" on question of workers deportation', 31 October, available at http://www.haaretz.com/news/yishai-migrant-workers-will-bring-diseases-to-israel-1.5056 (last accessed 20 January 2015)

Habte Selassie, B. (1989) *Eritrea and the United Nations* (Trenton, N.J.: The Red Sea Press)

Teklay Habteselassie (2004) 'I have no doubt that Sawa will be the fountain of development and commercial centre', *Teatek* (Be Ready), Asmara

Hart, D. K. (1994) 'The American Military, the Civic Tradition, and the Martial Virtue: Civic-Soldiers in a Civic-Army', available at http://isme.tamu.edu/JSCOPE94/Hart94.pdf (last accessed 20 January 2015)

Healy, S. (2007) 'Eritrea's Economic Survival', Summary record of a conference held 20 April, Africa Programme, Chatham House and Convenor of the Horn of Africa Group

Hippler, T. (2007) *Citizens , Soldiers and Armies: Military Service in France and Germany, 1789-1830* (London: Taylor and Francis)

Hirschman, A. (1978) 'Exit, Voice and the State', *World Politics* 31 (1): 90–107

Hirt, N. (2013) 'The Eritrean Diaspora: Saviour or Gravedigger of the Regime? Diaspora Response to the Imposition of UN Sanctions', GIGIA Working Papers, No. 236

Hirt, N. and Mohammad, A. S. (2013) '"Dreams don't come true in Eritrea": anomie and family disintegration due to the structural militarization of society', *Journal of Modern African Studies* 51 (1): 139–68

Hogan, P. (2009) *Understanding Nationalism: On Narrative, Cognitive Science, and Identity* (Columbus: Ohio State University Press)

——— (2014) 'The sacrificial emplotment of national identity. Pádraic Pearse and the 1916 Easter uprising', *Journal of Comparative Research in Anthropology and Sociology* 5 (1): 29–47

Howe, H. (2001) *Ambiguous Order: Military Forces in African States* (Boulder, Colorado: Lynne Rienner)

HRW (2009) 'Eritrea Service for Life: State Repression and Indefinite Conscription in Eritrea', New York. April

——— (2011) 'World Report 2011: Eritrea, Events 2010', available at https://www.hrw.org/world-report/2011/country-chapters/eritrea (last accessed 20 January 2015)

——— (2013) 'World Report 2013: Eritrea, Events 2012', available https://www.hrw.org/world-report/2013/country-chapters/eritrea (last accessed 20 January 2015)

——— (2014a) '"I Wanted to Lie Down and Die": Trafficking and Torture of Eritreans in Sudan and Egypt', 8 May, available at http://reliefweb.int/report/sudan/i-wanted-lie-down-and-die-trafficking-and-torture-eritreans-sudan-and-egypt (last accessed 20 January 2015)

——— (2014b) '"Make Their Lives Miserable" Israel's Coercion of Eritrean and Sudanese Asylum Seekers to Leave Israel', September, available at https://www.hrw.org/report/2014/09/09/make-their-lives-miserable/israels-coercion-eritrean-and-sudanese-asylum-seekers (last accessed 20 January 2015)

——— (2014c) 'World Report 2014: Eritrea, Events 2014', available at https://www.hrw.org/world-report/2014/country-chapters/eritrea (last accessed

20 January 2015)

—— (2014d) 'Denmark: Eritrea Immigration Report Deeply Flawed European Governments Should Rely on UN Reports', Support UN Inquiry, 17 December, available at https://www.hrw.org/news/2014/12/17/denmark-eritrea-immigration-report-deeply-flawed (last accessed 20 January 2015)

—— (2015) 'Letter to the UK Independent Chief Inspector of Borders and Immigration on Flawed UK Country Information and Guidance Reports on Eritrea', 1 July http://www.unhcr.org/refworld/docid/49de06122.html (accessed 14 January 2011)

Humphris, R. (2013) 'Refugees and the Rashaida: human smuggling and trafficking from Eritrea to Sudan and Egypt', March, *New Issues In Refugee Research*, Research Paper No. 254

Huntington, S. P. (2006) *Political Order in Changing Societies* (New Haven and London: Yale University Press)

IAGCI (2015) 'Report by the IAGCI on Eritrea Country Information and Guidance Reports produced by the UK Home Office', 13 May, available at http://icinspector.independent.gov.uk/wp-content/uploads/2015/06/Eritrea-report-IAGCI-19-May-2015.pdf (last accessed 20 January 2015)

ICG (2010) 'Eritrea: The Siege State', Africa Report, No. 163, 21 September

—— (2013) 'Eritrea: Scenarios for Future Transition', Africa Report, No. 200, 28 March

—— (2014) 'Ending the exodus', Africa Briefing, No. 100, Nairobi/Brussels, 8 August

IFAD (2011) 'The State of Eritrea National Agriculture Programme', Programme Design Report, East and Southern Africa Division Programme Management Department, available at http://www.ifad.org/operations/projects/design/102/eritrea.pdf (last accessed 20 January 2015)

—— (n.d.) 'Enabling the rural poor to overcome poverty in Eritrea', available at http://www.ifad.org/operations/projects/regions/Pf/factsheets/eritrea.pdf (last accessed 20 January 2015)

ILO (1957) 'Convention Concerning the Abolition of Forced Labour', No. 105

—— (1998) 'Forced Labour in Myanmar (Burma): Report of the Commission of Inquiry appointed under article 26 of the Constitution of the International Labour Organization to examine the observance by Myanmar of the Forced Labour Convention, 1930 (No. 29)', Geneva: ILO, Part IV, Examination of the case by the Commission

—— (2009) Forced Labour Convention, 1930 (No. 29), available at http://www.ilo.org/wcmsp5/groups/public/@asia/@ro-bangkok/documents/genericdocument/wcms_346435.pdf (last accessed 20 January 2015)

—— (2011) International Labour Organisation, Direct Request (CEACR) adopted 2010, published 100th ILC session (2010) Forced Labour Convention, 1930 (No. 29) Eritrea (Ratification: 2000), available at http://www.ilo.org/dyn/normlex/en/f?p=NORMLEXPUB:13100:0::NO::P13100_COMMENT_ID:2337201 (last accessed 20 January 2015)

IMF (2003) 'Eritrea: 2003 Article IV Consultation Staff Report; Public information notice on the Executive Board Discussion; and Statement of the Executive Director of Eritrea', IMF Country Report No. 03/165, June

Index of Economic Freedom (2011) available at http://www.heritage.org/Index/pdf/2011/Index2011_Full.pdf (last accessed 20 January 2015)

International Encyclopaedia of the Social and Behavioural Sciences (2001) Smelser, N. J. and Paul B. Baltes, Paul B. (editors in chief), available at http://www.sciencedirect.com/science/referenceworks/9780080430768 (last accessed 20 January 2015)

Ira, K. and Lantier, Alex (2008) 'Fighting erupts over Eritrean armed incursion into Djibouti', 18 June, available at: https://www.wsws.org/en/

articles/2008/06/djib-j18.html (last accessed 20 January 2015)

Isaias Afwerki (1990) 'Melstat Wana Tsehafi Nhitotat Hizbin Tegadeltin. Sagem', Official Organ of the EPLF, Special Issue, 2, (10), October

—— (1994) 'Eritrea Profile', 21 May

—— (1996) 'Glutz Zete Mis President Isaias' (Open Dialogue with President Isaias), *Hidri*, Special Issue, no. 4, 1 June

—— (2001) 'Arbaéte Seátat mis President' (Four Hours with the President), *Hiwyet*, No. 19

—— (2002a) 'Kale Meteyik' (Interview with the president), *Hadas Eritra*, 11 May

—— (2002b) Interview in *Hadas Eritra* on the Establishment of the Warsai-Yikealo Development Campaign, May

—— (2003a) *Dimtsi Hafash* (Interview with President Isaias Afwerki), 18 April

—— (2003b) 'Kale Meteyik ms President Isaias Afwerki' (Interview with President Isaias Afwerki) by Elias Amare and Mike Seyoum, Barentu, 23 January

—— (2003c) TV Interview with President Isasias, available at http://www.shaebia.org/hatewil/President_Part1.pdf (accessed 28 April 2003)

—— (2004) 'Kelemeteyik mis president Isaias Afwerki' (Interview with President Isaias Afwerki) *Teatek* (Be Ready), magazine published to commemorate the tenth Anniversary of Sawa and national service No 7, July

—— (2006) 'President Isaias Afwerki', Sawa, 19 July, available in http://www.shabait.com/staging/publish/article_005252.html (accessed 21 July 2006)

—— (2006) 'President conducts seminar for participants of second National Youth Festival and 20th round of National Service Programme', 20 July, available in http://www.shabait.com/staging/publish/article_005256.html (accessed 21 July 2006)

—— (2008) 'Interview with President Isaias Afwerki on the occasion of tenth anniversary of Sawa Military Camp and National Service', *Te'atek*, No. 7: 3–13

—— (2009) 'Eritrean President Afworki on Relations with Somalia, United States, Others', *Al-Sharq al-Awsat* Online, 26 May 2009, available at http://www.biyokulule.com/view_content.php?articleid=1924 (last accessed 20 January 2015)

—— (2012) 'President Isaias' speech at the opening of the 5th National Youths Festival', Sawa, 13 July, available at http://www.dehai.org/archives/dehai_news_archive/jun-dec12/0424.html (last accessed 20 January 2015)

—— (2014) English translation of President Isaias Afwerki's comments on the new Eritrean Constitution, 30 December, available at http://www.madote.com/2015/01/english-translation-of-president-isaias.html (last accessed 20 January 2015)

Iyob, R. (2004) 'Shifting Terrain: Dissidence versus Terrorism in Eritrea', United States Institute of Peace, Terrorism in the Horn of Africa, Special Report, January, available at http://www.usip.org/sites/default/files/sr113.pdf (last accessed 20 January 2015)

Jackson, R. H. and Rosberg, C. G. (1982) *Personal Rule in Black Africa: Prince, Autocrat, Prophet and Tyrant* (Berkeley: University of California Press)

Jacobsen, J. and Landau, L. (2003) 'The Dual Imperative in Refugee Research: Some Methodological and Ethical Considerations in Social Science Research on Forced Migration', *Disasters* 27 (3): 185–206

James, W. (1943 [1910]) 'The Moral Equivalent of War', *International Conciliation*, No. 27: 8–20, Washington, D.C., Carnegie Endowment for International Peace

James, W. (1943) *Essays on Faith and Morals* (New York: Longmans, Green and Co.)

Janowitz, M. (1964) *The Military in the Political Development of New Nations* (Chicago: University of Chicago Press)

—— (1967) 'The Logic of National Servic', in Tax, S. (ed), *The Draft: A Handbook of Facts and Alternatives* (Chicago and London: The University of Chicago Press), pp. 73–90

—— (1983) *The Reconstruction of Patriotism: Education for Civic Consciousness* (Chicago: University of Chicago Press)

Johnson, J. J. (ed.) (1962) *The role of the military in underdeveloped countries* (Princeton: Princeton University Press)

Jones, E. (1985) *Red Army and Society: A sociology of the Soviet military* (Boston, MA: Allen & Unwin)

Journalism Group (2012) 'Eritrea tops list of world's worst press censors', New York, 2 May, available at http://www.theguardian.com/world/2012/may/02/eritrea-worst-press-censor

Kaplan, R. D. (2003) 'The Tale of Two Colonies', *The Atlantic Monthly*, April, available at http://www.theatlantic.com/past/docs/issues/2003/04/kaplan.htm (accessed 15 April 2011)

Keetharuth, S. B. (2013) 'Report of the Special Rapporteur on the situation of human rights in Eritrea', Human Rights Council, Twenty-third session Agenda Item 4, 28 May

—— (2014) 'Report of the Special Rapporteur on the situation of human rights in Eritrea', Human Rights Council Twenty-sixth session Agenda item 4, 13 May

—— (2015) 'Report of the Special Rapporteur on the situation of human rights in Eritrea', Human Rights Council, 19 June

Keller, S. (2005) 'Patriotism as Bad Faith', *Ethics* 115 (3): 563–92

Kemenade, L. V. (2011) 'African Nation Eritrea Refuses to Acknowledge Drought; People Suffer in Silence', available at http://www.huffingtonpost.com/2011/07/30/famine-in-africa_n_913987.html (last accessed 20 January 2015)

Keynes, J. M. (1922) *A Revision of the Treaty* (London: Macmillan)

Kibreab, G. (1996) *People on the Edge in the Horn: Displacement, Land Use and the Environment in the Gedaref Region, Sudan* (Oxford: James Currey)

—— (2008) *Critical Reflections on the Eritrean War of Independence* (Trenton, N.J.: The Red Sea Press)

—— (2009a) *Eritrea: A Dream Deferred* (Oxford: James Currey)

—— (2009b) 'Forced Labour in Eritrea', *Journal of Modern African Studies* 47 (1): 41–72

—— (2009c) 'Eritrean-Sudanese Relations in Historical Perspective', in Reid, R. (ed.), *Eritrea's External Relations: Understanding its Regional Role and Foreign Policy* (London: Chatham House), pp. 71–97

—— (2013) 'The national service/Warsai-Yikealo Development Campaign and forced migration in post-independence Eritrea', *Journal of Eastern African Studies*, 2013 (7): 4: 630–49

—— (2014) 'Critical Observation on the Report of the Danish Immigration Service's Alleged Fact finding Missions to Ethiopia and Eritrea', August and October, available at http://fithinews.com/docs/Commentary_26_March_2015.pdf (last accessed 20 January 2015)

—— (2015) 'Some Reflections on the UK Home Office's Country Information Guidance Eritrea: National (incl. Military) Service & Illegal Exit, March 2015', London 25 March, available at http://asmarino.com/articles/4363-some-reflections-on-the-uk-home-office-s-country-information-guidance-eritrea-national-incl-military-service-illegal-exit-march-2015 (last accessed 20 January 2015)

—— (2017) 'Sexual Violence in the Eritrean National Service', *African Studies*

Review: 1-21.

Kinsley, P. (2015) 'Ten Truths about Europe's Migrant Crisis', *The Guardian*, 10 August

Krebs, R. (2006) *Fighting for Rights: Military Service and the Politics of Citizenship* (Ithaca and London: Cornell University Press)

Kwiatkowska, B. (2000) 'The Eritrean/Yemen Arbitration: Landmark Progress in the Acquisition of Territorial Sovereignty and Equitable Maritime Boundary Delimitation', *IBRU Boundary Bulletin*, 66–86

Kymlicka, W. (1997) *Contemporary Political Philosophy: an Introduction*. Oxford: University Press

Landinfo, Country of Origin Information Centre (2015) 'Report Eritrea: National service, Norway' available at http://www.landinfo.no/asset/ 3235/1/3235_1.pdf (last accessed 20 January 2015)

Leeca Lata (2006) 'The Search for Peace: the Conflict between Ethiopia and Eritrea', Proceedings of Scholarly Conference on the Ethiopio-Eritrea Conflict. Oslo, Norway

Lerner, D. and Robinson, R. D (1960) 'Swords and Ploughshares: the Turkish Army as a Modernising Force', *World Politics* 13 (1): 19–44

Lior, I. (2014) 'For One Eritrean Asylum Seeker in Israel, Hope for a New Life', 2 February, available http://www.haaretz.com/israel-news/. premium-1.571871 (last accessed 20 January 2015)

—— (2015) 'Israel will deport Eritrean, Sudanese refugees to Africa under new policy', 31 March, available at http://www.haaretz.com/news/national/. premium-1.649688 (last accessed 20 January 2015)

Locke, J. (2013) [1693] *Thoughts on Education* [Extr.] with Intr. Essay by J. Gill. Charleston, South Carolina: Nabu Press.

Lyons, K. (2015) 'Britain refusing asylum to Eritreans on back of discredited report', *The Guardian*, 10 September

Machiavelli, Niccolo (1518 [1998]) *The Discourses*, B. Crick (ed.), trans. L.J. Walker (Harmondsworth: Penguin Books)

Mandela, Nelson (1953) 'No Easy Walk to Freedom', Presidential Address by Nelson R. Mandela to the ANC (Transvaal) Congress 21 September 1953, available at http://www.sahistory.org.za/archive/no-easy-walk-freedom-presidential-address-nelson-r-mandela-anc-transvaal-congress-21-septemb (last accessed 20 January 2015)

Markakis, J. (1990) *National and Class Conflict in the Horn of Africa* (London: Zed Press)

McBride, A. M. and Sherraden, M. W. (2006) *Civic Service Worldwide: Impacts and Inquiry* (London: Routledge)

McCann, D. (2004) *Soldiers of the Pátria: A History of the Brazilian Arm, 1889– 1937* (Stanford: Stanford University Press)

McConnell, T. (2009) 'Eritrea national football team vanishes', *The Times*, 16 December

Mead, M. (1967) 'National Service System as a Solution to a Variety of National Problems', in Tax, S. (ed), *The Draft: A Handbook of Facts and Alternatives* (Chicago and London: The University of Chicago Press), pp. 99–113

—— (1971) 'Women in National Service', *Teacher College Record* 73 (September): 59-62

Mekonnen, D. R. and Estefanos, M. (2011) 'From Sawa to the Sinai Desert: The Eritrean Tragedy of Human Trafficking', Social Science Research Network, available at http://papers.ssrn.com/sol3/papers.cfm?abstract_id=2055303 30 Nov (last accessed 20 January 2015)

Millman, J. (2013) 'Ruthless Kidnapping Rings Reach From Desert Sands to U.S. Cities', *The Wall Street Journal*, 1 March

Ministry of Education (2013) 'Eritrea: Basic Education Statistics 2012/2013',

Asmara, Eritrea, December

Montague, J. (2014) 'A National Team Without a Country: Eritrea's Soccer Team Flees Together, and Arrives in the Netherlands', 21 May, available at http://www.nytimes.com/2014/05/22/sports/soccer/eritreas-soccer-team-flees-together-and-arrives-in-the-netherlands.html (last accessed 20 January 2015)

Montesquieu (1989 [1748]) *The Spirit of the Laws: Cambridge: Cambridge Texts in the History of Political Thought* (Cambridge: Cambridge University Press)

Moskos, C. C. (1988) *A Call to Civic Service: National Service for Country and Community* (New York: Free Press)

Mosley, J. (2014) 'Eritrea and Ethiopia: Beyond the Impasse Briefing Africa Programme', April 2014, AFP BP 2014/01

Muhmuza, R. (2013) 'A look at Eritrea, an isolated African nation', Kampala, AF correspondent, 8 October, available at http://news.yahoo.com/look-eritrea-isolated-african-nation-133218801.html (last accessed 20 January 2015)

Müller, T. R. (2008) 'Bare Life and the Developmental State: Implications of the Militarisation of Higher Education in Eritrea', *Journal of Modern African Studies* 46 (1): 11–31

Mussie Tesfagiorgis (2010) *Africa in Focus: Eritrea* (ABC-CLIO)

Nadel, S.F. (1946) 'Land Tenure on the Eritrean Plateau', *Africa* 16 (1): 1–22

Nathanson, S. (1993) *Patriotism, Morality, and Peace* (Lanhanm, Maryland: Rowman & Littlefield Publishers)

Obadare, E. (2010) 'Statism, Youth and Civic Imagination: A Critical Study of the National Youth Service Corps Programme in Nigeria', CODESRIA, Dakar

OCHA (2012) 'Eritrea, Eastern Africa', available at http://www.unocha.org/eastern-africa/about-us/about-ocha-eastern-africa/eritrea (last accessed 20 January 2015)

Oryada, A. J. (2012) 'Eritrean players seek asylum in Uganda', 5 December, available at http://www.bbc.co.uk/sport/footfall/20610675 (last accessed 20 January 2015)

Oucho, J. O. (2008) 'African Diaspora and Remittance Flow: Leveraging Poverty?' University of Warwick, available at https://www2.warwick.ac.uk/fac/soc/crer/research/mariecurie/afrobrain/oucho/publications/african_diaspora_and_remittance_flows_11.pdf (last accessed 20 January 2015)

Oxford Analytica (2013) 'Eritrea seeks to ease isolation by new bilateral ties', 18 July, available at http://www.dehai.org/archives/dehai_news_archive/2013/jun/att-0457/Eritrea_attempts_to_Ease_Isolation_Oxford_Analytics.pdf (last accessed 20 January 2015)

Oxford Latin Dictionary (1982) (Oxford: Oxford University Press)

Pateman, R. (1990) *Eritrea: Even the Stones are Burning* (NJ Lawrenceville: The Red Sea Press)

Perraudin, F. (2015) '"Marauding" migrants threaten standard of living, says foreign secretary', *The Guardian*, 10 August

Perry, R. B. (1921) *The Plattsburg Movement* (New York: E.P. Dutton)

Petros Ogbazghi (2011) 'Personal Rule in Africa: The Case of Eritrea', *African Studies Quarterly* 12 (2): 1–25

Plaut, M. (2007) 'Eritreans risk death in the Sahara', 25 March, available at http://news.bbc.co.uk/1/hi/world/africa/6492961.stm (last accessed 20 January 2015)

—— (2014) 'Ethiopia-Eritrea: no war, no peace has to end', 15 March, available at https://martinplaut.wordpress.com/2014/03/15/ethiopia-eritrea-no-war-no-peace-has-to-end/ (last accessed 20 January 2015)

Plaut, M. and van Reisen, M. (2015) 'Will Eritrea's drought turn into famine?'

14 December, available at https://martinplaut.wordpress.com/2015/12/14/will-eritreas-drought-turn-into-a-silent-famine/ (last accessed 20 January 2015)

Pool, D. (2001) *From Guerrillas To Government: Eritrean People's Liberation Front* (Ohio: Ohio University Press)

Pool, A. (2013) 'Ransoms, Remittances, and Refugees: The Gatekeeper State in Eritrea', *Africa Today* 60(2): 66–82

Poole, A. (2015) 'Ransoms, Remittances, and Refugees: The Gatekeeper State in Eritrea', *Africa Today* 60 (2): 66–82

Provisional Government of Eritrea (1993) 'Proclamation No. 37/1993 Issued to define the structure, power and functions of the Provisional Government of Eritrea'

Putnam, R. (2000) *Bowling Alone: The Collapse and Revival of American Community* (New York: Simon & Schuster)

Quinn, B. (2012) 'Eritrea's flag-carrying runner seeks asylum in UK to flee repressive regime', *The Guardian*, 15 August

Rakowska-Harmstone, T. (1979) 'The Soviet Army as the Instrument of National Integration', in Erickson, J. and Feuchtwanger, E. J. (eds), *Soviet Military Power and Performance* (Hamden, Conn: Archon Books)

Redeker Hepner, T. and O'Kane, D. (2009) 'Introduction: Biopolitics, Militarism and Development in Contemporary Eritrea', in Redreker Hepner, T. and Okane, D. (eds), *Biopolitics, Militarism and Development in Eritrea in the Twenty-First Century* (Oxford: Berghahn)

Reid, R. (2009) 'The Politics of Silence: Interpreting Stasis in Contemporary Eritrea', *Review* of *African Political Economy* 120: 209–21.

—— (2011) *Frontiers of Violence in North-East Africa* (Oxford: Oxford University Press)

Reporters Without Borders (2014) 'Press Freedom Index', 12 February, available at http://www.capitaleritrea.com/reporters-without-borders-2014-press-freedom-index/ (last accessed 20 January 2015)

Reuters (2000) 'Eritrea refugees pour into Sudan from Ethiopia war', 19 May, available at http://www.refworld.org/pdfid/3ae6a6c90.pdf (last accessed 20 January 2015)

Right-to-Remain (2015) 'The reality of risk in Eritrea: "Everybody is scared to talk … but I am tired of being silent", 19 August, available at http://www.righttoremain.org.uk/legal/the-reality-of-risk-in-eritrea-everybody-is-scared-to-talk-but-i-am-tired-of-being-silent/ (last accessed 20 January 2015)

Rousseau, J. (2005 [1761]) *The Plan for Perpetual Peace, On the Government of Poland and other Writings on History and Politics: The Collected Writings of Rousseau*, Vol. 11, Masters, Roger D. and Kelly, Christopher (eds) (Hanover and London: University Press of New England)

Rozakis, C. L. (1976) *The Concept of Jus Cogens in the Law of Treaties* (Amsterdam: North-Holland Publishing Company)

Rusom Kidane (n.d.) 'Tragic stories from young Eritrean asylum-seekers and refugees', available at http://www.ehrea.org/future.php (last accessed 20 January 2015)

Said, E. (1994) 'Representations of the Intellectual', The 1993 Reith Lectures, 23 June, First Vintage Books Edition, April 1996, available at http://www.mohamedrabeea.com/books/book1_10178.pdf (last accessed 20 January 2015)

Sebhat Ephrem (1995) 'Precedence to national sovereignty', *Eritrea Profile*, 18 November

—— (2008) 'Nay Aserte Seatat Kale Meteyek ms Kubur General Sebhat Ephrem in Teatek' (Ten Hours Long In-Depth Interview with General

Sebhat Ephrem), 18/19 July

Shabait.com (2010) Eritrea: 23rd Round National Service Graduate and 4th Eri-Youth Festival Officially Opened, July 16

—— (2014) Eritrea: 6th National Youth Festival, Shabait, 18 July, available at http://www.shabait.com/news/local-news/17543-6th-national-youth-festival-opens (last accessed 20 January 2015)

Sheen, D. (2014) 'Where was God when Israel deported African refugees?', 19 June, available at http://www.huffingtonpost.com/david-sheen/where-was god-during-isra_b_5500889.html (last accessed 20 January 2015)

Sherman, R. (1980) *Eritrea: The Unfinished Revolution* (New York: Praeger)

Sherraden, M. and Eberly, D. (1990) 'Introduction', in Eberly, D. and Sherraden, M. (eds),

The Moral Equivalent of War? A Study of Non-Military Service in Nine Nations (New York: Greenwood Press), pp. 1–6

Sherwood, H. (2012) 'Israel PM: Illegal African Immigrants threaten identity of Jewish State', *The Guardian*, 20 May

—— (2014) 'Hundreds of Eritreans enslaved in torture camps in Sudan and Egypt,' *The Guardian*, 11 February

Shinn, D. H. (2012) 'Eritrea, Arms Embargo and Regional Relations', *International Policy Digest*, August

Slavery Convention, 1926, Amended by Protocol, 1953, in Brownlie, I. and Goodwin Gill, G. (eds) (2010) *Brownlie's Documents on Human Rights* (Oxford: Oxford University Press)

Smith, D (2012) 'Ethiopian raid on Eritrean bases raises fears of renewed conflict', *The Guardian*, 16 March

Stapleton, T. (2013) *A Military History of Africa* (Westport: Praeger Publishers)

Stevis, M. and Parkinson, J. (2016) 'African Dictatorship Fuels Migrant Crisis Thousands flee isolated Eritrea to escape life of conscription and poverty', *Wall Street Journal*, 20 October

Student Council (2001) 'Statement of the Student Council of the Students' Union of Asmara University'

Styan, D. (1996) 'Eritrea 1993: The End of the Beginning?', in Allen, T. (ed.) *In Search of Cool Ground: War Flight and Homecoming in East Africa* (James Currey/Africa World Press)

Tarnopolsky, N. (2013) 'Israel built a new border wall to prevent migrants from "smuggling in terror"', 5 December, available at http://www.globalpost.com/dispatch/news/regions/middle-east/131204/israel-new-border-wall-egypt-terrorism-immigration-project-hourglass (last accessed 20 January 2015)

Te'ateq (2004) Special Issue, 10th Anniversary of the Sawa Military Camp and the National Service, No. 7, July

Tekle, A. (1995) *Eritrea and Ethiopia: From Conflict to Cooperation* (Trenton, NJ.: The Red Sea Press)

Temesgen Kifle (2007) 'Do Remittances Encourage Investment in Education? Evidence from Eritrea' *Journal of Africa Studies* Vol. 4, no. 1 available at http://quod.lib.umich.edu/g/gefame/4761563.0004.101/--do-remittances-encourage-investment-in-education-evidence?rgn=main;view=fulltext (last accessed 20 January 2015)

The Constitution of Eritrea (1997)', ratified by the Constituent Assembly, 23 May

The Economist (2006) 'Eritrea: A myth of self-reliance Eritrea's people pay the price for their Government's pride, 27 April

—— (2015) 'Asylum-seekers turned away', 12 December, The Heritage Foundation, 2015 Index of Economic Freedom, available at http://www.heritage.org/index/country/eritrea (accessed 14 January 2016)

The Local (2014) 'Danish report on Eritrea faces heavy criticism', 1 December 2014

Tilly, C. (1975) *The Formation of National States in Western Europe* (Princeton: Princeton University Press)

Transparency International (2015) 'U4 Expert Answer, Corruption in Eritrea', available at http://www.u4.no/helpdesk/helpdesk/query.cfm?id=117 (accessed 4 December 2011)

Treiber, M. (2009) 'Trapped in Adolescence: The Postwar Urban Generation', in O'Kane, D. and Redeker Hepner, T. (eds), *Biopolitics, Militarism and Development in Eritrea in the Twenty-First Century* (Oxford: Berghahn)

Trevaskis, G. K. N. (1960) *Eritrea: A Colony in Transition: 1941–52* (Oxford: Oxford University Press)

Tronvoll, K. and Mekonnen, D. R. (2014) *The African Garrison State: Human Rights and Political Development in Eritrea* (London: James Currey Publishers)

UK Home Office (2012) 'Eritrea Country of Origin Information (COI) Report', 17 August 2012

—— (2015a) Statistic – National Statistics, 27 August, available at https://www.gov.uk/government/publications/immigration-statistics-april-to-june-2015/asylum#nationalities-applying-for-asylum (last accessed 20 January 2015)

UK Home Office (2015b) 'Country Information and Guidance Eritrea: Illegal Exit March 2015', Annex B: Letter dated 1 April 2010 from British Embassy in Asmara, available at https://www.gov.uk/government/uploads/system/uploads/attachment_data/file/412716/CIG_-Eritrea_-_Illegal_Exit_-_March_2015_-_v1_0.pdf (last accessed 20 January 2015)

UK Home Office (2015c) 'Country Information Guidance Eritrea: National (incl. Military) Service & Illegal Exit', March

United Nations (2001) Common Country Assessment (CCA) Eritrea, Vol. 1, available at http://www.er.undp.org/content/dam/eritrea/docs/Legal/cca_pub_eritrea.pdf (last accessed 20 January 2015)

UN Commission of Inquiry on Human (2015) 'Report of the commission of inquiry on human rights in Eritrea,' Geneva, 4 June, available http://www.ohchr.org/EN/HRBodies/HRC/CoIEritrea/Pages/ReportCoIEritrea.aspx (last accessed 20 January 2015)

UN News Centre (2014) 'Modern slavery: UN rights experts welcome new international agreement on forced labour', 13 June, available at http://www.un.org/apps/news/story.asp?NewsID=48037#.VS-Q4ZTF9XY (last accessed 20 January 2015)

—— (2015) 'UN refugee agency concerned by abduction of Eritrean asylum-seekers in eastern Sudan', 5 June, available at http://www.un.org/apps/news/story.asp?NewsID=51076#.VlB-AGThB8c (last accessed 20 January 2015)

UNDP (2011) 'Human Development Report 2011 Sustainability and Equity: A Better Future for All' available http://hdr.undp.org/sites/default/files/reports/271/hdr_2011_en_complete.pdf (last accessed 20 January 2015)

—— (2014) 'Human Development Report 2014 – Eritrea HDI values and rank changes in the 2014 Human Development Report', available at http://hdr.undp.org/sites/all/themes/hdr_theme/country-notes/ERI.pdf (last accessed 20 January 2015)

UNCR (2004) 'UNCR position on return of rejected asylum seekers to Eritrea', Geneva, January

UNHCR (2005) 'Draft Evaders in Eritrea', PRL23.1/Eritrea/RB, 11 March

—— (2009) 'UNHCR Eligibility Guidelines for Assessing the International Protection Needs of Asylum-Seekers from Eritrea,' April

—— (2012) 'Press Release. One survivor, 54 die at sea attempting the voyage to Italy from Libya', 10 July, available at http://www.unhcr.org/4ffc59e89. html (last accessed 20 January 2015)

—— (2013) 'UNHCR concern at refugee kidnappings, disappearances in eastern Sudan', 25 January, available at http://www.unhcr.org/510275a19. html (last accessed 20 January 2015)

—— (2015) 'UNHCR country operations profile – Sudan', available at http:// www.unhcr.org/cgi-bin/texis/vtx/page?page=49e483b76&submit=GO (last accessed 20 January 2015)

UNICEF (2009) 'UNICEF Humanitarian Action Eritrea in 2009', available at http://www.unicef.org/har09/files/har09_Eritrea_countrychapter.pdf (last accessed 20 January 2015)

—— (2011) 'Eritrea and Southern Africa', available at http://www.unicef. org/arabic/hac2011/files/HAC2011_4pager_Eritrea.pdf (last accessed 20 January 2015)

—— (2016) 'Powerful photos reveal Ethiopia's worst drought in Decades', 25 May, available at http://www.unicef.org.au/blog/may-2016/powerful-photos-reveal-ethiopia-drought (last accessed 20 January 2015)

UN Office for the Coordination of Humanitarian Affairs (2003) 'Eritrea 2004: Consolidated Appeals Process', Geneva

—— (2012) 'Eritrea, Eastern Africa, 2012. Eastern Africa Eritrea', available at http://www.unocha.org/eastern-africa/about-us/about-ocha-eastern-africa/eritrea (last accessed 20 January 2015)

—— (2013) 'Eritrea. Eastern Africa.',Aaailable at http://www.unocha.org/ eastern-africa/about-us/about-ocha-eastern-africa/eritrea (last accessed 20 January 2015)

US Department of State (2002) 'International Religious Freedom Report, Eritrea', available at www.state.gov/j/drl/rls/irf/2002/13820.htm (last accessed 20 January 2015)

—— (2010 and 2011) 'Country Reports on Human Rights Practices, Eritrea', available at http:// www.state.gov (last accessed 20 January 2015)

—— (2011) 'Country Reports on Human Rights Practices – Eritrea', 24 May 2012, available at http://www.unhcr.org/refworld/docid/4fc75aa141.html (accessed 1 October 2012)

—— (2014) 'Eritrea 2014 Human Rights Report', available at http://www. state.gov/documents/organization/236568.pdf (last accessed 20 January 2015)

Van de Giessen, E. (2011) 'Horn of Africa', Institute of Environmental Security, The Hague, January, available at http://www.environsecurity.org/espa/ PDF/ESA_HOA.pdf (last accessed 20 January 2015)

Van Gennep, A. (2010 [1909]) *The Rites of Passage* (London: Routledge Chapman & Hall)

Vertovek, S. (2007) 'New Complexities of Cohesion in Britain: Super-diversity, Transnationalism and Civil Integration', Commission on Integration and Cohesion

Walzer, M. (1980) *Radical Principles Reflections of Unreconstructed Democrat* (New York: Basic Books)

—— (1983) *Spheres Of Justice: A Defense of Pluralism and Equality* (New York: Basic Books)

—— (1990) 'What does it mean to be "American?"', *Social Research* 57 (3): 633–54

War Resisters International (2009) 'HRW report denounces conscription in Eritrea', 16 April, available at http://www.wri-irg.org/node/7300 (last accessed 20 January 2015)

Welch, C. E. (1991) 'The military and social integration in Ethiopia', in Dietz, Elkin, J. and Roumani (eds), *Ethnicity, Integration, and the Military* (Boulder,

Col.: Westview Press), pp. 151–78

WFP (2004) 'A Report from the Office of Evaluation', 28 January–10 March 2004, available at http://documents.wfp.org/stellent/groups/public/docu ments/reports/wfp065383.pdf (last accessed 20 January 2015)

WFP (2000) Eritrea Emergency Food Assistance to Victims of Crop Failure due to Drought, Project No: EMOP 10261.01, 25 June, Final draft, available at http://reliefweb.int/report/eritrea/emergency-food-assistance-victims-crop-failure-and-drought-eritrea-emop-622700 (last accessed 20 January 2015)

WHO (2013) 'Country Cooperation Strategy', available at http://www.who. int/countryfocus/cooperation_strategy/ccsbrief_eri_en.pdf (last accessed 20 January 2015)

World Bank (2002a) 'Obstacles to the Expansion of Eritrea's Manufacturing Sector', Final Report, Pilot Investment Climate Assessment, World Bank/ International Financial Corporation

—— (2002b) 'Technical Annex for a Proposed Credit of SDR 48.1 million (US $60 million equivalent) to the State of Eritrea for an Emergency Demobilisation and Reintegration Project', 22 April

—— (2004) 'Document of the World Bank', Report No: 28571-ER

—— (2011) 'Eritrea – Nutrition at a glance', available at http://documents. worldbank.org/curated/en/2011/04/17689731/eritrea-nutrition-glance (last accessed 20 January 2015)

—— (2012) 'Eritrea–Nutrition at a Glance', available at http://www-wds.worldbank. org/external/default/WDSContentServer/WDSP/IB/2013/05/09/000445729 _20130509145630/Rendered/PDF/771620BRI0Box0000eritrea0April02011. pdf (last accessed 20 January 2015)

—— (2015a) 'Eritrea's Economy', 22 September, available at http://www. worldbank.org/en/country/eritrea/overview (last accessed 20 January 2015)

—— (2015b) 'Ease of Doing Business in Eritrea', available at http://www. doingbusiness.org/data/exploreeconomies/eritrea/ (last accessed 20 January 2015)

—— (2015c) 'Eritrea: Overview', available at http://www.worldbank.org/en/ country/eritrea/overview (last accessed 20 January 2015)

World Bulletin (2014) 'Denmark: Anger over bid to curb asylum for Eritreans', 2 December, available at http://www.worldbulletin.net/news/149687/ denmark-anger-over-bid-to-curb-asylum-for-eritreans (last accessed 20 January 2015)

Yemane Desta (2006) 'Designing Anti-corruption Strategies for Developing Countries: A Country Study of Eritrea', *Journal of Developing Societies* 22: 421–49

Younkins, E. W. (2000) 'The Common Good Demystified', *Ideas of Liberty* May, pp. 48–9

Zonszein, M. (2015) 'Israel to deport Eritrean and Sudanese asylum-seekers to third countries', 31 March, *The Guardian*, Tel Aviv, available at http:// www.theguardian.com/world/2015/mar/31/israel-to-deport-eritrean-and-sudanese-asylum-seekers-to-third-countries (last accessed 20 January 2015)

Afar 6, 17, 104, 107–8tabs., 118–20, 125, 184, 187
Afghanistan 147, 152
African Development Bank 5, 128
Afwerki, Isaias 7–9, 16, 28, 57, 68, 70, 83, 94, 173
    attitude to higher education/intellectuals 135–8, 140
    as prime architect of ENS 17, 44–52, 54, 65, 77–9, 96, 177
    stance on corruption 123
    views on ethnic, religious and regional identity 85–6, 97–101, 115
Afwerki, Isaias, personal rule strategies 128
    blackmail of zone commanders 41–2
    control of state institutions 4, 17, 36–43, 52, 123, 178
    creation of counter ground force 39, 42
    creation of Presidential Guard units 42
    see also constitution: Afwerki's refusal to implement; People's Militia
agricultural production 19, 32, 67–8, 70
    impact of ENS on 129–31, 174, 188
    see also livelihoods of families: role of subsistence agriculture in
America see North America; United States of America
Amnesty International 148
ancestry, myths of common 17, 34, 95–6, 170, 180
Andemariam, Gerezgiher (Wuchu) 39–41
Asmara 6, 40, 42, 46, 48, 63, 69, 105, 123, 125, 150–51, 155, 157, 160, 164, 182, 187
    British Embassy 115–16
    training camp 20

    see also University of Asmara
asylum seekers 4, 7, 9–11, 59, 144–6
    in European Union (EU+) 5, 59tab., 142, 147–51, 185–6, 190
    sports teams/athletes 61
    underage 185–6, 190
    see also human trafficking of refugees/asylum seekers; Israel: mistreatment of asylum seekers in; sexual violence/abuse: against asylum seekers/refugees; smuggling
Australia 146, 149–50

Bedouin tribe 62, 124, 143, 185
Bellamy, Edward 24, 55, 95
Bertelsmann Stiftung's Transformation Index (BTI) 124, 131
Bloch, Alice 10–11
border war (1998–2000) 12, 36, 39–40, 50, 58, 66, 89, 96–7, 113, 125–7, 137, 156, 158, 163, 165–6, 170, 187
    ENS as contributor to 47–8
    Eritrea/Ethiopia Claims Commission 45–6, 48
    as excuse for militarisation 14, 21, 44–6
    no-war-no-peace relationship 63–4, 130–32, 146
    peace agreement 46, 55, 57, 99, 179
    third offensive 2, 19, 48, 51, 56
Bourne, Randolph 24–5
Brazil 84–5
Bryman, Alan 9–10

Carr, Edward E 17, 26–7, 75–6, 78
citizenship 1, 15, 91, 94, 101, 114, 184
    American 34, 111
    concept of citizen-soldier 23
    good 22, 25, 91–2, 182
    supranational 28
    see also common good

civic militia *see* People's Militia
civil rights 23, 49, 75, 88, 127 *see also* human rights
civil society 23, 37, 79, 110, 137
Cohen, Eliot 29, 95
Coleman, James 10, 26, 106
common enemy 17–18, 25–7, 35, 75–6, 78, 181
common good 1, 12, 19, 73, 86, 93, 97–8, 114
  disputed notions of 15–16, 24
  national service as commitment to 1, 14, 22–3, 27, 52, 63, 70, 75, 77, 79–80, 89–91, 182, 186, 190
constitution 77, 88n4
  Afwerki's refusal to implement 12, 77&n1, 88
Constitutional Commission 12
corruption in Eritrea 120–21, 128
  Transparency International Corruption Perception Index 121–2&tab., 123
corruption/abuse of power in ENS/ EDF 5, 73, 75, 79, 93, 123–4, 179–80, 182–3, 187–8
  buying out of national service 5, 112, 115–16, 124, 126
cronyism/favouritism 40, 115, 124–6, 128, 139, 141, 188
  exploitation of conscript labour 4, 43, 67–70, 75, 183, 190
  influence over location of assignment 5, 112, 116, 124–5, 187
  see also under defence capability, impact of compulsory conscription on; human trafficking; smuggling; WYDC

Dawson, David 29–30, 114
defence capability of Eritrean military 1–2, 4, 12, 40, 177
  EPLF 17, 54, 56
  see also Eritrean Defence Force: military manpower
defence capability, impact of compulsory conscription on 35, 43–4, 47–56, 60, 62–4, 66, 73, 178–9
  desertion on 65–6
  mismanagement and corruption on 66–9, 72, 178
  warsai/yikealo conflict on 69, 71–2, 179–80
demobilisation, lack of 14, 36, 55–6, 58, 62, 109–10, 113, 127, 132, 137, 156, 158, 165, 168
  impact on private sector 131

National Commission for the Demobilisation and Re-integration Programme (NCDRP) 57, 60
democracies/democratic societies 7, 15, 34, 84, 88, 142, 145, 152
democratic values/process 22, 39n1, 83, 87–8, 99, 142, 184–5
deserters/draft evaders 4, 8–9, 20, 49, 52–5, 58, 62, 65, 74, 127, 182–3, 185
  decision to 'vote with their feet' 4, 55, 58, 110–11, 178, 190
  'shoot to kill' border policy 60, 62, 152
  views on ENS and national unity and cohesion 100–106, 109–10, 180–81, 183
  views on transformative effect of ENS 88–93, 100–101, 175–6, 183
  see also asylum seekers; refugees
Desta, Yemane 122–3
Djibouti 44, 46–7, 99, 173
drought 172–4

Egypt 141, 142, 144, 160
Egypt/Israeli border wall 145, 151, 185
  Sinai desert 5, 62, 124, 128, 135, 142–3, 150–52, 157, 159, 171
Enegwea, Gregory 33–4
Ephrem, Sebhat 7–9, 17, 28, 39–41, 43, 48–9, 64–5, 78, 85, 96–7, 99
equality 1, 5, 24, 70, 77, 88
  lack of 71–2, 90
  unitary conception of 81
equality of bearing the ENS burden 112, 114–15, 124, 126
  among different ethnic/religious communities 119–20
  among female conscripts 118–20, 188
  impact of power imbalance on 117–8, 120–21, 123–4, 127, 186–7
  see also corruption/abuse of power in ENS/EDF; forced equality, principle of
Eritrean Defence Force (EDF) 38–9, 41, 51, 123–124, 178
  autonomy of 4, 37, 41–2, 177, 179
  military manpower in 43, 49–50, 52–6, 60, 62–4, 66
  organisational structure/ leadership of 8, 36–42, 178
  professionalisation/ professional-ism of 4, 37, 41–2, 179
  technical capability of 4, 41–2
  see also defence capability of ENS; institutionalisation of military; Ministry of Defence

Eritrean economy, impact of ENS on 1, 10, 14, 40, 147, 166, 173, 188–90
shortage of consumer goods 132
see also agricultural production; food security/insecurity; labour shortage; livelihoods of families
Eritrean economy, role of diaspora in 145–7
Eritrean Islamic Jihad Movement (EIJM) 46, 99
Eritrean Liberation Front (ELF) 40, 54, 94 *see also* Eritrean People's Liberation Front
Eritrean military *see* Eritrean Defence Force
Eritrean National Service (ENS)
age range for conscription 36, 61, 139, 156, 163, 166, 179, 187, 189
compulsory/open-ended 3–4, 14, 21, 31–2, 35–6, 43, 50, 54, 63, 66, 110–11, 177
historical background to 2, 4, 11, 14, 18
lack of accountability within 68, 116, 136, 190
perceived transformative effects of 2, 16, 19, 22, 70, 81, 85, 88–91, 97, 101–3, 108, 110, 114, 165, 176, 183, 185
punishment/abuse within 52–3, 55–6, 73, 81, 179, 181, 190
structure of 3, 14, 19, 190
universality of 2–3, 44–5, 47, 95, 103, 112, 114, 124, 147, 154, 164, 171, 177, 183, 188–9
see also demobilisation, lack of; exceptions/exemptions from national service; mobilisation
Eritrean National Service goals and objectives 1–4, 8–9, 14, 19, 25, 27, 35, 66, 97, 141, 177
rationale behind 2, 4, 17–18, 47–9, 75–6, 177
post-conflict reconstruction 1, 3, 12, 14, 86, 93, 97, 113, 126, 138, 181
transmission of core EPLF values 2, 4, 8, 47, 69–71, 75–6, 81–2, 85, 87–91, 93, 132, 180–82
see also nation building, ENS as tool of; national unity, ENS as vehicle of; Proclamation No. 82/1995
Eritrean People's Liberation Army (EPLA) 38, 43, 50–51, 54, 56, 178
Eritrean People's Liberation Front (EPLF) 2, 8, 51, 56–7, 71–3, 94, 97, 124, 135–7, 164, 177–8, 181, 186
leadership/Central Council 12, 17, 40n2, 41, 54, 77, 80

notion of nationhood 83–4
perceptions of civilian youth 18–19
role in PGE 11–12
see also under defence capability of Eritrean military; Sawa Military Camp
Eritrean war of independence *see* thirty years' war
Ethiopia 11, 14, 34, 62, 86, 179 *see also* border war 1998-2000
Ethiopian occupation *see* border war (1998-2000): third offensive
ethno-linguistic composition of Eritrea 17–19, 96, 183
Etzioni, Amitai 15–16, 25, 28, 55, 95, 100, 105, 108–9, 184
Evers, William 24, 27–8
exceptions/exemptions from national service 2, 34, 36, 44–6, 112–14, 116, 168, 179, 188

Food and Agriculture Organisation (FAO) 129–30, 146, 161–2, 189
food security/insecurity 129, 153–4, 161–2, 166, 169, 171, 189
restriction of food aid 161, 172–4
forced conscription 1, 3–4, 12, 22–5, 28, 32–3, 36, 40, 49, 54–5, 58, 65, 67, 164
penalty for non-compliance 113
see also youth, impact of open-ended ENS on; forced labour: degeneration of ENS into
forced equality, principle of 112, 114–15, 119, 123–4, 126, 186
forced labour
degeneration of ENS into 12, 33, 44, 49, 52–3, 55, 58, 62–5, 67, 69, 109, 111, 132
international laws on 31–3
philosophical debates on 1, 4, 12, 22, 30–31
see also ILO; slavery, national service as form of
France 29, 59tab., 95, 114
asylum seekers in Calais 152, 157, 159
freedom of press, expression 87–8, 115–16, 123, 136–7
banning of independent media 40n2
French Revolution 24, 81–2, 96, 114

G-15 change-seeking forces 40n2–42
gender equality 132–3
gender-based division of labour 168
Gide, Debesai 20, 119
Great Britain *see* United Kingdom
Gulf States 146, 150–51, 157, 159

Habteselasse, Teklay 39, 41, 72
Hagos, Mesfin 39, 41
Hedareb 103, 107tab., 119, 125, 184, 187
Hippler, Thomas 23–5, 27, 58, 81–2, 96, 112, 114
Hirt, Nicole 37, 40
household income *see* livelihoods of families
human rights 9, 27–33, 68, 88, 142, 144, 148, 165, 167
    UN Commission of Inquiry on Human Rights in Eritrea 110, 135
    UN Human Rights Council 149
Human Rights Watch (HRW) 52, 55, 57–8, 61, 65, 126, 142–4, 148, 154, 169
human trafficking of refugees/asylum seekers 5, 40–41, 128, 133, 135, 151–2, 171–2, 185
    role of corrupt military officials in 124, 141–3, 145, 150, 160
    use of torture/violence 124, 142–4, 156

ILO
    Forced Labour Convention 30–31
    Abolition of Forced Labour Convention 31–3
independence, Eritrean 1, 11–12, 16
institutionalisation of military 4, 37–8, 41–2, 52, 86, 98, 177
internally displaced people (IDP) 10, 56, 62, 65, 141, 152
International Crisis Group (ICG) 41, 123–4, 132, 146, 178
International Fund for Agricultural Development (IFAD) 130, 146, 154
International Law Commission 31–2
International Monetary Fund (IMF) 5, 57, 128, 131, 163, 189
Israel 5, 62, 110, 128, 142, 151, 157, 159, 185
    defence force of 84
    mistreatment of asylum seekers in 144–5
Italian colonialism 17–19

James, William 17, 24–8, 34, 55, 78, 95, 100
Janowitz, Morris 25, 28, 55, 84
Jehovah's Witnesses 3, 113

Kenya 11, 34, 61, 151
Kesete, Semere 137–8
Kiloma training camp 20–21

labour shortage 20, 129–32, 163, 172, 189–90

    impact on family labour allocation 154–5, 160–61, 163–6, 168, 170, 172, 174, 188
Landinfo 6–7
liberation struggle 1, 43, 78, 177
    core values of 4, 8, 12, 16, 18, 35, 47, 69, 71, 73, 77, 92, 179, 182
    marginalisation of heroes 39–40
    see also EPLF; thirty years' war
Libya 5, 62, 128, 135, 141–3, 145, 151–2, 157, 159–60, 171, 185
lineage *see* ancestry, myths of common
livelihoods of families 2, 5, 8–9, 63, 129, 158, 161–2, 164, 166, 169, 178, 188–9
    importance of income diversification for 154–7, 160, 162–3, 170, 188
    loss of breadwinners 73, 156, 160, 163–4, 167–71, 174, 189
    role of remittances in 68, 145–6, 149–50, 154, 156–7, 160, 171, 176
    role of subsistence agriculture in 153–4, 157, 160–62, 168–70, 189
    see also labour shortage: impact on family labour allocation
Locke, John 36

Mai Nefhi college 21n19, 140–41
martyrdom as core value 76–7, 81, 88, 97, 155–6, 158, 164
mass media, state controlled 7, 9, 43, 78, 86
    Te'atek 7, 44, 90
    see also freedom of press, expression
Mead, Margaret 100, 114
Mediterranean Sea 5, 62, 128, 138, 142, 150–52, 157, 159–60, 171, 185
Menqaê 136–7
menqasaqesi (travel permits) 69, 124–6
migration 62
    forced 8, 65, 110–11, 147, 151
    rural-urban interface 35
Meiter training camp 20–21
militarisation and securitisation 5–6, 47–8, 129–30, 132, 166, 189
    of education 5, 128, 134–6, 138–41
    see also People's Militia
Ministry of Defence 3, 8–9, 39, 42, 58, 64, 90, 113, 129 *see also* Ephrem, Sebhat
mobilisation 14, 33, 56, 66, 81, 54–5, 63, 66, 111, 114, 130, 132
    threat of war as pretext for 14, 44, 46, 57, 83, 98–9, 127, 130
Montesquieu, 23–4, 52, 54, 95, 114
Moskos, Charles 17, 25–6, 34, 55, 95–6, 100, 184

nation building, ENS as tool of 1–3, 12, 18–19, 35, 84, 86, 96–7, 140
importance of core values for 81, 93, 181
national identity 1–2, 12, 17–19, 84, 180
building/consolidation of 75–6, 78
guüzo (the hike) and 20–21
national service
as institution of modernisation 23, 75, 84
as sociological mixer 94–5, 103, 105–6, 108–9, 184
national service, philosophical debates 4, 9, 15, 22, 24–5, 35, 55, 114, 176
on civic duty 22–3, 75, 114
on national unity 95–7, 100, 106, 111
on universality 28–30, 84, 94, 100
see also forced labour; patriotism: sacrificial; *posse comitatus*, feudal institution of; slavery, national service as form of; social capital
national unity, ENS as vehicle of 1–3, 5, 12, 17, 19, 21–2, 35, 75, 81, 93, 110, 180–81, 185
and homogenisation of polity 33–4, 83–5, 94, 96, 98–106, 111
see also under deserters/draft evaders
nationalism 83–4, 170
patriotic 85, 97
sacrificial 16–18, 24, 26–7, 71–3, 75–8, 80–82, 86, 91, 93, 98, 179–80
see also patriotism
Netanyahu, Binyamin 144–5
New Zealand 146, 149
Nigeria 35, 84, 99
National Youth Service Corps (NYSC) 33–4, 96
North America 29, 146, 149–50, 159 *see also* United States of America
Norway 11, 59tab., 134, 147
Norwegian Country of Origin Information (COI) Centre 6–7 *see also* Landinfo

patriotism 17, 23, 27, 52, 65, 71, 83–6, 90–92, 95–6, 101, 164, 181
sacrificial 5, 12, 76–8, 81, 175, 180
unpatriotic taboos 126
see also nationalism: patriotic
People's Front for Democracy and Justice (PFDJ) 7, 14, 19, 32, 40n2, 51, 67, 77, 83, 85, 87, 93, 97, 170
cultural hegemony of 141

leadership 17, 131, 183
People's Militia (*Hizbawi Serawit*) 20, 23, 36, 42, 132, 189
pluralistic societies 15
such as Eritrea 87, 99, 106, 111, 115
political education 81, 86–88, 103
posse comitatus, feudal institution of 22, 29–30, 36, 49, 73
poverty 95, 141
impact of ENS on 8, 153–4, 158, 162, 166–9, 172, 182, 189
president of Eritrea *see* Afwerki, Isaias
private sector 121
government animosity towards 127
impact of ENS on 130–31
Proclamation No. 82/1995 on ENS 1–3, 35, 55, 58, 76–8, 83, 88, 97, 109, 112–13, 118, 127, 139, 164, 166, 188
on defence capability 43, 49
on duration of service 14, 21, 32, 36, 44–6, 60, 66
Provisional Government of Eritrea (PGE) 2, 14, 86
provisional government proclamations No. 11/1991 on ENS 2–3, 44–6, 58n5
No. 37/1993 11–12
see also Proclamation No. 82/1995 on ENS
Putnam, R 26, 83, 106

Rashaida group 17, 62, 107tab., 118–20, 125, 143, 172, 187
reconstruction of the nation *see* nation building
refugees 9–11, 59tab., 134, 142–6, 159, 190 *see also* asylum seekers
detention centres/transit centres/ refugee camps 62, 152, 159–60, 185
see also internally displaced people
Reid, Richard 6, 17–18, 21, 41, 80, 96, 140–41
research restrictions in Eritrea 6–9, 38
use of snowball sampling 9–11
Roman Empire 23, 29
Rousseau, Jean-Jacques 23–24
Rwanda 83, 145

Sahara desert 5, 62, 128, 135, 143, 151–2, 157, 159–60, 162, 171, 185
Saho group 6, 17, 107–8tabs., 119–20, 125, 184, 187
Saudi Arabia 155, 157
Sawa Military Camp 5, 13map, 112, 116, 124–6, 133, 135, 156, 164, 187n1, 189
admission of school students at 15, 20–21, 133, 139–40

commanders/leadership of 8, 19, 22,
    39–41, 48, 62, 178
discipline at 21, 28, 53
EPLF political socialisation/
    indoctrination at 79–83, 85–8,
    101, 183–4
establishment of/first conscripts
    14–15, 19–20, 58, 72, 39, 126
Fifth Youth Festival 97–8
language of training at 85
percentage of women students at
    118–19
purpose/nature of training 3, 19, 21,
    47, 70, 85, 90, 98–9, 103
see also sexual violence/abuse: at
    military training camps; Summer
    Work Programme; *warsai;*
    Warsai-Yikealo School; yikealo
sexual violence/abuse 62, 133, 172
    against asylum seekers/refugees
        134-5, 142–4, 152, 172
    and impact of ENS on women's
        rights 134, 139–40
    at military training camps 63, 67,
        72, 90, 93, 125, 128, 132–5, 139,
        189–90
slavery, national service as form of 1,
    4, 22–3, 29, 32, 49, 58, 60, 62, 66,
    68, 110, 113, 125, 127, 169 *see also*
    forced labour
smuggling 5, 40–41, 62, 124, 128,
    141–2, 145, 152, 157–60, 170–72
    involvement of high-ranking
        officials in 150–51, 160
social capital
    erosion of 33, 78–9
    impact of ENS on 65, 73–5, 77, 106,
        110–11, 145, 185–6
    relationship between war and 17,
        25–6, 80
    social cohesion 26–8, 75–6, 78–9,
        84, 86, 98, 100–101, 110
    ENS as vehicle of 5, 17, 21, 93–6,
        102–4, 109–11
    in Nigeria 33–4
    see also national unity, ENS
        as vehicle of; trans-ethnic/
        religious/regional cohesion
social fabric, impact of ENS on 5, 9, 12,
    141, 175
    children 133–5, 161–8, 171
    disrespect for cultural/religious
        practices 174
    family health/wellbeing 5, 118, 149,
        153, 156–60, 162–5, 167, 170–72,
        176, 188
    psychological pain 172, 174–5
    survival of elders 165–6, 168–9

see also Eritrean economy, impact
    of ENS on; food security/
    insecurity; livelihoods of
    families; youth, impact of open-
    ended ENS on
Somalia 51, 83, 173
South Africa 11, 34, 151
Soviet Union 50, 84
Sudan 51, 81, 141, 170–3, 175, 178,
    185–6, 190
    asylum seekers/refugees in 5, 11,
        56, 60, 62, 139, 150–52, 156,
        158–60
    Eritrean disputes with 46–7, 99
    human rights violations in 141–5
    Islamist state of 99
    Khartoum 143, 159–60, 185
    see also under human trafficking of
        refugees/asylum seekers
Summer Work Programme (SWP) 3, 20,
    132–3, 137–8
Sweden 11, 59tab., 147
Switzerland 11, 59tab., 147

tegadelti 53, 69, 80–82, 92–93 *see also*
    yikealo
Tesfai, Alemseged 71, 77, 80, 82
thirty years' war (1961–1991) 19, 35,
    42–3, 50, 66, 69, 79, 88–90, 92, 96,
    177
    fighting capability of EPLA/EPLF
        56–7, 179–80
    post-conflict reconstruction 1–3, 12,
        14, 18, 86, 93, 97, 113, 126, 138,
        181
    role of EPLF leadership in 17
    see also liberation struggle:
        core values of; nationalism:
        sacrificial; *yikealo*
Tigray People's Democratic Movement
    (TPDM) 51, 178
Tigray People's Liberation Front
    (TPLF) 56
Tigrinya group 17–18, 57, 78, 84–6, 92,
    105, 107, 115, 117–18, 120, 184, 187
torture 31, 42, 52–3, 149, 181
    by *halewa sowra* (guards of the
        revolution) 81
    of women 133–4
    see also under human trafficking of
        refugees/asylum seekers
trans-ethnic/religious/regional
    cohesion 18, 20, 26, 28, 33–5, 78,
    83–4, 119–20
    friendship bonds among *agelglot*
        5, 94, 103, 106–108&tabs., 111,
        183–4
    see also national unity, ENS as

vehicle of: homogenisation of polity

Uganda 61, 145, 151
Umoden, Gabriel 33–4
UNICEF 161–2, 171, 173, 189
United Nations 5, 11, 110, 128, 165, 172
  Office for the Coordination of Humanitarian Affairs (OCHA) 130, 161, 173
  imposition of sanctions against Eritrean government 146, 173
UN High Commissioner for Refugees (UNHCR) 56–7, 133, 142, 147–8, 159, 185
United Kingdom (UK) 8, 11, 29, 58, 61, 114, 152, 157, 159, 181
  Home Office 7, 116, 148–9
United Kingdom Border Agency (UKBA) 115–16
United Kingdom Upper Tribunal (Immigration and Asylum Chamber) 149, 191
United States of America 17, 29–30, 34, 94–5, 100, 111, 114, 184
  Department of State 161
  University of Asmara 136, 140–41, 165
  closure of 15, 124, 127, 138–40
  student defiance at 15, 137–40

virtues 4, 23, 71
  civic 33, 96
  martial 23–5, 27, 35, 84, 91–2, 181–2

Walzer, Michael 24–5, 28–9, 55, 95, 100, 111, 114
war veterans *see yikealo*
warsai 20
  hostile relationship with *yikealo* 4, 19, 43, 53, 69–73, 75, 90, 127, 179–80
  transmission of core values to 2, 8, 19, 70, 85
  virtues and vices learned 4, 75, 91–2, 181–2

Warsai-Yikealo Development Campaign (WYDC) 10–11, 77, 82
  failure of/corruption within 63, 66, 92–3, 117, 120, 123
  introduction of 21, 36, 57, 113, 125, 127, 165–6
  as instrument of reconstruction/tranformation 14, 70, 81, 83, 88, 90–91, 100, 113
  sustainability of 115
Warsai-Yikealo School 20, 118, 140, 180
Wi'a
  detention centre 138
  training camp 20–21, 135
Woldeyohannes, Filipos 40–41
World Bank 5, 57, 121, 128, 130–31, 146, 153, 162–3, 165, 171, 174, 189
World Food Programme 129–30, 146, 160–62, 189

yikealo 2, 4, 8, 18
  abuse of power/exploitation of conscripts among 4, 63, 70, 72, 75, 90, 93, 127
  as incarnation of revolutionary values 19, 69–71, 90, 179
  privileged/corrupt members of 4, 70, 73, 90, 93
  see also sexual violence against female conscripts; *warsai*: hostile relationship with *yikealo*
youth, impact of open-ended ENS on 15, 24–5, 28, 54, 153–5, 164, 189
  education/careers 5, 12, 15, 22, 29, 63, 73, 79, 125, 127, 141, 153, 160, 167, 188
  lack of remuneration 2, 16, 21, 33, 36, 60, 63–8, 73, 127, 129, 132, 166, 170, 179
  high flight propensity 1, 14–15, 20, 60–64, 142, 156, 171, 175, 190
  morale 53–4, 60, 65, 68–9, 72, 110, 171
  see also forced conscription; social fabric, impact of ENS on
youth unemployment 3, 34, 127

EASTERN AFRICAN STUDIES

These titles published in the United States and Canada by Ohio University Press

Revealing Prophets
Edited by DAVID M. ANDERSON
& DOUGLAS H. JOHNSON

East African Expressions of Chistianity
Edited by THOMAS SPEAR
& ISARIA N. KIMAMBO

The Poor Are Not Us
Edited by DAVID M. ANDERSON
& VIGDIS BROCH-DUE

Potent Brews
JUSTIN WILLIS

Swahili Origins
JAMES DE VERE ALLEN

Being Maasai
Edited by THOMAS SPEAR
& RICHARD WALLER

Iua Kali Kerya
KENNETH KING

Control & Crisis in Colonial Kenya
BRUCE BERMAN

Unhappy Valley
Book One: State & Class
Book Two: Violence & Ethnicity
BRUCE BERMAN
& JOHN LONSDALE

Mau Mau from Below
GREET KERSHAW

The Mau Mau War in Perspective
FRANK FUREDI

Squatters & the Roots of Mau Mau 1905-63
TABITHA KANOGO

Economic & Social Origins of Mau Mau 1945-53
DAVID W. THROUP

Multi-Party Politics in Kenya
DAVID W. THROUP
& CHARLES HORNSBY

Empire State-Building
JOANNA LEWIS

Decolonization & Independence in Kenya 1940-93
Edited by B.A. OGOT
& WILLIAM R. OCHIENG'

Eroding the Commons
DAVID ANDERSON

Penetration & Protest in Tanzania
ISARIA N. KIMAMBO

Custodians of the Land
Edited by GREGORY MADDOX,
JAMES L. GIBLIN & ISARIA N.
KIMAMBO

Education in the Development of Tanzania 1919-1990
LENE BUCHERT

The Second Economy in Tanzania
T.L. MALIYAMKONO
& M.S.D. BAGACHWA

Ecology Control & Economic Development in East African History
HELGE KJEKSHUS

Siaya
DAVID WILLIAM COHEN
& E.S. ATIENO ODHIAMBO

Uganda Now • Changing Uganda Developing Uganda • From Chaos to Order • Religion & Politics in East Africa
Edited by HOLGER BERNT
HANSEN & MICHAEL TWADDLE

Kakungulu & the Creation of Uganda 1868-1928
MICHAEL TWADDLE

Controlling Anger
SUZETTE HEALD

Kampala Women Getting By
SANDRA WALLMAN

Political Power in Pre-Colonial Buganda
RICHARD J. REID

Alice Lakwena & the Holy Spirits
HEIKE BEHREND

Slaves, Spices & Ivory in Zanzibar
ABDUL SHERIFF

Zanzibar Under Colonial Rule
Edited by ABDUL SHERIFF
& ED FERGUSON

The History & Conservation of Zanzibar Stone Town
Edited by ABDUL SHERIFF

Pastimes & Politics
LAURA FAIR

Ethnicity & Conflict in the Horn of Africa
Edited by KATSUYOSHI FUKUI &
JOHN MARKAKIS

Conflict, Age & Power in North East Africa
Edited by EISEI KURIMOTO
& SIMON SIMONSE

Propery Rights & Political Development in Ethiopia & Eritrea
SANDRA FULLERTON
JOIREMAN

Revolution & Religion in Ethiopia
ØYVIND M. EIDE

Brothers at War
TEKESTE NEGASH & KJETIL
TRONVOLL

From Guerrillas to Government
DAVID POOL

Mau Mau & Nationhood
Edited by E.S. ATIENO
ODHIAMBO & JOHN LONSDALE

A History of Modern Ethiopia, 1855-1991(2nd edn)
BAHRU ZEWDE

Pioneers of Change in Ethiopia
BAHRU ZEWDE

Remapping Ethiopia
Edited by W. JAMES,
D. DONHAM, E. KURIMOTO
& A. TRIULZI

Southern Marches of Imperial Ethiopia
Edited by DONALD L. DONHAM
& WENDY JAMES

A Modern History of the Somali (4th edn)
I.M. LEWIS

Islands of Intensive Agriculture in East Africa
Edited by MATS WIDGREN
& JOHN E.G. SUTTON

Leaf of Allah
EZEKIEL GEBISSA

Dhows & the Colonial Economy of Zanzibar 1860-1970
ERIK GILBERT

African Womanhood in Colonial Kerya
TABITHA KANOGO

African Underclass
ANDREW BURTON

In Search of a Nation
Edited by GREGORY H. MADDOX
& JAMES L. GIBLIN

A History of the Excluded
JAMES L. GIBLIN

Black Poachers, White Hunters
EDWARD I. STEINHART

Ethnic Federalism
DAVID TURTON

Crisis & Decline in Bunyoro
SHANE DOYLE

Emancipation without Abolition in German East Africa
JAN-GEORG DEUTSCH

Women, Work & Domestic Virtue in Uganda 1900-2003
GRACE BANTEBYA
KYOMUHENDO & MARJORIE
KENISTON McINTOSH

Cultivating Success in Uganda
GRACE CARSWELL

War in Pre-Colonial Eastern Africa
RICHARD REID

Slavery in the Great Lakes Region of East Africa
Edited by HENRI MÉDARD
& SHANE DOYLE

The Benefits of Famine
DAVID KEEN

CPSIA information can be obtained
at www.ICGtesting.com
Printed in the USA
BVOW06*2100270517

485325BV00004B/12/P